Runaway

Runaway

Skye Sinclair

with

Diane Taylor

**HODDER &
STOUGHTON**

First published in Great Britain in 2008 by Hodder & Stoughton
An Hachette Livre UK company

1

Copyright © Skye Sinclair

The right of Skye Sinclair to be identified as the
Author of the Work has been asserted by her in accordance
with the Copyright, Designs and Patents Act 1988.

A CIP catalogue record for this title is available from the British Library

Hardback ISBN 978 0 340 95336 5
Trade paperback ISBN 978 0 340 96229 9

Typeset in Sabon by Hewer Text UK Ltd, Edinburgh
Printed and bound by Clays Ltd, St Ives plc

Hodder & Stoughton policy is to use papers that are natural,
renewable and recyclable products and made from wood grown in
sustainable forests. The logging and manufacturing processes are expected
to conform to the environmental regulations of the country of origin.

Hodder & Stoughton Ltd
338 Euston Road
London NW1 3BH

www.hodder.co.uk

Author's Note

This book is dedicated to my children, who don't have my genes but will always have my heart; to all my godchildren and to all the people who are special in my life – they know who they are.

In order to protect the privacy of the many people I have known over the years, names and other details have been changed in every instance, throughout the book.

Contents

PROLOGUE

I was crouched on my hands and knees, scrubbing an endless corridor with a toothbrush. It was a pointless task but was seen as the right sort of punishment for a girl like me. I was fourteen years old and was locked up in an institution called the Blue Door Centre. It was one step down from youth remand, and was a kind of last-chance saloon for delinquent girls who had caused the authorities too much hand-wringing. Most of the others who were holed up in this fortress had been involved in serious crimes. My only crime was running away.

Even at fourteen, I was very good at running away from children's homes, but the Blue Door Centre wasn't like anywhere I'd been before. It was a high-security unit, and when I'd arrived, a burly, foul-smelling member of staff had said, 'You'll never get out of this place: all the doors and windows are bolted. You're stuck here until we decide you can leave.' I had taken an instant dislike to this man, and had vowed that I would find a way to break free.

I couldn't breathe properly unless I was free to roam, to climb trees and ride horses. My need for freedom was as basic as oxygen. But for my mother, her boyfriend, Michael, and too many social workers, police and teachers to count, pinning me to one place was the endgame. I felt worse than an ensnared tiger. I was tired of being cooped up in institutions like this. It didn't matter where adults had tried to confine me, I had always found a way to squeeze myself out of windows, slither down drainpipes or scale high fences.

Escaping from the infamous Blue Door Centre was, however, a different matter entirely. It was one of the most deadly places I had found myself in. The staff were cruel with strong, rigid bodies that looked as if they were made from the same material as the sturdy window bars. The heavy front door could only be opened by tapping in a pin number, and the other doors were triple-locked.

Over the years I had developed a technique of giving myself pep talks to help me through the toughest times. Times like now, when I was locked up, and the many occasions when adults had been cruel to me. Right now, though, in the Blue Door Centre, I was pouring every ounce of mental energy into finding a way to escape. I was so frustrated about my imprisonment that I couldn't stop smashing my toothbrush against the floor over and over again. 'How could I not have found a way out of here yet?' I chastised myself.

I'd never felt quite so trapped. I'd been here for three weeks now, probably the longest I'd stayed anywhere. Claustrophobia was making my chest feel tight and was sending waves of panic up from my stomach. I shuffled along the corridor, moving my bucket of water with me. Floor-cleaning duty was one of the many acts of drudgery assigned to us. Scrubbing the toilets, the bedrooms, burnt pans in the kitchen – all these tough, repetitive tasks were designed to break our spirit. The strategy didn't work for me, though. Inside, I may have been gasping for air, but I would never stop fighting and I would never give the staff the satisfaction of seeing my distress. I remained calm and expressionless in their presence, only coming to life when I was alone with the other girls, with whom I felt an instinctive connection.

A couple of the girls had also been condemned to corridor-scrubbing duty. Usually we were under surveillance by the metal-bodied staff, but now and then they went off for tea breaks and we would allow ourselves a few moments of wildness, skidding along the polished corridors at top speed, throwing water from our buckets at each other as we ran. When the staff returned, we would spring back to our subservient positions on the floor.

I finished scrubbing the corridor and moved myself and my bucket of grey water towards the entrance hall. I watched the front door swing repeatedly open and shut as a procession of official-looking people tapped in the pin to enter or exit. Each time the door clicked shut my heart sank.

Suddenly a plan flashed into my mind like a fork of lightening. Still on my hands and knees, I crawled across the hallway, continuing to clean the floor diligently so as not to arouse my jailers' suspicions. In the entrance area, there was an inner door a few feet away from the heavy front door. This was not locked. I propped my bucket against it to keep it open, then busied myself with cleaning the square of floor between the inner and outer doors. One of the members of staff who was supposed to be supervising me signalled to his fellow jailer that he was going for a cigarette. His friend agreed to join him.

All I had to do now was wait. My heart was beating very fast. If my plan was going to work, I knew I had to act quickly. Poised like a greyhound in the starting blocks, I waited patiently for the front door to buzz. The second the lock released on the door, I sprinted past the visitor, a non-descript, grey-haired woman, almost knocking her over. I ran faster than I'd ever run in my life. To the woman who had unwittingly set me free, I must have looked like a blurred squiggle, getting smaller and smaller as I disappeared down the long drive.

Freedom and adrenaline surged through my veins in a heady cocktail. I couldn't believe my luck when I saw a large delivery van on its way out of my prison. It slowed down, waiting for the heavy metal gates at the foot of the drive to open. During my interludes of freedom, I had spent a lot of time playing on vans and lorries with other children. I knew exactly how to jump on to them while they were moving and how to open their back doors. I swung inside this one. It had been delivering fruit and vegetables, and smelt of damp cabbage, at that moment the best smell in the world. I heard the gates swing open for the van; then it picked up speed and the Blue Door Centre was behind me for ever, I hoped.

As soon as I felt the van stop, I leapt out and bolted into the bushes at the side of the road. Because I'd left the van, I knew that the immediate danger had now passed, but I also under-stood that the staff at Blue Door would have immediately contacted the police, who would be searching for me. I decided that my only option was to hide. I darted through the undergrowth, celebrating my return to life in the open air, and shook myself vigorously like a wet dog to make sure that I had shed all the toxic residue of the Blue Door Centre.

The tight pain in my chest had vanished now that I was no longer imprisoned. Euphoria kicked in. I didn't imagine that many people made it out of the Blue Door Centre. Pure jubilation rushed to my head, making my brain tingle in a way no drug in the world could. I didn't care about food or warmth or comfort. All that mattered was that I was free again.

I knew that if I stayed in the area, the police would inevitably find me, but I decided to lie low in the undergrowth for a few hours before making a move. My friend Sarah, who was eighteen, lived in nearby Southampton, so I hitched a ride to her place. As soon as it was dark, I crept into her back garden, climbed up on to her porch and threw a stone at her bedroom window to attract her attention. I often called on her late at night like this, so she wasn't surprised to see me.

'You've got to help me,' I panted. 'I need to get out of the country fast. Can you lend me your birth certificate? I'll make sure you get it back. There won't be any comeback – I'll say I took it without you knowing. I've run away from Blue Door and everyone's after me. If I've got a birth certificate showing I'm eighteen, I can get myself a temporary passport from the post office and get out of here.'

She agreed without hesitation, and so the following morning her name and age, along with my photo and a forged doctor's signature went onto a temporary one-year passport, which was stamped for me with an unsuspecting smile by the woman sitting behind the post-office counter. She hardly even glanced at me to see if I really was eighteen. I walked as calmly as I could out of the post office and then whispered a triumphant 'Yes!' under my breath.

Now I had a fake passport, my freedom had taken on an entirely new dimension – I could go anywhere I wanted. My stomping ground had always been the corridors of council estates in Southampton, the woods and forest around my home or the streets of London, but I had always sensed that my future would not be lived out in England. I couldn't see myself settling down with a husband and children in suburbia behind a white picket fence. The world seemed like a very exciting place and I wanted to see all of it. Running my thumb back and forth across the tough plastic cover of my new passport, a thrill of pleasure shuddered through my veins. I knew that now I could run much, much further than ever before.

LOVE AND HATE

My mother and father's story together began with a passionate affair in 1957. In fact, their love for each other led to newspaper headlines. My father, Cyril, was a semi-professional footballer and played in various different countries. He came from a working-class background, while my mother's family placed themselves at the posh end of middle class.

Social standing wasn't an issue for either of them when they first set eyes on each other at a football match, which he was playing in and she was watching with her friends. It was certainly an issue for my mother's parents, though, and they strongly disapproved of the pair seeing each other, considering my father to be beneath my mother. My parents were young and impetuous, and convinced that love would conquer all, they moved in together. Neither of them could have been more than eighteen at the time. My father was classically tall, dark and handsome, with a reputation as a playboy, while my mother's delicate, elfin features and slender frame prompted comparisons with Audrey Hepburn. She was always immaculately and fashionably dressed, and stood out from her peers.

Very soon, though, the inevitable happened and my mother, Susan, got pregnant. My father declared that he would do the honourable thing and marry her, but in those days couples had to be twenty-one before they could marry without parental permission. There was no way that my mother's parents were going to permit the union. So fierce was my parents' love for each other that they went to court to challenge the law and won! It was 1959 and the case made it into the newspapers, which used headlines like 'Nice one, Cyril' to hail their legal victory. My parents were euphoric that the courts had endorsed their love – unlike my mother's parents, who were of course deeply unhappy. It made relations between them and my mother even more strained, although they did stay in touch.

Sadly, the baby my mother was carrying was stillborn. Next, my brother Jay was conceived. My mother was just twenty when he arrived – far too young to be tied down with a baby. A year after he arrived, on April 27th, 1961 I came along. By then, my mother had spent almost three years pregnant. None of the babies were planned, and I think that by the time I came along she was really fed up of the whole baby business. Rather than sterilising bottles and changing nappies, she wanted to be out dancing and having a good time. She had always been a terrible flirt and she missed having lots of male attention. From the start I believe that she saw Jay and me as millstones round her neck.

Apparently, I was very reluctant to come out of the womb, and arrived overdue. Perhaps I knew what was in store for me. Initially, though, there was no sign of trouble. My mother told me later that I was a wonderful baby who sat and smiled all day long.

Some of my mother's relatives came from Scotland, and my father's from France; there was also some American Indian blood on my mother's side, so genetically I was pretty mixed. I had jet-black hair, the deepest brown eyes and berry-brown skin. I always looked very striking next to other children, with their pale complexions and dirty-blond hair. From an early age I was independent and liked my own company. I amused myself by chatting away in my cot or crawling into the corners of my bedroom. My mother often told me off for climbing out of my cot because I wanted to explore.

Home was a three-bed council house in Lidgate Green, on the Thornhill estate in Southampton. It had a large garden surrounded by high walls. My mother was good at keeping house and everything was always clean and ordered with smells of bleach and furniture polish wafting through the air. We were banned from the living room for most of the day in case we made a mess.

As soon as I could move around by myself, I started to explore anything and everything. According to my mother, when I was two years old I scaled the garden wall, bursting with curiosity to know what was on the other side. The next-door neighbour happened to be in her garden at the time and screamed when a daredevil toddler teetered into view. She was terrified that I was going to tip over the top of the wall, breaking every bone in my body in the process, and so she scooped me into her arms before any harm was done.

As an attempt to restrain me, when I was two or three years old, my mother put me in reins. I remember how much I couldn't bear them and always tried to find a way to wriggle out. She often dressed me up in ribbons and bows, but as soon as I was old enough to talk and run around, I craved shorts and threadbare T-shirts. She was forever licking a tissue and using it to wipe traces of food or mud off my face. I hated her doing that and would twist and writhe to get away whenever she tried to make me look 'respectable'. Sometimes I banged my head against the bars of my cot in sheer frustration about being held in captivity.

When my father's brother got married, it was decided that I would be a bridesmaid. I'm sure that at the age of three I looked very cute in a fussy white dress with a garland of flowers in my hair, but wearing these clothes felt stiff and unnatural to me. Everyone was wearing prissy dresses and hats and pressed suits, and I wanted to get away from it all. When my mother's back was turned, I scaled an oak tree in the yard of the church where the wedding was taking place, almost losing my footing a couple of times because of my cumbersome dress. I sat hidden in the leaves and sturdy branches, inhaling the damp, woody smell. I looked at the frilly hats and carnation buttonholes bobbing around below me and decided I wanted to sit up there forever. Needless to say, this plan didn't appeal to my mother when she spotted me.

'Louise, what on earth are you doing up there? Your beautiful dress will be completely ruined. Get down here this instant.'

I thought my dress looked much better smeared with greeny-yellow lichen, but of course my mother was furious.

By this point, acid acrimony had stripped the love clean away from my parents' marriage, like a locust feasting on sugarcane. There was simply no evidence remaining that there had ever been any affection between them. Some of my earliest and most powerful memories are of violent fights between my mother and father. The sound of the hate in their voices often woke me at night.

Late one evening when their shouts had woken me yet again, I crept downstairs to try to discover why they were making such horrible noises. I was appalled when I saw them fighting with each other. I didn't realise that grown-ups did that sort of thing. I ran in, filled with shock that the two people who looked after me could be doing that to each other. Although I was only three years old, it was clear to me that they hated one another, but why? I couldn't make any sense out of it and tears sprang to my eyes.

I threw myself in between the two of them, thinking I could stop them from fighting, but my gesture was futile. My mother pushed me out of the way. I fled back upstairs sobbing. I was baffled by their behaviour. Although I was only little, I knew that something between my parents was terribly wrong. I felt completely hopeless because I was powerless to stop them. After that, I kept well out of the way when they were fighting.

Around this time my father got a hamstring injury and had to give up his football career, so took a job as an engineer on the *QEII*, which meant that he was away a lot. My mother believed that he then embarked on a series of affairs, and it's certainly true that their shaky relationship was damaged further by his prolonged absences and the awful atmosphere of mistrust.

We saw very little of my father once he got the job, and it was left to my mother to do most of the childcare. I'm sure she found it hard having to be responsible for two young children when what she really wanted was to lead a carefree existence and go out dancing until all hours. It was very important to my mother to be admired and approved of by men. Sometimes when we were out shopping, she started flirting with men she had never met before. Although I was very young, I knew that what she was doing was wrong. I didn't dare say anything because I knew she would shout at me, but I recall thinking, 'Why is she behaving like this?' During my father's absences she embarked on a series of affairs, often with the pursers and other staff from the big ships that docked in Southampton, including the *QEII*.

When my father did come home, he brought us presents. One time when he went off to sea, I asked him if he'd bring me back a box record player. I was thrilled when he returned home three months later with one securely tucked under his arm. I wasn't used to being listened to and having my requests granted, and I was overjoyed that he'd remembered something I'd asked him what seemed to me ages and ages ago.

'Oh, thank you, Daddy, thank you,' I said, flinging my arms round his neck.

He also bought me some rock 'n' roll records and I played them over and over again. He usually returned from sea with some kind of present for Jay and me. It was a real treat because my mother never bought us anything. I never felt that I was special or precious to my mother. In fact, I can't remember her being anything other than cold towards Jay and me.

By the time I was four, I understood enough to know that my mother didn't like me. I tried as hard as I could to be good, but nothing seemed to make any difference. I had no idea what I was doing wrong. I saw other mothers cuddling their children and playing with them in their back gardens. My mother never did that with us, though. We always seemed to be in her way.

One night I woke up burning hot. My throat was so sore I couldn't swallow and my head was pounding. I crept into her bed, looking for some comfort, and put my leg over hers in the hope that she would cuddle me.

She pushed me away and said crossly, 'Don't come near me.'

Her rejection made me feel a deep physical pain, as if she'd fired an airgun pellet right into my stomach. Each time my mother made it clear she neither liked me nor wanted to get too near to me I retreated a little more inside myself. After a while I stopped asking for cuddles and kisses. It was less painful not to get these things than to ask for them and be pushed away.

'I think she wishes she never had us,' I whispered to Jay one day.

He was much more timid than me and was terrified of getting into trouble. 'Don't say things like that,' he said anxiously. 'If she hears you, she'll go mad.'

When we were still very young, my mother took a job at the Silhouette Club in Southampton, first as a barmaid and then as a croupier. Later she worked in a famous Southampton nightclub called the Guinea Gourmet. Working in clubs suited my mother well. She loved to dress up, and in these places, wearing a glamorous silk dress and bright-red lipstick, with her hair elegantly coiled in a chignon at the nape of her neck, she could pretend that instead of being an impoverished mother of two demanding young children living on a council estate, she was in fact a starlet on the verge of being discovered by a film director.

And of course she got plenty of attention and flattering compliments from men in clubs. One of the men she encountered at work was called Alex. Sometimes she met him in the afternoons and dragged Jay and me along with her. I liked him because we usually went to the Wimpey and he bought us big, frothy milkshakes, which were a treat.

Once when we hadn't seen him for a while, I innocently asked my mother what had happened to Uncle Alex. My father was at home at the time and realised straight away that I was referring to one of my mother's boyfriends. My father was furious with my mother, and they had a blazing row about who had behaved worse when it came to cheating.

Whenever my father returned from sea my parents fought. They often had violent fights in front of me. I winced and cried as I watched my father punching my mother in the face. On one occasion I recall her crouched sobbing in the corner with a bloodied nose and a big bruise to one eye, which had turned black by morning. She grabbed a pan off the stove and whacked him with it.

As usual, I had no idea what they were fighting about, but I was terrified. Jay and I were crying because there was nothing we could do to stop the two of them tearing each other apart. I was sure that one of them would end up dead.

'Stop, please stop,' I cried, but they paid no attention.

I became hysterical and started to scream. It was horrible feeling so powerless. Jay was flapping in and out of the room like a chicken that had just had its head cut off. Like me, he was too young to know what to do. Both of us were wailing helplessly. In the end, the violence subsided, but I spent each day in terror waiting for the next fight, which came just a few days later. This one wasn't quite so brutal, but still left Jay and me in tears and seeking shelter in our bedrooms.

The atmosphere was always unpredictable in our house. One minute everything was quiet and calm, and the next there would be a bitter and mighty explosion. I longed to be in a peaceful place with no fighting. Jay and I spent our time tiptoeing around in the hope that we wouldn't upset anyone or trigger an outburst.

I had a little radio by my bed and sometimes put it on to drown out the shouting. At other times I crept miserably out of my bed and sat on my windowsill gazing up at the moon. I loved that peaceful, creamy-coloured disc and decided that it was my friend. In the absence of human confidants at home, I began to chat to the moon whenever it showed its face.

I became convinced that the two people who told me they were my mother and father weren't actually my parents at all. I had a fantasy that one day a fairy godmother would turn up on the doorstep and say, 'Louise, there's been a mix-up. These two people aren't really your parents at all. Here are your real parents.' At that point she would produce two kind, beaming adults who would open their arms and envelop me in a big, warm hug.

'So sorry about the mix-up,' my real mother would say.

In my mind she was a shadowy figure without a proper face, but I could make out enough to see her huge smile. The mother I lived with hardly ever smiled.

I was sure that my real parents would never hit each other or raise their voices, and that I would live a calm and peaceful life full of love. I waited and waited for my fairy godmother to turn up, but of course she never did.

I instinctively felt that I didn't belong to the parents I lived with, or they to me. I knew that I wasn't like them and didn't fit in. In a strange way, the moon became a surrogate source of comfort to me. I switched on Radio Luxemburg. 'Rock Around the Clock' was played all the time when I was small, and I climbed up on my windowsill and danced for the moon. When I sat in my room listening to my music, I could briefly forget about the misery of my home life.

One night, when I was still just four years old, instead of simply staring at the moon, I decided to try and get a bit closer to it. I had just started infant school and was far too young to be wandering around by myself late at night, but I was a fearless, curious child and the thought that I might be putting myself in danger never crossed my mind. I slipped quietly out of the back door while my parents were having yet another argument and ran through the council estate in what I thought was the direction of the moon.

As I wandered, I felt glad to be away from the shouting and out in the peaceful streets. I had no idea where I was, but it didn't matter to me. After about twenty minutes I reached a dual carriageway. A driver spotted me and called the police. I vividly remember dazzling blue and white lights heading towards me, and startled, I ran into the hedge at the side of the road.

A few moments later a police officer carrying a big torch approached me. 'Hello. It's very late for a little girl like you to be out by yourself. What's your name? Do you know where you've come from?' he asked.

I shook my head. He lifted me into the patrol car and took me around the streets asking if I recognised where I lived.

After we'd driven through a few streets, I recognised the house in Lidgate Green and pointed to it. 'That's it!' I cried.

The officer climbed out of his patrol car and knocked on the door. My father answered and turned white when he saw me standing in my nightdress with a police officer. He couldn't believe that I had slipped out and wasn't tucked up in bed. After that, my parents made sure the back and front doors were double-locked at night.

That wasn't the last time a police officer came to our house: every so often the fights between my parents were so bad that the police were called. At times, during violent rows, my mother temporarily fled the house, usually late at night, hurrying Jay and me along the dark, quiet streets with her to seek refuge at the home of one friend or another. I felt very close to the moon then as our footsteps echoed on the pavements. I decided that its light was there to guide me, and I was mesmerised by it.

One of the few happy memories I have from that time are the walks my mother took me and Jay on in the woods near our home. We went with one of her friends, who also had children, and while the two women chatted about the disappointments and miseries of their lives, we children ran off, picking blackberries and climbing trees. It was on these walks in the woods that I first began my lifelong love affair with horses. Groups of gypsies lived in the woods and they kept some of the ponies tethered to trees. Although I wasn't tall enough to stroke their heads or feed them apples, I loved patting their smooth, sleek bodies and inhaling their distinctive smell.

'Oh, please could I have a pony?' I begged my mother.

'Don't be ridiculous. Where on earth would we get that sort of money?' my mother snapped, and went back to chatting with her friend.

I tried to spend as much time as I could around the ponies. They always seemed calm and peaceful, and I was sure that they would never let me down in the way that adults did.

I think that I was born with the urge to be wild and free. I felt much more comfortable outside surrounded by the vast expanse of the sky and the dense woods than cooped up inside my parents' three-bedroom council house. Like my American Indian ancestors, I had an instinctive affinity with the natural world. I got to know the woods like the back of my hand on the outings with my mother. Little did I know, but that knowledge would become very useful to me later on.

As the rows between my parents intensified, I noticed that my mother started to meet boyfriends more frequently while my father was away. She still met Alex, but now there were others too. When she met them on a weekend or when Jay and I weren't at infant school, she had no choice but to drag us along with her.

After our usual visit to the Wimpey with Alex, we all went to a nearby hotel. My mother sat Jay and me down on a sofa in the reception area and said irritably, 'Wait here. I'll be down soon.' Then she and Alex disappeared into the lift, giggling.

We waited patiently for about twenty minutes; then I began to get restless. 'I'm going to look for Mum,' I said to Jay.

'She told us not to move,' he replied anxiously. He did everything he could to stay out of trouble and was an extremely obedient little boy.

'I don't care what she said – she shouldn't have left us like this. I'm going to find her.' I marched over to the lift and tried to work the buttons, but I didn't understand what to do and, sighing, went back to sit with Jay.

The hotel was used by sailors when their boats docked and so there were lots of slightly rough-looking men wandering around. Anything could have happened to two young children perched uncertainly on the sofa in the reception area. Wasn't Mum at all concerned? I felt upset and scared while we sat waiting for her.

'She doesn't want us, and she doesn't love us,' I said gloomily to Jay.

He didn't reply.

After an hour my mother emerged with Alex. Both of them looked slightly dishevelled and flushed.

'Right, time to go home,' said my mother abruptly, giving Alex a tender, lingering kiss goodbye. I couldn't remember her ever treating Jay or me so lovingly.

Not long after, my parents began divorce proceedings. It was even more horrible than their arguments. The first time I heard the word 'divorce' was when my father appeared at the house and told us he was moving out of the family home. Suddenly tears rolled down his cheeks.

'What's the matter, Daddy?' I asked, puzzled. I had never seen my father cry before and it looked odd seeing this big, strong man weak with emotion. I ran up to him and cuddled him. 'Please don't cry, Daddy,' I said, sobbing myself now.

He explained to me what a divorce was. I had never heard of mothers and fathers splitting up. Even though I knew mine couldn't stand the sight of each other, it seemed a very strange thing to do.

Later that night I crept downstairs because I heard my name being mentioned when my parents were having yet another argument.

'I'll keep the kids,' said my mother sourly. 'After all, I'm the one who's really brought them up. You're away the whole time, sailing on the high seas with your fancy women.'

'No, I'll have the kids!' my father shouted. 'You've never wanted them. You talk to me about fancy women, but what about all those boyfriends you pick up from the boats and the clubs? You only want the children so you can keep this council house.'

My mother raised her voice in return, but I didn't want to listen to any more. I ran back upstairs, tears springing from my eyes. All my mother cares about is the house, I thought, feeling totally devastated. Although she spent a lot of time shouting at me and Jay, it had never crossed my mind that she cared more about a property than us. Although I was sure my father loved me, I imagined that he wanted the house too.

The more I found out about the way adults did things, the less I liked them. Nobody wanted me and I had no one to turn to. If my mother and father had plunged a knife into my heart, I don't think it would have hurt as much as those cruel words. I flung myself on to my bed, too upset to switch on Radio Luxemburg or to dance for the moon. I had no idea that things were about to get much worse.

THE GABLES

The fight between my mother and father for custody of Jay and me, and therefore of the house, ended up in court. Most unusually, Jay and I were actually brought into the court-room and asked which parent we wanted to live with. I had no idea what a court was. We were led into a room with lots of dark wood panelling and a musty smell. There were a few men wearing old-fashioned grey wigs and black cloaks that made them look like bats. Everybody had very serious expressions on their faces and suddenly I felt terrified. I was sure I'd seen rooms like this on TV, and after people went into these kinds of rooms they got locked up in jail. I wanted to get out of there as fast as possible, but an official-looking woman was leading Jay and me into the centre of the room. There was no escape.

'She's an unfit mother who drinks far too much,' my father said to a man who was sitting by himself on a high bench. He was wearing similar clothes to the others but in brighter colours. I wondered fleetingly if he was playing dressing-up, but his expression was also very serious.

'And he's an aggressive son of a bitch,' countered my mother.

The man on the bench turned to Jay and me. 'Now, children, we don't always do this, but we're going to ask you a question. Which of your parents would you like to live with after their divorce? Would you like to live with your mummy or your daddy?'

The woman who had ushered us into the court whispered, 'That's the judge. He's in charge, so tell him who you'd like to live with.'

I thought the man had a kind face and had no hesitation in speaking up. 'I want to live with my daddy,' I said boldly.

There were a few murmurs in the room. I suppose most little girls would have said they wanted to be with their mother, but I was certain that my father was kinder than my mother, and I thought I'd have more chance of doing whatever I wanted if I lived with him. He was so much more easygoing. I looked across at my mother. She seemed quite relieved. I understood later that, whatever my dad had said about wanting to hang on to the house, really she craved freedom and that Jay and I were standing in her way.

When Jay was asked, he just shrugged his shoulders. He looked first at my mother and then at my father, and said meekly, 'I don't mind.'

I glanced at him scornfully. I knew he didn't want to hurt their feelings, but I thought he was mad not to speak up. 'They'll probably put you with Mum, and you know how strict she is, always shouting and complaining,' I whispered. 'You could do what you want living with Dad.'

He just shrugged and looked away.

Next, my father stood up and said that he was giving up his job at sea so that he could be closer to his children. He explained that he was taking a position at the local Pirelli tyre factory and would employ a live-in nanny to look after us if the court gave him custody.

The judge nodded. 'I think we'd better adjourn proceedings while we consider this,' he said, again looking serious. He turned to Jay and me, and said, 'We're going to take a few weeks to think about whether it would be best for you to live with your mummy or your daddy. You will become wards of court until we have made our decision. That means someone else will look after you for a little while until the decision is made.' Then he gathered his papers and stood up.

'All rise,' said a woman who was also wearing a black cape.

I thought she meant we had to float up to the ceiling. I had no idea how any of us would manage that. But everybody just stood up, kept their feet firmly on the ground and started talking to each other.

I just hoped the judge would decide quickly. My mother and father spent a long time that day talking to official-looking people.

'There are a lot of arrangements that need to be made,' said my mother, pressing her perfectly painted lips together. She didn't say anything more on the subject.

We went back home and played outside with the other children on the estate. Everything seemed very normal.

The next morning, however, my mother shook me awake. I was sure it was earlier than usual. Most mornings the light splashed through my curtains, making cheerful patterns on the opposite wall, but today all I could see was a thin, watery light like gruel.

'Come on, Louise, you need to hurry. We have to get across town by eight.'

I had no idea why there was this sudden urgency. I hated

getting up in the morning at the best of times, so I wasn't happy to be dragged out of bed before it was properly light. My mother wasn't generally an early riser either, so I knew that something important was happening. She seemed to be taking extra care to make sure I looked smart and presentable. I watched as she packed some of my clothes into a small suitcase and felt a mounting sense of alarm. I didn't like not knowing where she was taking me.

'Where are we going, Mum?' I asked, as she hurried me out of the front door.

'You're going to stay somewhere for a little while until Daddy and I sort out the divorce,' my mother said, as tears started to roll down my cheeks.

Although I was very unhappy at home, I was scared of being looked after by someone else. What if they're worse than my family? I thought.

'Your brother's going to stay with Grandma and Grandpa.'

'Why can't I go with him?' I said, the tears falling faster now. Although my grandparents were very strict, I enjoyed going to their house because they had a big garden with woods at the bottom, which I could explore without anybody bothering me. I felt very hurt that they had chosen Jay and not me. Once again a powerful sense of being unwanted washed over me. He was much more of a goody-goody, and I supposed that that was why he was allowed to stay within the family while I was thrown out to strangers.

They must think I'm really bad not to want to look after me, I thought to myself. I was very upset because I always tried to be good. Just because I loved climbing trees and running around outside didn't make me bad, did it? Adults obviously thought those things were naughty. I didn't think

I'd ever be able to understand the way grown-ups thought about anything.

My mother clamped her lips tightly shut and I knew she wasn't going to say anything more. She was wearing a line of bright lipstick, which looked as if it had sealed up her mouth.

The place she was taking me to was a bus ride away. On the journey, she sat bolt upright. As usual she looked immaculate. As the minutes went by, I got more and more scared. I was probably going to be taken somewhere terrible, and there was nothing at all I could do about it. I started to cry again. I wanted to jump off the bus and run away, but I had no idea where I could run to.

We got off the bus in a part of Southampton I didn't recognise and walked a few hundred yards to a building surrounded by black wrought-iron gates. As we walked towards the gates, I wondered if I was starting junior school. I knew about it from some of the six- and seven-year-olds I played with on the estate. They had told me that school was 'great' – much better than infants – and that they got to do really grown-up things there, like reading books and writing their own stories. There were lots of young children running around and playing outside, and I decided that I had guessed right about starting school. I felt slightly relieved: if I was just being taken to school, then my mother would collect me at the end of the day and take me home. Then I remembered that she'd packed a suitcase for me and my heart sank. I wasn't going to be coming home later today.

I was terrified by the time we arrived at the big, heavy gates. 'They're going to lock me in. Please can we go home? Please?' I looked up imploringly at my mother. 'I'll be good. I won't

give you any trouble.' I planted my feet firmly on the ground
and refused to move.

Impatiently my mother gripped my hand and dragged me
forwards through the gates. 'Come on, Louise, don't be a silly
girl. You're only going to be here for a few days and then I'll
come and collect you.'

We approached a solid black front door with a polished
brass knocker. My mother rapped it decisively and a woman
with bleached-blonde hair piled up on top of her head
appeared. She looked as if she was in her mid-fifties and
was wearing a starched white apron. I looked at her grey-blue
eyes and could see no trace of a smile.

'Hello. Come on in – no point hanging around on the
doorstep. You must be Louise. I'm Miss Billington,' said the
woman tartly. She must have seen my cheeks were wet with
tears but made no attempt to comfort me. 'Say goodbye to
your mother now. We don't encourage parents to come in,'
she said briskly.

My mother gave me a quick hug. 'Don't worry, Louise, I'll
be back to collect you very soon,' she said, and hurried off
down the path.

I looked helplessly at my mother's retreating figure. I
prayed that she would turn round and say, 'It's all been a
terrible mistake – you're coming home with me,' but she
strode off without even a backwards glance.

The place my mother had brought me to, I soon discovered
from the other children, was not a school but a children's
home called The Gables. She had never left me anywhere
before, so for the first few days I looked forward to her
coming to collect me. I had no reason to believe that she
wouldn't be back very soon.

There were lots of toys and a little playground with swings, slides and a sandpit. We were fed banana sandwiches, corned beef and lumpy porridge. I ate what I was given because my mother had always told me never to waste food. Some of the other people who worked at the children's home were nicer than Miss Billington. There was a plump, smiley woman called Brenda, who looked very old to me, though she was probably in her fifties. She often gave me a cuddle and told me to be 'a good kid'. My mother had always been very strict with us and made sure that we were polite to adults, never forgetting to say 'please' and 'thank you'. I knew how to behave and so looked at her solemnly and said, 'I know how to be a good girl. My mummy has taught me my manners.'

After a few days, when there was no sign of my mother, I started to feel really frightened. I panicked that maybe I would be confined to the Gables for ever.

'What am I doing here? Where's my mum?' I asked Miss Billington.

She shrugged and said unhelpfully, 'I'm sure your mother will be back soon. Stop being so impatient.'

Back in my room, I threw myself down on the bed and cried and cried. How could my mother have said she'd be back very soon and then not turn up? I felt as if my whole world had fallen in, crushing me so that I could hardly breathe. Although life at home wasn't perfect, at least I had some idea of what would be happening each day. Now I had no control over anything.

Every day I peered through the gaps in the wrought-iron gates at the bottom of the drive, looking for my mother, but she didn't come. Suddenly it dawned on me that maybe I was being punished for something. I knew that I loved running around outside and didn't always come inside for tea the minute my mother called, but surely that wasn't naughty enough to lead to a punishment like this. I racked my brains trying to think of what I could have done. Even though I was only little, I was sure that I wasn't a bad person, so why I was being treated this way? Then I remembered the time I'd mentioned Alex in front of my father a few weeks before. That must be why Jay was allowed to stay with our grandparents while I had been sent away. I vowed to keep my mouth shut after that. It was just too risky to say anything that may possibly be a secret in front of grown-ups. It seemed they had a lot of secrets that I just couldn't understand.

I decided that my mother was probably never going to come back for me, but I still ran to the gates every day and poked my nose through, hoping against hope that she would appear in the street in her high heels and smart coat. I was even missing the harsh line of lipstick she wore, which usually made me shudder because it looked so fake. My life at home in Lidgate Green was the only one I knew. I loved playing out with the other children on the estate, I loved looking after our mongrel dog and our two white rabbits, and I loved climbing onto my windowsill to dance for the moon. I didn't want to stay another minute at The Gables. I wanted to go home.

As I stood by the gate watching and waiting and hoping to see my mother again, tears dripped down my cheeks. My devastation was total. My mother was supposed to be the person whom I could trust most in the world, yet she had completely let me down. If I couldn't trust my own mother, who could I trust? I felt terribly alone, as if my entire life had been swept away in a flood and I had been left with just a broken body, which somehow I had managed to salvage.

After I'd dried my tears, I vowed never to cry again in front of adults, who I decided were all enemies. Miss Billington and my mother had obviously conspired between them to betray me. I presumed that the other staff at the children's home were also in on the plot. I realised that I would never again be able to trust an adult and resolved that from now on I would somehow survive by myself. I felt the betrayal very pro-foundly, and it probably shaped many subsequent events in my life.

Once I had made the decision to rely only on myself, I lost interest in playing with the other children. I decided that if I was on my own in life, at least I would know where I was, and if I expected nothing from other people, I could never again be let down. I found this thought oddly comforting.

Four weeks later Miss Billington, as unsmiling as ever, called me into her office. I trembled, wondering if yet again I'd done something naughty without realising. But she hadn't summoned me to tell me off. To my amazement, when I entered her office, I saw my father standing beside her. I couldn't believe that at last I was being rescued. I had told myself that I was unlikely ever to see my mother, father or brother again.

I flung myself into his arms and cried, 'Daddy, Daddy, please take me home with you. Don't make me stay here any longer. I hate it here.'

'Don't worry, Louise, you don't need to stay here any more. Everything's been sorted out. The judge has said that I can look after you and your brother.'

My heart leapt. All the time I had been in the children's home I'd concentrated my disappointment on my mother. The fact that it was my father who collected me reinforced these feelings further.

He smiled, wrapped me up in his arms and cuddled me tenderly. 'Sorry about all this, Louise. Everything's been very difficult while we've been trying to sort out the divorce,' he said, looking sad.

I was overjoyed to see him, but sending me away to a children's home at such a young age had had a very profound effect on me. In the moment when I had watched my mother hurrying off down the path of The Gables and over the days that followed, when I had frantically looked through the gates to see if she was coming back to collect me, something inside me had changed for ever.

I believe that children are born as open, trusting creatures holding their arms out for love. If instead of warmth and honesty and affection they receive harshness and untruths from the adults around them, a hard shell develops to insulate them from further hurt and betrayal. The greater the disappointments, the tougher the shell becomes and the more difficult it is for adults to penetrate the scar tissue beneath the protective coating. By the time I walked away from The Gables with my father, that is what had happened to me.

'NO STRAWBERRIES FOR YOU'

Jay and I moved back into the house in Lidgate Green with my father and Lynn, the woman he had employed to look after us. She was lovely. She had a two-year-old son and seemed to adore children. She was always soft and kind to me, and treated me like her own daughter. Soon Lynn became my father's girlfriend, but life carried on as normal for me. My father was contented and easygoing with Jay and me. Lynn became a mother to us, feeding us, washing our clothes, cleaning the house and chatting to us about how our day at infant school had been. I don't remember seeing my mother at all during this period.

Sadly, my happy life with Lynn and my father lasted only a few months. She and my father began to argue, and eventually she and her son moved out. My father struggled to cope with looking after us on his own, and it was impossible for him to hold down a job, look after us and run the house.

I was devastated that the calm, happy time we'd enjoyed when Lynn had first moved in was over and that once again things were uncertain. Dad went back to court to explain his difficulties. I felt a prickle of fear at the thought of being taken back to The Gables. Instead, the court ruled that Jay and I had to go into foster care until a more permanent arrangement could be made.

As we left court, my father said with a sad smile, 'I think your mother may be coming back to look after you. But not just yet. She has a few things to sort out first, so you'll be staying with different families for a while.'

'Oh, please let us stay, Daddy,' I begged. 'I'll do everything. I know how to clean up, and I can make myself cornflakes and milk. We can survive on that, can't we?'

'No, Louise. I'm sorry, love, but this is the way we have to do it. Don't worry, I'll still see you at weekends.'

My mother and father came to an informal agreement that he would see us at weekends when he wasn't working and she would have us the rest of the time.

Once again I felt as if my world had fallen in. I think my father did genuinely want to look after us but once he'd tried it he realised that he wasn't cut out to have full responsibility for us and that was why he went back to court and asked them to step in.

The next day a woman with grey hair and thick glasses knocked on our door. My father answered and I heard the two of them talking quietly in the hall.

'Louise, this is Mrs Willis. She's a social worker and she's going to take you to stay with a new family for a little while. Just until we get things sorted out. A different family has been found for your brother. But don't worry, everything will be fine. I'll be living somewhere else and your mother will be moving back in here to take care of you.'

I cried and clung to my father's legs and once again begged him to change his mind. Jay looked very pale but said nothing.

'I'm sorry, Louise. You know I'd keep you if I could, but at the moment it just isn't practical. I have to earn a living – you know that.'

Mrs Willis, who looked cold and unsympathetic, prised my fingers away from my father's legs, took hold of Jay's hand and mine, and marched us off towards the brown Mini she had parked outside. My father had packed our suitcases and he carried them out to the car.

Jay and I climbed into the back seat, and I watched out of the rear window as we drove away and my father became a tiny dot in the distance. Fresh tears trickled down my cheeks.

'No need to get so upset, Louise – you're going to a lovely family,' Mrs Willis said matter-of-factly.

I didn't like her businesslike tone, and continued to gaze out of the car window as she drove us through the streets. Everything I could see was blurred because I was crying so much. To comfort myself, I went back to my familiar daydream of my fairy godmother turning up on the doorstep with my real parents by her side.

A little while later, we pulled up on a residential street and Mrs Willis opened the car door and told me to get out. Because I was dropped off first, I didn't see where Jay was to be taken. I had been right not to trust Mrs Willis. At the front door, the mother of the family greeted me unsmilingly. I took an instant dislike to her, which intensified when I saw her carefully counting the cash Mrs Willis handed over.

'It's not much when I've got another mouth to feed, is it?' she said grumpily.

'You know that's our standard allowance, Mrs Berry. Right, I must be off – I have to drop this young man off with his foster family. Be a good girl, please, Louise, and don't cause any bother for Mrs Berry.'

I sighed. Why did the social worker assume that I would be a bad girl? I hadn't done anything wrong.

Mrs Berry introduced me to her three children and told us to run off and play. An hour later she called us for tea. She doled out plates of egg and chips to all of us, which I wolfed down because I was starving. It was the height of summer and I remember the backs of my legs feeling sticky with sweat against the plastic chair I was sitting on. For dessert, Mrs Berry began serving out bowls of plump, sweet-smelling strawberries. My mouth watered. I held out my hands to take the next bowl she passed around, but she snapped, 'No strawberries for you, Louise. The social don't pay us enough to feed you with luxuries like strawberries. You can have jelly.'

I didn't want her to see how much she'd upset me, so although my lip quivered, I managed not to cry. I sat blankly spooning the synthetic-tasting jelly into my mouth, while the rest of the family enjoyed their ripe strawberries and cream. Claire, one of the Mrs Berry's children, felt my pain and covertly slipped a strawberry under the table for me. Her kindness lifted my spirits.

Despite Claire's compassion towards me, I was relieved that my stay with this family didn't last long. A couple of weeks later I was moved to another foster family, who put me in a bed with three other children, one of whom wet the bed. I hated having to share this damp, smelly bed and longed to be back in my own room in Lidgate Green.

The eldest girl in this family was fifteen and she bullied me mercilessly, forcing me to go and steal sweets from the local corner shop for her. One time I refused and she grabbed my hand and shoved it through the gaps in a gate, behind which a ferocious Alsatian barked. Then she threatened to push my hand into the dog's mouth. I was terrified, but I was determined not to show the girl, or the dog, my fear. Miraculously the dog didn't bite me.

I cried into my pillow every night and longed to be rescued. I could see the foster families cared little for me. Life with my father at home in Lidgate Green had been so much better and I prayed that a way would be found for him to care for us. My hopes were dashed a few weeks later, when as my father had predicted, my mother moved back to Lidgate Green and grudgingly looked after us again.

My mother had tasted freedom as a single woman and had liked it, so her dissatisfaction at finding herself once again responsible for two young children was palpable. She was rarely in a good mood, and I tried to spend as much time as possible out of her way.

Our next-door neighbours Tony and Shirley were both very kind. Shirley seemed to have a good understanding of my home situation. I often played in their garden and would evidently look starved of love as she would sometimes envelop me in a big, motherly hug. Having grown accustomed to my mother's lack of warmth, I now baulked at being so physically close to another human being. I simply didn't know how to receive and process love. Instead of feeling grateful for Shirley's affection, I would stand woodenly waiting for the spontaneous embrace to end.

I felt much more comfortable with children and animals. They were more honest. With adults, I never quite knew if I could believe the words spilling out of their mouths. I imagined the words to be like snakes trying to wrap themselves round me and trip me up. The more I grew to loathe adults, the easier I found it to show animals love.

When one of my rabbits gave birth to a little pile of babies, I watched horrified as she bit the head off one. 'We've got to stop her,' I cried, trying to drag the already limp remains of the baby out of its mother's mouth.

'That's how nature works – it's all very practical,' said Tony, who was in our garden at the time. 'The mother rabbit knows she won't have enough milk to feed all the babies and it's kinder to kill the baby now than let it slowly starve to death.'

I understood that nature sometimes had to be cruel to be kind and I watched with grim fascination as the mother turned away from her lifeless baby. I wondered if my mother's apparent lack of love for me was also due to the laws of nature, but it didn't seem to make as much sense with her: she managed perfectly well to feed and clothe me; she just didn't seem to love me.

Not long after, our dog gave birth to eight puppies. Mirroring what the mother rabbit had done, my mother took four of the puppies, placed them in a wicker basket and marched next door to a neighbour who had a gas oven. The neighbour knew what to do and placed the supine puppies in the oven, wrapped them in newspaper and switched on the gas.

When I looked at my mother in horror, she shrugged and said, 'There were too many of them. The dog could never have fed them all. This was the most sensible thing to do.'

I couldn't understand how my mother could do such a thing. Surely we could have fed the puppies? I ran out of the neighbour's house, screaming, 'How could you kill those poor little puppies?'

My mother clamped her lips tightly shut and said nothing.

My love of animals also extended to rats, which I went through a phase of keeping as pets. My mother, like many people, found this abhorrent. I felt very protective of these small, efficient creatures. When my mother saw me cuddling a rat, she would try to beat it with a stick. Invariably the rat scampered off and I took the beating. So accustomed was I by now to her ways, I only felt relief that the rat had got away unharmed.

My mother also displayed an obvious preference for Jay over me, which made me feel more distant from her than ever. I remember she bought him a Chopper bike but got nothing for me. I longed to own a bike like that, but she snapped that I wasn't old enough and would probably ride straight on to a main road and get myself killed. Jay jealously guarded the bike, locking it in the garden shed and refusing to let me use it.

I don't remember Jay ever trying to protect me from my mother's sharp tongue, even though I stuck up for him when criticised. Although he was a year older than me, I was the one to protect him when he was bullied at school. I always made sure that if I got sweets I shared them with him, although he rarely did the same for me. We had never been close, but now that we had both started junior school, each day we seemed to drift further and further apart.

One day when I was nine and Jay was ten my mother saw Jay being beaten up by a bigger boy outside our house. Instead of intervening to protect her son, she said to Jay, 'Don't just

stand there like a wimp – give him a good punch on the nose.'
Jay's humiliation in front of the boy who was beating him up
was plain to see. The next day my terrified brother told me
that a couple of children who had witnessed the incident had
taunted him by repeating my mother's words over and over
again. I tried to stand up for him whenever I could, and had
been horrified that my mother could behave like that towards
her own child. It upset me just as much when she was cruel to
him as when she was cruel to me because I knew he wasn't as
strong.

Every so often we went to visit my mother's parents who
lived in the New Forest. My mother's father, James, was an
eminent professor of marine biology, and for a while had his
own TV programme. Like my parents' marriage, his own
was rather loveless. My grandmother had fallen pregnant
with my mother and they had been forced to marry. My
grandmother showed little affection to my mother. Much
later I understood that the reason my mother found it so
hard to show us love was because she had never received any
herself. Her parents had often blamed her for the misery of
their relationship.

My grandmother, a prim and proper woman with her grey
hair coiled into a perfect bun, was desperately disappointed
that her daughter had gone down so far in the world that she
now lived on a council estate. 'The children have picked up
shockingly common accents,' she complained to my mother.
'You mustn't say "ain't", Louise; it's "am not",' my grandmother chided me over and over again.

She loathed me, but she adored my polite, docile brother.
Everybody seemed to prefer Jay to me. I felt powerless to
change the opinions of all these grown-ups, and felt very hurt

they had decided I was bad, even though I was convinced I was not.

My grandparents' garden was full of wild cats, and in the garden shed that my grandfather used as an office there were all kinds of stuffed scorpions and deadly spiders like tarantulas, which he had collected on various trips to Africa. Some children might have been scared by these stiffened creatures gazing blindly at them, but not me – I loved them. My grandfather had forbidden me from touching them in case I damaged them, which made doing so when his back was turned even more thrilling.

My grandfather also had beehives at the bottom of the garden, close to the apple trees, which hung heavy with fruit in the autumn. As I walked past one day, the bees swarmed out and surrounded me. Of course I was terrified and began to scream.

'Stop screaming, it'll distress them,' said my grandfather irritably. He seemed more concerned about his bees than about me, even though I can only have been six at the time.

When one of them stung me inside my ear and I cried, he said harshly, 'Don't be such a baby.'

It is little wonder to me now that my mother showed us no affection when she can have been brought up on so little herself.

Day to day, she veered between indifference and anger towards Jay and me. Indifference was of course better because it meant we could do as we pleased. She was more likely to let behaviour she didn't like pass when she was involved with a boyfriend. Over the three years since my parents' divorce we saw a succession of boyfriends come and go, most of whom paid little attention to Jay and me.

We saw my father at weekends. Often he went to the pub with his friends and left Jay and me sitting outside on the wall with a bottle of Coca-Cola and a packet of crisps. I was always happy to see him, but because we were no longer living with him, he suddenly felt very distant. He was not involved in the daily events of our lives and was very busy with his job and his new girlfriend. A year or so after we moved back in with our mother he went back to working on ships and was away for long periods. We saw him much less frequently after that.

He had never really intervened when my mother told us off when he was living under the same roof as us, so he certainly wasn't going to start doing so now. Besides, he had little knowledge of what went on in the house in Lidgate Green. My memories of him are not unhappy, but they are blurred because the divorce exiled him to the margins of our lives.

Mostly, I associated him with treats, which my mother never gave us. On Saturday nights he often took us to a local social club, which had a family night. There was a children's room, where we could play snooker and use the one-armed bandits. I loved going there because Jay and I could play freely, while my father chatted to his friends at the bar. Nobody told us off or tried to spoil our fun, and we always behaved very well.

For her part, my mother seemed relieved that she and my father were no longer together, and that she was free to go out with other men openly. I remember that she sometimes wandered around the house in her bra and knickers in front of her various boyfriends. From a young age I knew that other people's mothers didn't do that kind of thing and I often begged her to put some clothes on.

Sometimes when Jay and I came home from school and knocked on the front door there was no answer, even though our mother was supposed to be in. We had to force open a window and climb through because her failure to answer the door invariably meant that she was in bed with a boyfriend. Often Jay and I caught glimpses of an unfamiliar man trying to scurry down the stairs and do up his trousers at the same time.

My mother's favouritism towards Jay continued, and I occasionally wondered if it was because I was a girl. She was always a man's woman, saving all her affection for the opposite sex. Even the babysitters she arranged for us when she went out to work were teenage boys, with whom she could banter. The main activity for her and the few female friends she had was the pursuit of men.

One of the things that tormented me the most during my childhood was the sight of my mother, who was terribly vain, grabbing the loose skin on her stomach, a legacy of three pregnancies, and shouting, 'Look what you've done to me, you two. You've destroyed my beautiful body. I wish I'd never had you kids,' she would continue, still pulling scornfully at the flesh. 'You've brought nothing but trouble into my life.'

She would do this frequently, both when she was walking around semi-naked and when she was fully dressed and simply wanted to show us. Apart from the chewed-up, stretch-marked flesh around her belly button, her body was perfect, but she was unable to come to terms with the fact that her once-smooth, taut stomach was gone for ever, and she blamed us for it.

In some ways, even now it feels difficult to imagine a more devastating blow that a parent can inflict on a child. Jay would go quiet, but I would become enraged. 'Don't blame us – we didn't ask to be born, and we didn't spoil your stupid stomach on purpose,' I would retort. 'You should have thought about your stomach before you went ahead and had children.'

Whenever I felt under attack I couldn't stay quiet like Jay did and hope that the whole thing would blow over. I met rage with rage. Neither Jay's approach nor mine seemed to make any difference to my mother's outbursts. I felt desperately rejected. My mother seemed to go out of her way to wound me, and always succeeded in causing me pain. It was impossible not to feel worthless as my mother lobbed more and more negative emotions in my direction.

There was never any kindness or care, none of the little treats of childhood or play time that other children seemed to enjoy with their mothers. My friends at school used to boast about the money the tooth fairy had left for them when they had placed a tooth under their pillow. When one of my teeth came out, when I was perhaps seven, I fleetingly considered putting it under my pillow but knew that my mother would never play along with the tooth-fairy game. I looked at my perfect little white tooth and then threw it as hard as I could out of the window.

I vowed that as soon as I was old enough, I would run away and live my life without adults constantly shouting at me and telling me that I was bad when I was sure I'd done nothing wrong. I didn't realise that the time to run would come sooner than expected.

MICHAEL

When I was seven, a new man called Michael crashed into my mother's life. Things were never the same again.

I won't forget the first time he walked into the house. He was a tall, smarmy man dressed in a suit and smart shoes and he spoke with an upper-crust accent, which I was to discover later was an affectation, as he had the same humble council-house origins as us. On this first meeting, I paid very little attention to him, assuming that he was just another fleeting male presence in my mother's life. He and my mother were gazing into each other's eyes and couldn't keep their hands off one another. Jay and I hung around in the background, invisible to either of them.

To my surprise, though, Michael wasn't temporary. He turned into one of my mother's live-in lovers pretty quickly when, a couple of months after I first set eyes on him, he moved in with us. Soon afterwards the lovey-dovey affection between him and my mother vanished. It was replaced with vicious rows, which often culminated in noisy love-making sessions upstairs. I didn't fully understand what sex was, but I knew it was something where the man and woman's bodies wriggle around very close together. It disgusted me, and it didn't seem to match up with all the rows.

If we had guests to stay, I was sometimes expected to give up my room and sleep in a makeshift bed at the bottom of my mother and Michael's bed. I don't know if they assumed I was asleep or didn't care that I might have been awake, but the agitated sounds and movements going on under the bedclothes made me feel physically sick. Often I used to creep to the window, hide behind the curtains and look up at the moon, urging it to give me the strength to get through the nightmare of hearing my mother and Michael having sex.

'Can you fly me away somewhere, Moon?' I used to silently plead.

My nose would be pressed firmly against the windowpane, my eyes screwed shut and my hands over my ears, in the hope that by some magical means I would be transported to a gentler, kinder place, but I remained trapped in the bedroom.

My life in Lidgate Green before Michael came along had been starved of love and lacking in consistency, but it hadn't been hell. That soon changed.

Almost as soon as Michael unpacked his suitcase, he took over the running of things and ruled the roost sergeant major-style. He had been in the military and transplanted the discipline that had been drummed into him directly into our lives. I couldn't understand the point of having so many rules. I knew it was wrong to hurt other people and I tried my best never to do that, but I couldn't understand why I had to obey all Michael's stupid rules. I secretly wished he'd stayed in the military and ordered people around there, instead of making our lives a misery.

Our shoes had to be polished until they shone, and if he

spotted even a single smudge, we had to do them all over again. He put a lock on the phone and wouldn't allow Jay or me to answer it. Even my mother wasn't allowed to use the phone. We were forbidden from taking a biscuit or even a glass of water unless Michael gave us permission. He insisted that all the tins in the pantry were lined up as tidily as privates on parade, with their labels uniformly displayed. If his perfectly ordered shelves got messed up, he yelled at us. Our shoes and coats had to be hung up neatly in our bedrooms, and if we failed to polish our shoes, we were in serious trouble when he carried out his daily inspection of them.

My mother changed. She had always stood her ground in arguments with my father and had never allowed other boyfriends to walk all over her, but there was something different about Michael. He had some kind of power over her that sapped her strength and spirit. He mixed his nastiness with just enough tenderness to keep her hooked. He employed a 'good cop, bad cop' act. Much later I learnt that this is a classic form of behaviour for men who are violent against women.

Once he'd moved in, he began telling Mum over and over again that she was worthless, and after a while she started to believe it. I hated seeing the conflict and felt very scared and helpless whenever my mother and Michael got into a fight. When all this started, my instinct was to try to get between them to stop them, as it had been with my mother and father, but I was a small, skinny, wiry child and both Michael and my mother could physically overpower me with ease. Instead, I ran to my bedroom whenever I could and clamped my hands to the sides of my head or turned the radio on loud to try to drown out the noise. I prayed every day that he would leave the house in the morning and never return, but my wish wasn't granted.

I hated to see adults fighting, and I vowed that if this was what love between men and women was about, I didn't want any part of it when I grew up.

When he wasn't attacking my mother, Michael was string- ing her along with promises of a blissful future together in which they'd move to Spain and open a pub. For a long time my mother believed the rubbish that spewed out of his mouth. Although he often spoke of the fancy jobs he was going to get, and considered himself to be superior to other people, he worked in a fairly lowly job as a coach driver.

He lashed out at my mother on the flimsiest of pretexts. Out of frustration at her powerlessness, she started to whack Jay and me. Before Michael arrived she had shouted at us all the time but she hadn't beaten us. My mother hit me across the head once and broke one of her perfectly manicured nails. She blamed me for it and after that used a wooden spoon, a stick or a belt to beat me. All three of them stung badly and made my skin sizzle with pain. I tried to dodge the blows, so my mother's chosen weapon often caught me on the back of my legs.

At first Michael didn't touch me – he left it to my mother to discipline me by hitting me – but when he saw that my spirit was not broken, he set about trying to destroy it permanently.

'You're much too soft with her,' he accused my mother. 'I'll show you how it's done.' He took off his belt and whipped me hard with it on my back. I curled up in a ball on the floor, wishing I was dead, but he didn't stop. The pain was unbearable, and even though I desperately tried to keep quiet so he wouldn't see how much pain he was causing me, I couldn't help but scream. I was terrified that Michael was going to continue hitting me until he killed me. After a couple of minutes he stopped. I was in too much pain to move and lay sobbing on the grey kitchen linoleum. When the pain began to subside, I crept up to my room. The lash wounds and weals on my back had left bloodstains on my T-shirt, which I attempted to rinse out.

After that, I tried to keep out of Michael and my mother's way, but still the beatings came. Almost anything I did was grounds for getting hit by my mother or Michael, or both. I had been given some rabbits by Tony and Shirley next door and often fed them dandelions. If I fed them at the wrong time of day, I received a swipe across the head. If my bedroom was slightly untidy or I left a book in the living room, I was hit.

I knew that none of these acts were terrible crimes and that my friends' parents didn't bat an eyelid when they did such things. As a child, the dividing line between good and bad is very clearly marked. I felt an enormous sense of injustice when I was beaten for doing things I didn't consider to be wrong. At the best of times children can feel very powerless in the world of adults, but for me, this feeling was magnified a hundredfold by my mother and Michael's cruel and illogical behaviour.

I was determined not to let them see how upset they made me, but in the privacy of my bedroom I shed many tears. I don't think a day went by that I didn't get a beating. I became an expert at detaching myself from my emotions when the blows rained down on me. I loved being in the woods and forest near our home, and while I was being hit, I tried to transport myself there in my mind, stroking the ponies I loved and climbing trees.

Mealtimes created particular flashpoints: if I accidentally

put my elbows on the table or scooped my peas up with my fork, I received a slap across the head. And Michael force-fed me liver, which he knew I hated. 'This costs money,' he would snarl, as he shoved the horrible, slippery meat down my throat, making me gag. Once he had forced the liver into my mouth, he would clamp his big, rough hand over my lips to prevent me spitting the foul stuff out. One of Michael's most common refrains was 'I bought the food that fills your stomachs, you ungrateful children.' His origins were humble and he came from a family of eight children, so he couldn't bear waste, but took his philosophy to extremes.

I found out later that my mother received benefits from social services that paid for most of what we ate. But that didn't deter Michael. Because he supplemented what my mother purchased, he monitored what was eaten with more vigilance than a guard in a high-security prison. We had to eat a cheap brand of margarine, but for himself he kept a stash of Anchor butter, which we weren't allowed to touch. He treated himself to steak and chocolate biscuits, which Jay and I weren't allowed. He even marked the butter packet, as well as the biscuits, so that he could see if one of us had used some while his back was turned. If any of us dared to use his upmarket Imperial Leather soap instead of the cheap stuff he gave us, we received a beating.

More distressing than the brutal things Michael did to me and Jay was the fact that my mother always stood by and never intervened however bad things got. One time Michael hit me so violently that I passed out for a couple of minutes. I came round lying on the floor to hear my mother saying irritably to him, 'Next time don't hit her around the head – hit her somewhere else on her body.'

While I lay on the floor, dazed, she appraised me coolly, like a joint of meat in a butcher's shop, and seemed unconcerned that Michael might have given me a serious head injury. Why did she even have me? I wondered silently, as I lay on there, holding my head to try to soothe the agonising pain from Michael's beating. However much I tried to toughen my spirit so that I could repel these cruelties, it never entirely worked. I was more deeply hurt by my mother's comments than by the physical pain Michael had inflicted on me. I curled up in the foetal position on the floor and rocked back and forth.

I couldn't understand why I was treated so badly, because I rarely did anything wrong. Whenever we were at home Jay and I felt as if we were tiptoeing on eggshells, and both of us did our best to avoid the seemingly endless wrath of Michael and my mother. Looking back, I understand that both of them were nursing enormous disappointments in their lives and were venting their anger on us. Michael dreamt of being rich and successful, and my mother dreamt of being attached to someone rich and successful. Neither of them could bear the fact that despite their greedy ambitions they remained in a modest council house doing poorly paid, humdrum jobs.

At the time, though, I understood nothing of their actions, and felt hugely frustrated that my mother tolerated the way Michael treated her and didn't stand up to him. I remember one occasion when she was cooking Michael his breakfast. He liked his eggs cooked in a very specific way; the fat that the eggs were fried in had to be flicked on top of the eggs before they were served to him. One day, although my mother had done her best to meet his peculiar request, her efforts failed to satisfy him. When she placed his plate of eggs in front of him, he inspected it critically and then exploded, his mean features contorting into even harsher shapes.

'How many times do I have to tell you, woman? I'm not putting up with substandard eggs!' His face was twisted into an expression of pure evil. He picked up the plate of eggs and aimed it at my mother. She ducked just in time and the eggs splattered against the wall, silently sliding on to the linoleum.

Instead of challenging Michael and telling him to make his own eggs in future, she remained in the position she had ducked in, probably protecting herself in case he started beating her. With Michael my mother was like a floppy, wrung-out cloth. Why doesn't she stand up to him? I wondered.

I watched the eggs lying in a gelatinous heap on the floor, and giggled nervously. Michael didn't see the funny side. He gave me a deft, brutal swipe across the head with his arm for daring to mock him. The pain took my breath away. I saw stars and the horrible buzzing started up in my head again. Even so, I was determined not to give him the satisfaction of seeing me cry. I refused to let him think he had beaten me. Perhaps this defiance came from seeing my mother and brother so weakened by his actions.

Michael would frequently accuse Jay of being 'more like a girl than a boy'. 'You're a wimp,' he'd sneer, when he saw him skulking silently around the house, desperately attempting to avoid any sort of confrontation. Despite being extremely well behaved, Jay was not spared the beatings, and so would try to make sure he was tucked away in his bedroom or out taking the dog for walks as often as he could.

Michael's behaviour enraged me, and unlike Jay, I wasn't prepared to keep my head down in the vain hope that he wouldn't notice me. I often challenged him and paid for it with more beatings than Jay received. One day I came home from school and saw him standing in the kitchen looking me up and down. I watched his lips curl as he prepared to make a snide remark, and decided to get in first. 'We don't want you here. You're not my father,' I blurted out recklessly. It was worth the beating that followed to look him in the eye and say that. I was proud to show him that he couldn't break my spirit the way he had with my meeker mother and brother. I felt it was a badge of honour that although he hurled all kinds of verbal abuse at me, he never branded me a wimp.

I had never been the sort of child who liked to sit indoors; I had always wanted to be active and busy and out in the fresh air. After Michael arrived, it became much more important to me to get away and I would stay out for as long as possible. Whatever the weather, I preferred being outside to sitting in the same room as Michael and my mother, who would argue constantly. I was overjoyed to be away from the fighting and not to have the sound of adult voices ringing in my ears and telling me what a bad girl I was. I played out with the other children on our estate or spent hours by myself walking through the woods, petting the ponies, climbing trees or nibbling berries.

I also found myself a little bolthole sitting on top of the porch that framed our front door. To get to it, I had to climb out of my bedroom window and jump a couple of feet across and down. If I'd misjudged it, I would have fallen and hurt myself badly, but luckily I always made it safely. I'd take my little portable radio and a bundle of comics, and spend hours up there. It was bliss. If Michael or my mother ever caught me, they screamed for me to climb back inside. I did as I was told, but as soon as their backs were turned, I crept back out to my safe place. On the roof, I could hardly hear Michael and my mother arguing. Their voices were drowned out by the birds' singing and the swaying of the trees in the wind. Up there, I was safe and happy, and quite literally no one could touch me.

Down below, on our estate, there was plenty of violence. Husbands beat wives, and both beat the children, particularly after the parents had had a few drinks. One day when I was perched on the porch roof reading a comic, I saw a man from the estate beating up his heavily pregnant wife. She curled into the foetal position to try to protect herself and the baby from his blows, but he seemed possessed and when she begged for mercy he hit her more. Then he grabbed hold of her ponytail and dragged her along the ground.

'Stop it! Stop it!' I screamed. 'She's pregnant.'

The man looked up scornfully and carried on beating the poor woman. I was just a little girl and there was nothing I could do. I'd seen enough violence at home and I couldn't bear to see any more. I clambered off the porch roof and swung myself back through my bedroom window. I drew the curtains tightly shut and clamped my hands over my eyes so that I didn't have to see any more.

Because Michael and my mother wanted us out of the house as much as possible, Jay and I always ended up round at our friends' houses after school to watch the children's TV programmes we loved, like *Blue Peter* and *Scooby Doo*. The TV had pride of place in the living room, but we were banned from watching it during the day. When I went round to friends' houses and watched their parents speak to each other and to the children quite normally, without yelling or raining blows down on them, I began to suspect that something was very wrong in my own home. Until I saw that not every child lived the way I did, I had assumed that every family was like mine. Certainly, many of the kids on our estate were hit by their parents, but none seemed to have as miserable a time as Jay and me.

The walls were thin in the council houses and all the neighbours could hear when my mother and Michael were fighting and when they beat us, but child abuse wasn't spoken about when I was young in the way that it is now. Although I know the neighbours could hear our screams, many of them probably accepted Michael's explanation that we were wayward kids who needed disciplining.

My friend Pauline, who lived a couple of doors away and was in my class at school, occasionally commented on having overheard the violence in our house. 'I heard you getting hit last night. It sounded bad,' she said, looking concerned.

'It's OK,' I replied, shrugging.

From the day my mother had abandoned me in the children's home, I had decided that the only way I could survive hardship was to lock all the pain away inside me. Admitting to anyone that bad things were happening to me seemed like a sign of weakness and an admission of defeat. 'Just keep your mouth shut and everything will be OK,' I kept on telling myself.

Consequently, I didn't like to confide in Pauline that my ears were still singing with pain from the blows to my head inflicted by both Michael and my mother the night before. Both of them often targeted my head when they punched me, leaving me with perpetual, unpleasant tinnitus, which I have to this day.

But Pauline was persistent, not out of nosiness but because she was worried about me. 'I wouldn't fancy having Michael as my dad. He seems like a really horrible man,' she said.

'He's not my dad,' I said angrily. 'My dad's much nicer than Michael.'

Another of my friends was called Julie. Her family always seemed calm and happy in each other's company, and her father was teaching her how to play the guitar. It would have been obvious even to a block of stone just how much her parents loved her. Seeing this at firsthand jolted me into a realisation of just how bad my life at home was. I really hadn't realised that families could actually enjoy being under the same roof as each other.

To my delight, Julie's parents offered to take me on a caravanning holiday with them for a week in Devon one year. It was just before my eighth birthday and I jumped at the chance. My mother didn't hesitate to give her permission; the prospect of having me out of the way for a while obviously pleased her.

In my memory the sun shone permanently on that holiday, though it was a shock sitting round the dinner table with all of them, seeing them laughing and talking, rather than fighting and crying, which was what happened in our house. And it was bliss not to go to sleep and wake up to the sound of shouting adults.

Julie was mixed race and our skin turned the same shade of deep brown in the sun. I had often felt the odd one out among my blonde and mousey-haired friends, but when I looked at Julie, a similar image was reflected back as the one I saw in the mirror. It was comforting. I felt so much happier in Julie's family than in my own. We fished for shrimps and crabs with little nets and played endlessly in the sand. On that holiday I felt as if I had a protective glass wall around me, making sure that nothing bad could touch me and ruin the perfection. Everyone was very friendly towards us on the caravan site and I loved being there. I prayed that each day would stretch out and last for a week.

When Julie's parents began packing up to go home, I said, 'Could I stay on here by myself? I know I would be fine. I could eat the crabs and shrimps, and pick apples and pears off the trees.'

Julie's mother laughed. 'Of course you can't, love – your family will be expecting you back home and school will be starting again soon. I'm glad you enjoyed it so much, though.'

As we drove home in the car, I felt as if a big, black cloud had fallen out of the sky and wrapped itself around me so tightly that I could hardly breathe. Julie and her parents seemed perfectly happy to be going home, but for me, it felt like a kind of death.

It was on that holiday, my first experience of living in a caravan, that the idea was planted in my head that maybe I could run away and survive by myself.

RUNNING AWAY: THE BEGINNING

School was little better for me than home. Like my mother and Michael, many of the teachers told me I was bad because I wasn't as quiet and docile as some of the other children. The teachers often said, 'You're a bad girl. Why can't you behave nicely like your classmates?' Even though I didn't understand what I'd done wrong, I had it drummed into me so often that I was a bad child that I began to think, However hard I try to be good, they keep on telling me I'm bad, so I might as well *be* bad.

A big, brass bell was rung to signal the beginning and end of the school day, and one of my earliest and most unpleasant memories of school is of being hit on the shoulder with the bell by one of the teachers, Miss Williams for being naughty. I can't remember what I had done wrong, but I soon learnt that once a teacher brands you a 'rebel', rehabilitation is very hard.

One day Miss Williams, asked each child in turn what they wanted to be when they grew up. The responses were mostly predictable – doctors, teachers, police officers.

'And how about you, Louise?' Miss Williams asked a little tiredly, raising one eyebrow. She had pigeonholed me as a troublemaker and wasn't interested in probing below the surface to see if she could work out what lay beneath.

We had recently read a story about Dr Livingstone and his exploration of Africa. I also liked the sound of Dr Doolittle, who met many wonderful wild animals and had talked with them about all sorts of things. 'I want to be like Dr Doolittle and Dr Livingstone,' I declared. 'I want to go on lots of exciting adventures in Africa and have conversations with animals.'

'That's very interesting, Louise,' she said. It wasn't the sort of answer she was expecting and she seemed surprised that I had said something so different from the other children.

During my years at primary school I found the work relatively easy and proudly brought home school reports with mostly A and B grades. I thought that maybe the fact that I could do well at my schoolwork would impress my mother and Michael, and make them love me more. When my friends received similar grades, they were rewarded by their parents with Chopper bikes and other delights. The year that I was eight I had done particularly well in my end-of-year tests and raced home to show my report to Michael and my mother.

'Look, Mum, I've done really well at school,' I said to her breathlessly as I ran into the house.

My mother took the report out of my hands as if it was something slightly soiled and looked at it quickly. 'You need to do better than that, Louise. Why couldn't you manage all As?'

Once again I was crushed. Childhood achievements are no fun if nobody praises you for them. I knew that my mother couldn't really see the point in girls focusing too much on their education. She repeated over and over again her mantra for what I should achieve: 'When you grow up, don't marry for love; marry for money. That's more important than anything else.' It was something she had tried and failed to do herself.

Life at home continued to be grim. On the rare occasions when we were supposed to have a treat, it always seemed to go wrong. One day Michael announced that we were going on a family outing to the cinema. I was ecstatic.

'Oh, please can we go and see *Bambi*?' I said when we arrived at the cinema and I saw that it was on. I'd watched it before with a friend, but I loved anything about animals and was very keen to see it again.

'No,' Michael grunted. *The Good, the Bad and the Ugly* was also on and he said he wanted to watch that and we'd just have to put up with it. He went over the ticket counter, but discovered that Jay and I were too young to be admitted. He immediately flew into a rage. 'Put them on the bus and send them home – we'll have to watch it by ourselves,' he said to my mother.

I couldn't believe he could be so heartless. Even my mother was taken aback, and for once she stood up to him. 'Don't be ridiculous, Michael. They're far too young to go on the bus by themselves. Louise is only eight. I'll take them home.' She sighed, took our hands and led us to the bus-stop.

Soon afterwards the government called a general election. All the tenants on the estate had 'Vote Labour' posters in their windows, but Michael's read, 'Vote Conservative.' I didn't understand anything about politics, but I knew that his blue sign was different from everyone else's red sign. It stuck out like a sore thumb.

'Why's he put the blue poster up?' I asked our next-door neighbour Shirley.

'Because he's a dickhead,' she replied dryly.

Meanwhile the beatings at home intensified and I became more and more miserable. One time Michael pulled down my pants and whipped me on my bare bottom with his belt. I felt ashamed and humiliated, and instinctively knew that this was even more wrong than the beatings he usually gave me. My mother stood and watched the whole thing impassively and did nothing to help me or to stop Michael's blows.

When he had finished, I cried to my mother, 'How could you let Michael do that to me? You know it's wrong.'

My mother wouldn't meet my gaze. 'Maybe if you behaved better, Louise, Michael wouldn't have to punish you so much.'

I ran up to my room and managed to hold back the tears until I had shut the bedroom door firmly behind me.

As life became increasingly bleak at home, I retreated more and more frequently to the woods where my mother had taken us for walks when we were little. With just a hop, skip and jump, I could leave behind the red-brick houses and neat paths and run around there. I loved breathing in the clean, tree-scented air and sometimes lay on my back on a carpet of leaves gazing up at the sky through a crisscross of branches. I wasn't scared of being alone there, because the woods were very familiar to me and I loved being close to nature.

I would make a beeline for the woods as soon as I'd finished school for the day, and sometimes when I didn't feel like going to school – by the time I was nine I had started to miss the occasional day of school. I always left the house in my school uniform, but I had jeans and a T-shirt hidden behind the dustbin outside our house in case I decided to bunk off. Michael found my clothes in a crumpled ball in a carrier bag one morning and went wild at me, beating me across the head for treating my clothes so disrespectfully and for playing truant.

'Don't you dare miss school again,' he bellowed. He threw my crumpled uniform at me. 'Put that on and get yourself off to school right now.'

On those days when I played truant, I'd go into school at lunchtime if I felt hungry, wolf down my school dinner, get a quick summary from friends of what had been covered in lessons – so that I could relay some basic information to my mother and Michael that evening – and then dart back into the woods. I was constantly wriggling in and out of different clothes because I had to put my uniform back on to eat school dinner. Sometimes I even wandered into other local schools at lunchtime and picked up a meal there. Once, I was challenged by a dinner lady for wearing the wrong uniform.

'What are you doing in this school wearing another school's uniform?' the plump, overalled dinner lady demanded.

'Oh, my uniform got dirty yesterday and my mum hasn't had time to wash it yet, so she let me borrow my elder sister's uniform from the school she used to go to.'

I thought that was quite an impressive explanation, though it didn't hold much water with the dinner lady. Her triple chin wobbled with disbelief, but she let me sit down with my plate of watery mince and lumpy mashed potato. I perched on the edge of a chair so that I could make a quick getaway. I had my back to her, but could feel her small, beady eyes and sharp nose trained on me. As soon as I'd filled my stomach, I sprinted out of the dining room and back to the freedom of the woods.

Petrified of the beatings and harsh words that had now become an almost daily occurrence at home, I began to stay away for longer and longer periods. At first I stayed out until teatime, then until the middle of the evening. The woods were my favourite hiding place, but I occasionally hung out on the doorsteps of tower blocks, which were much warmer than the woods. On one such evening, in the depth of winter, there seemed to be a lot of comings and goings in the hallways of the particular tower block I had chosen, so I went to find shelter in the woods for a couple of hours. Even though I tried to cover myself with leaves, I just couldn't get warm. I lay shivering until I felt it was safe to return home. Mum and Michael sometimes left the back door open after they'd gone to bed and my plan was to creep up to my bedroom without them realising how long I'd been gone. If my mother and Michael were in the middle of a noisy lovemaking session, they wouldn't hear me tiptoe up the stairs. Unfortunately, that night the back door was locked, so I threw stones up at Jay's window in the hope that he would quietly open the door for me.

My heart leapt when I saw the light go on in his bedroom. Thank goodness he's heard me, I thought to myself. Then, to my horror, I saw the light in my mother and Michael's room go on too. My stomach lurched. Instead of helping me, Jay had betrayed me; the only person who could have been my ally against my mother and Michael was on their side. Michael's face appeared at the window. It wore the same twisted, evil expression as when he beat me. I started to run away, but he quickly sprinted down the stairs, opened the door and grabbed me.

'What time do you call this?' he hissed and snarled, dragging me inside and beginning to beat me with his belt. 'It's about time that you learnt to do as you're told. Your mother and I have been worried sick. We were just about to call the police and send out the search parties.'

When he'd finished, I ran to my room and sobbed under the sheets. I was in agony. When he hit me on the back with a belt, he made large, bloody weals in my skin. Before the injuries had a chance to heal up, he would always reopen the wounds with a fresh beating. As I lay on my bed trembling with pain and fear, Michael flung open my bedroom door and marched in. I thought he'd used up all his anger and energy hitting me, but he obviously had plenty left.

'Why can't you be more like your friends?' shouted Michael. 'They don't behave like you, they don't walk around in scruffy jeans and T-shirts the way you do, and they don't stay out all evening making their parents worried sick.'

I put my hands over my ears. I had started to hum whenever he or my mother launched into one of these attacks. It worked quite well at drowning out the sound of their voices. I practised and practised until I could no longer hear the cruel things that were being said to me. I'd trained my mind to block out what was happening. Eventually he left. I had escaped another beating, but not for long.

I knew I couldn't take much more of the beatings, or the way my mother and Michael insulted and humiliated me, so I started to stay out later and later. My main aim was to avoid seeing Michael and my mother at all. When I came home of my own volition, I tried to creep upstairs while they were watching TV or had gone to bed. One evening I had gone to the woods as usual and planned to return home at around 9 p.m., when I knew my mother and Michael would be watching a film on TV, but I fell into a deep sleep and was woken at dawn by the birds singing. I felt cold and stiff, but I had survived. I was just nine years old and was proud of myself for managing a whole night in the woods. I rubbed my eyes and walked home. When I got there, my mother and Michael were standing, white-faced, in the kitchen.

'And where do you think you've been?' screamed Michael. 'The police have been searching everywhere for you. Your mother and I have been worried sick.'

'Sorry, I . . . I . . . dropped off to sleep in the woods without realising,' I stammered.

'I'd better phone the police and tell them to call off their search,' he said, rolling his eyes. He raised his hand ready to thump me on the side of the head, but I managed to dodge him and bolted upstairs to my bedroom.

After my first overnight stay in the woods, I grew bolder and began to sleep out more and more often. I did still occasionally spend the night at home, particularly when it was very cold or rainy, but if the weather was mild or the day's beating had been particularly bad, I slept in the woods and crept back home early in the morning to have a wash, change my clothes and eat breakfast before going to school. Michael left the house early and my mother was usually still in bed, so if I was lucky, I managed to avoid seeing either of them.

Michael and my mother routinely called the police to report me as missing. Children of nine out on the streets by themselves get noticed easily by adults, so I was frequently brought home by the police. They never treated it as an emergency, because I was classed as a 'habitual runaway'. Nobody panicked because they were certain I'd turn up sooner or later.

Sleeping rough sounds like a shocking thing for a nine-year-old to do, but I lived in such terror of beatings and fights at home that the woods and the doorsteps of flats in tower blocks in Southampton didn't hold the same fears for me as they did for other children my age.

As my disappearances became more frequent, a stream of social workers were called in to try to sort me out, but Michael and my mother usually convinced them that they were wonderful, concerned parents and that all the problems lay with me. Any social worker worth their salt should have realised that something has to be seriously wrong in a child's life to make them choose to flee a clean, comfortable bed and sleep rough on the cold, filthy ground, but they all seemed to accept that I was a 'problem child' who needed to be disciplined. Although I loved my freedom, I certainly didn't love the times I spent away from home when I was freezing and hungry and scared. It was simply better than the alternative.

Most social workers never asked me the right questions. They assumed I was 'bad' and concentrated on the symptoms, rather than the cause of my troubled state of mind and told me I needed to start behaving myself. By and large neither they nor the police probed below the surface to find out what was really going on in my life.

'Why are you so wild, why can't you behave nicely like other children,' was all they could think of to say to me. They didn't try to find out what was making a girl of nine run away so often. I don't believe that any child of that age would run away if they were happy at home.

There was one social worker, though, who understood. She was a kind, plump woman with bleached-blonde hair. She once took me out for a steak meal, which she paid for out of her own pocket. That impressed me because I knew it was something she didn't have to do. I think she genuinely wanted to help me.

'I can see right through Michael, you know,' she said over lunch. 'I have a pretty good idea of what's going on at home – no wonder you keep on running away.

'I don't think you're bad at all,' she continued. 'I think you're a very strong, brave little girl, not a bad one. Children are too easily labelled these days, and we social workers aren't listening properly to what they're saying.'

Although I liked this social worker, and I responded to her warmth and sincerity, I still felt I couldn't break my rules and start confiding in an enemy adult, so I nodded and smiled and said nothing. I loved being treated kindly by an adult, though; it felt like being brushed with silk.

Soon after our lunch she was moved to another department and I never saw her again. Maybe if I'd continued seeing her, I might eventually have trusted her enough to confide in her. I often wonder how different my life would have been if I had.

I was often freezing cold when I slept in the woods or the tower blocks, and sometimes used the prickly, hairy doormats that people put outside their front doors as blankets. The mats were filthy and smelly, but it was warmer lying on one with another over me than sleeping on the chilled concrete floor. I always slept on the top floor because I knew that heat rises.

Sometimes I stole bread and milk from the milkman to keep the hunger pangs at bay. At times I was almost fainting with hunger and the bread and milk were a lifesaver.

I learnt many survival tips in the woods. I realised that if I stayed very still, the animals ignored me because they didn't consider me to be a threat. I often saw wild ponies, foxes and deer. In the mating season stags can get quite violent and I was once chased by one. Another time, a bull charged at me. I was absolutely terrified, but in both instances fear made me run faster than them, and with my heart beating so hard I thought it was going to burst, I climbed up a tree to make my escape.

Sometimes when I lay down to sleep in the woods I was so exhausted that I dropped off right away, but at other times my imagination ran wild and I would be convinced that a bogey-man would come and claim me. My heart would race when I heard some creature or other snapping twigs as it made its way through the undergrowth. Like a mantra I kept on telling myself that I would survive, and that sleeping out in the open air was preferable to staying at home and being a victim of the heated, violent rows between my mother and Michael.

Some of my survival skills were learnt through trial and error. I once ate some poisonous mushrooms. They looked innocent enough and I was starving, but I was soon retching and experiencing terrible diarrhoea. I felt as if my whole body was being pulled in a hundred different painful directions and I really thought I was going to die. The ponies could see that I was suffering and shied away. It seemed like an eternity of vomiting and groaning before the pains finally started to ease. Weakly I dragged myself to a stream and scrubbed my soiled clothes as best I could. I didn't eat mushrooms for years after that. This was the only time that the natural world really betrayed me. The rest of the time I survived well in this environment.

The more I stayed away from home, the stricter the rules became about when I had to return each evening, and so the harsher the beating. Of course, the worse the punishment, the more afraid I was of returning home. It was a vicious circle. 'I got lost,' was my lame excuse when I did decide to come home and couldn't avoid seeing my mother and Michael.

While blows from one or both of them rained down on my head, I tried to fix my mind on how happy I had felt climbing a tree, or trying to make friends with the wild ponies in the woods, or rescuing an injured bird. In the springtime I hid in the bushes and watched entranced as sticky foals were born and took their first shaky steps. Those moments of nature's extraordinary beauty kept me sane.

I often felt closer to horses and ponies than to humans, and like many other youngsters who lived in the area, I used to help out at local stables and stud farms. I loved inhaling the pungent smell of horses, watching their nostrils flare and grooming their sleek manes. I first learnt to ride when I was helping out at one of these stables. A stable hand explained the basics to me, and when I climbed on to the horse's back for the first time, it felt strangely familiar, as if I had done this in a previous life and knew exactly what to do. I didn't need much teaching and soon could ride as if I'd done so for years.

When all the jobs in the stable had been done, my treat was to ride one of the horses as fast as they wanted to go through the cool woods. The trees rustled softly as we passed, and the foxes and rabbits darted out of sight until the galloping horse had passed.

The actor Richard Burton had a stud farm in the area and I often used to help out with his horses. I never saw him, but I was much more interested in the horses than in a celebrity with a chequered love life. Attached to the stable was a room for the stable workers to take their breaks and make tea or coffee. I soon learnt how to squeeze myself through the small, high window, and sometimes when I didn't want to go home, I hid outside the stables until everyone had gone for the day, then climbed back into the room and spent the night there. I loved curling up on the squishy sofa with its faded floral patterns and horsey smell, and I often slept much more peacefully there than I did at home, where I had to block out the sounds of my mother and Michael's blazing rows, which were invariably followed by noisy sex.

One night when I was fast asleep in the stables, I was awakened by the sound of a thoroughbred black Arab stallion, the star of the stud farm, kicking wildly against his stable door. His job was to sire foals, and as far as I knew, he'd never been ridden. I looked at my watch. It was 4.30 a.m. The horses didn't usually wake me at that time and I wondered what was wrong. I rubbed the sleep out of my eyes and walked tentatively towards his stable. The stallion's agitation seemed to be increasing. I wondered if someone had tried to break into his stable. Cautiously I opened the door, but nothing appeared to have been disturbed. He must have got the scent of a mare, and with that smell lodged in his wide nostrils, it would have been intolerable for him to be cooped up.

Impulsively, I decided to climb on his back and take him into the paddock. I had a reputation for jumping on horses without a saddle, but usually it was the ponies I chose to mount. I put a halter on him because I couldn't find a bridle.

Then I led him into the field behind the stables. The sky was
very black, but the moon, which had remained my friend and
confidant over the years, lit my way.

The stallion was huge, probably about sixteen hands high. I
nimbly climbed the paddock gate to mount him. I trotted him
round for a few minutes. He calmed down and seemed very
tame and easy to handle. I decided it was boring being in such
a confined space with him, and always daring myself to do
things that were a bit more dangerous and exciting, I opened
the paddock gate. Instantly he was off, racing through the
woods at breakneck speed. I was riding him bareback, so had
to cling on to his mane for dear life. It was by far the most
thrilling and exhilarating experience I had ever had. I loved
the fact that I had no control over this animal, that I had to
yield to his will. Moving through the woods so quickly made
everything look very different. A blur of branches slapped my
face, but somehow I felt no pain. The stallion was the only
thing disturbing the sleep and silence of the woods.

He never did track down the mare he had scented, and after
an hour his pace began to slow. His energy was spent, his
shiny mane was drenched with sweat, and he was content for
me to lead him back to the stables. By now the moon was
retreating, pushed aside by a deep-orange sun, which moved
boldly up the sky. It illuminated the dew that hung from every
blade of grass and made the cobwebs in the trees shimmer. I
was bathed in a sense of peace I had never before experienced,
something that can only come from exertion and when everything is as it should be in nature's pecking order.

I began to spend more time than ever in the woods. When I
was forced to have contact with my mother and Michael, I
would hear an unpleasant jangling in my brain. When I ran

around the woods, petting the animals and inhaling the scent of wild flowers, the discordant sound vanished. I began to help out every day in the stables and told the stable manager that instead of paying me for my work, I would love to have one of the foals that a mare had recently given birth to. The foals were three-quarters Arab. When one of the foals was weaned at six months, I was allowed to have him. I called him Bourbon Starlight because he was brown with a little white patch on his forehead. He flared his nostrils like a true racehorse.

This horse was the first love of my life. I didn't keep him in the stables but tethered him in the woods and fed and groomed him myself. I gave him the best-quality bran, brushed him until he glistened, and before he was big enough to be ridden, I led him round the field with a halter. I don't think any horse could have been better cared for or more loved than Starlight Bourbon.

When winter arrived, it was important to me that he had the most nutritious hay. There were several inches of snow on the ground and the local farmers had all sold out of hay. I cycled fifteen miles in the snow to find a farmer who still had hay for sale, and then cycled all the way back with the gigantic bale balanced precariously on my back. I didn't have any gloves and by the time I returned to the stable, the skin on my hands had frozen to the handlebars. Prizing them away was pure agony, but it was worth every icy, slushy mile that I'd cycled just to see my beloved horse munching so contentedly.

Starlight Bourbon and the rest of the natural world restored some sort of balance to my soul and gave me the strength to deal with all the pain in my life. Now that I had my horse, I rarely slept in the tower blocks and usually passed the night in the woods or on the sofa in the stables. When Michael and my mother grounded me, I simply wriggled out of one of the windows, determined to be free again. Once, I even tried to get out through the cat flap, but it was too small for even my slight frame and exceptional skill at bending myself into different shapes.

The police continued to pick me up when I ran away and would call my mother to come and collect me. Dressed in her smartest clothes, she would come down to the police station and sob, 'I can't handle her. She's so wild, Officer. She comes from a good, loving home, so I don't understand why she's behaving like this. As soon as your officers pick her up and I take her back home, she's off again. Her brother doesn't do anything like that, so it can't be to do with the home environment. She's well-fed, well-dressed and well brought up. I'm really at a loss.'

Sometimes Michael accompanied her. He put on his fake upper-crust accent and made the same points as my mother but much more forcefully. A procession of different officers would nod sympathetically at their plight and make absolutely no helpful suggestions. Being apprehended by the police and returned to my mother and Michael never deterred me from running away again. In fact, it made me even more determined to escape.

Although I ran away continually, I still went to school most days, though I often felt I was learning much more about nature, the seasons and how to survive from my time in the woods than I could ever have learnt if I'd spent twenty years sitting behind a desk in a classroom.

By the time I was ten I was becoming more independent.

The more unloved I felt at home, the more determined I was to make my own way so that I didn't have to ask Michael or my mother for anything. But I was so focused on avoiding the beatings at Lidgate Green that I was caught completely off guard when something terrible happened to me just yards from home.

THE MILKMAN

As part of my plan to be more independent from my mother and Michael, I was forever looking for odd jobs. There weren't many that a child of ten could do, so I was over-joyed when I got a job working for a greasy old milkman with one ear called Jim. I had to get up at 5 a.m. every day, but I didn't mind. Working and earning money made me feel very grown-up, and if I hurried from one doorstep to the next with the bottles of milk under my arm, I didn't feel the cold.

A boy called Patrick also worked for Jim. Patrick and I got along well, and the time passed quickly as we made jokes to each other and told stories. Jim didn't seem to mind the two of us chatting away as long as the milk got delivered. I liked Jim because he had given me a job and was paying me money, and he seemed very easygoing.

One morning Patrick was ill and didn't come to work. All morning Jim kept staring at me and I sensed that something was wrong. I had no idea why he was looking at me that way, but I felt very uneasy. He said little and I wondered if he was annoyed with the way I was doing the work and was about to sack me.

At the end of the milk round, as usual Jim and I went to a storeroom on our estate to drop off the crates. I had gone to the room many times with him and Patrick. It was a damp, windowless room with a cold stone floor covered in dust. When the crates were piled up, there wasn't much space to walk around. My job was to pile the crates against the wall. I was stooping to pick them up and stack them neatly when suddenly I heard a key being turned in the lock. I froze. Why on earth would Jim want to lock the door? I didn't know what he was planning to do, but I knew instinctively that I was in great danger.

My heart pounding in my ears, I turned round suspiciously. He was walking towards me slowly and deliberately, and was breathing very fast. He began tickling me and laughing as if he was doing the funniest thing in the world. I wasn't laughing at all and kept trying to dart out of his way.

'Stop messing about,' I said crossly.

I couldn't understand why he was behaving so strangely. He had never done anything like this when Patrick was around. Next, he started rubbing his old, slack body up against me.

'Get away from me!' I screamed.

I was more scared than I'd ever been in my life. When Michael and my mother beat me, I was terrified, but at least I knew what was coming. Locked in the storeroom with Jim, I had no idea what was going to happen next. All I knew was that it was something very bad and something that he shouldn't be doing.

Roughly he pushed me up against the wall. I could smell stale cigarettes on his dirty clothes and feel his foul breath all over my face. He unzipped his trousers and pulled my knickers down, then tried to force his penis inside me. In agony, and sobbing now, I fought and struggled and tried to bite him. My heart was beating very fast. I had heard plenty of stories about bogeymen and thought he must have turned into one.

I continued to struggle and cry, and as he couldn't hold me still long enough to do what he wanted, he ended up rubbing his penis against my stomach, grunting and pushing faster and harder. Eventually he stopped, hurriedly fastened his trousers and strode towards the door. A revolting sticky substance like snot was dripping down from my belly button. He unlocked the door and then turned to look at me scornfully. I was trembling with shock and was frozen to the spot.

'Don't you ever tell anyone what happened,' he said, narrowing his eyes. He walked back towards me and gripped my arm tightly to emphasise that he meant what he said. 'In any case, you're just a kid, so no one would believe anything you say. If you ever tell anyone about this, you'll end up going to prison – that's if I don't kill you first.'

He walked back out to his milk float looking as if he hadn't a care in the world, while I pulled up my knickers and jeans, still shaking with fear. I knew nothing about men and sex, so didn't understand what had just happened. All I knew was that it was something horrible and that I was going to make sure it never happened again. I wished I had someone I could ask for an explanation of what he'd done – did all men behave like that or only some of them? – but I had no one. I knew that most children would have run to their parents, but I was sure that my mother and Michael would either not believe me or blame me. Either way, I would end up getting a beating. I couldn't think of anyone else I could confide in, and in any case I was terrified that Jim would carry out his threat if I did tell anyone.

I sank to the floor, still too shocked to move. I had a strange sense that somehow I had had a lucky escape, and that if he had succeeded in ramming his revolting penis into me, he would have caused me some terrible internal injury. I shivered, feeling very alone. Eventually I wiped away my tears and found the strength to stand up and struggle home. I was desperate to get into the bath and scrub all traces of him off my body.

When I got back, Michael had thankfully left for work, my mother was still asleep, and Jay was getting himself ready for school. I walked past him without saying a word and locked myself in the bathroom. I ran a steaming-hot bath, climbed in, then lay back and shut my eyes.

I couldn't believe that Jim, who had always been so pleasant to me, could have suddenly turned into a monster. I vowed never to be alone with a man ever again. I decided that there wasn't a single trustworthy adult in the world and that most of them stuck together against children like me. Nearly everyone that I knew had betrayed me in some way. I still liked our neighbours Shirley and Tony but because I was away from home so much I rarely saw them now.

The only person you can rely on is yourself, I said to myself over and over again. For some reason it comforted me. I picked up a scrubbing brush and a bar of soap, and scoured my skin to remove Jim's sour breath, his fetid sperm and stale sweat. Every now and again I burst into tears, but eventually I felt I had no tears left.

I climbed out of the bath and wrapped a towel tightly round my body. Now I know exactly what these penis things are and that they can inflict pain, I thought to myself, I'll have to learn how to avoid them in future.

I never wanted to see the clothes I had been wearing again, so I threw them in the bin. I put on a clean pair of jeans and a new T-shirt. If I don't look like a girl, maybe I'll be safer, I thought. Choosing the most boyish clothes I could find, I pulled on a dark jacket and pushed a cap firmly down over my head, hiding my long, dark hair.

I was keen to get out of the house before my mother woke up and so headed for the woods. I fed the ponies some apples and laid my cheek against one of the mares, breathing into her mane. I knew that she would never let me down.

I never went back to work for Jim, and whenever I saw a milk float in the street I ran away as fast as I could in case it was his. After the attack, I suffered terrible nightmares. They were always the same: I was running through the woods and Jim was chasing me, but some invisible force was slowing me down, preventing me from getting away. Every time I looked round Jim was getting closer and closer, and I'd cry out, 'Stop! Don't hurt me. Please don't hurt me,' but it made no difference.

Sometimes my nightmares would stop, and I'd think I was getting over what he'd done to me, but after a while they always returned. I had managed to scrub all traces of Jim off my body, but I couldn't shake him out of my soul.

STANDING UP FOR NIGEL

In the weeks and months following the assault, I regularly began getting into trouble at school. Consequently, I tried to stay away as often as I could. At the time, I didn't understand how traumatised and unsettled Jim's attack had left me because I'd tried my best to shut it out of my mind. Why can't I get over it? I wondered. The attack had made me angry not just with Jim but with all adults. I completely gave up trying to please them, and tried to get as far away as possible. I felt completely let down by them and thought they had no understanding of all the hurt sloshing around inside my head like a deep, muddy puddle.

At primary school, I had only played truant occasionally, but as I moved into secondary school, I was absenting myself regularly. Older children are much less visible on the streets than younger ones, so the older I got, the more able I was to blend in with the crowd. I had also become more streetwise about hiding from people in authority and was rarely spotted.

The more the authorities battled to get me to stay in school, the harder I tried to avoid being there. My repeated absences made the teachers begin to threaten me with expulsion. If they wanted to encourage me to come to school and learn, it seemed like a peculiar way of going about it. Not to have to go to school was, after all, exactly what I wanted. As soon as I realised that certain kinds of behaviour would get me thrown out of school, I tried to dream up as many escapades as possible to get myself expelled.

Inside my head, something had snapped. I was getting angrier and angrier at the way I had been treated. I was so used to being beaten by Michael and my mother that I barely noticed all the wounds and bruises on my head, back and arms. They had become as much a part of me as my hands and feet. Even so, I vowed that they were not going to beat me any more and I was determined that no man would ever do to me what Jim had. I didn't know how to explain how hurt I was feeling inside, and in any case I had no one to explain my feelings to, so all the pain inside my head came out in various forms of rebellion. I had often said to myself that there was no point in trying to be good when everyone told me I was bad. Now I took this idea even more to heart and went out of my way to cause trouble. I'll show them what bad is, I said to myself.

When I was twelve, I started to play more elaborate pranks at school. One day I was in an after-school detention with a boy called Mark. We whispered and giggled together and hatched a plan to saw off the legs of the chair the headmaster sat on in morning assembly. The headmaster was a bully and a tyrant, and was unpopular with staff and pupils alike. His manner was pompous, and he demonstrated few signs of humanity. The prank seemed like a way of humiliating him the way he had so often humiliated so many of us.

When Mark and I were released from detention, we crept into the woodwork room and collected a saw. Then we tiptoed into the assembly hall and climbed on to the stage where the headmaster sat. Gleefully we sawed almost through the legs of his chair. It looked intact, but we knew exactly what would happen as soon as he lowered his bulky body on to it.

The next morning Mark and I were uncharacteristically punctual for school. We filed dutifully into assembly with the other children, our stomachs fluttering with excitement and anticipation. After we had all walked to our seats, he nodded to everyone to sit down and he did the same. Immediately his chair collapsed and he landed in an ungainly heap on the floor. The pupils and the teachers roared with laughter.

Instinctively he knew that I was behind this stunt. When he'd picked himself up off the floor, he yelled, 'Louise, into my office now.'

Once there, he grabbed his bamboo cane and started hitting me on the hand. His face reddened with exertion, and he looked as if he was enjoying every moment. I was determined not to give him the satisfaction of letting him win. I wrestled the cane out of his hands and used it to hit him all over his body. I was like a wildcat, too quick and strong for him to subdue. He yelled for his secretary, and between them they finally managed to wrest the cane from my hands. Then the police were called. Before they arrived, I grabbed his typewriter and flung it at him. It missed and went through his office window.

'You're expelled!' he yelled at me, trying to regain some authority over me.

'Good!' I shouted, and flounced out of his office.

That night I slept in the woods, knowing that I would receive a particularly vicious beating if I went back home. The

next day hunger forced me home. The police and the school
had contacted Michael and my mother, who beat me black
and blue. Despite the beating, I was relieved to have been
expelled, but it wasn't long before the education authority
sent me to another school and the whole circus began again.

Because of the countless beatings I had received at home, I had
developed a strong instinct to protect the underdog. If I saw a
child being bullied, I waded in, often fighting with the
oppressor because I knew that the weaker child was unable
to stand up for himself. Bullies had always disgusted rather
than scared me.

At my new school, there was a child called Nigel who had
Down's syndrome. He was a sweet and gentle boy, and smiled
all the time. Although he couldn't join in with everything we
did, we all felt very protective towards him. He was an
extremely innocent, affectionate child, and he always hugged
me and gave me kisses. He was small for his age and had
blond hair. Even the really tough, thuggish boys melted a bit
when they saw Nigel because he was one of those angelic
children whom it was simply impossible not to love.

We were upset when we discovered that Nigel was being
moved from our school to an institution, particularly when
rumours spread, which we never managed to substantiate,
that he was going to be given electroconvulsive therapy, or
ECT.

I felt really strongly that Nigel shouldn't be moved to an
institution, especially if there was a chance he could be treated
badly. It just didn't seem fair. I knew that grown-ups went on
strike when they were unhappy about conditions in their
workplace and I couldn't see why children shouldn't do the

same if they had a grievance. As soon as an idea came into my head, I wanted to carry it out. The very next day I made some placards from cardboard with 'Save Nigel' on them and brought them to school.

I never sat back and considered the consequences of anything I decided to take on. Organising a school strike on behalf of Nigel was no exception. I knew that I needed to find the quickest possible way to gather all the pupils together so that I could put my plan into action. The fastest way to do this was to set off the fire alarm. It was very easy smashing the glass and pressing the red button. The pupils filed out obediently, along with some of the teachers, and waited in the playground. I knew I had to be quick before the teachers realised that there was no fire and herded everyone back into the classrooms, so I ran to the front of the crowd of pupils and shouted, 'Hey, everyone, you all know about Nigel, the Down's syndrome boy, who has been told he can't come to our school any more?' Lots of children nodded their heads and I handed out the makeshift placards to them. 'The only way we can save him is if we go on strike right now.'

The teachers watched open-mouthed. Lots of the pupils cheered and followed me as I sprinted out of the school gates before any of the teachers could stop me. About a hundred pupils joined me. The rest decided not to risk it. I felt exhilarated that I'd managed to get a respectable number of pupils to walk out with me. It felt well worth the trouble I knew we'd all get into.

Sadly, the uprising failed to keep Nigel at the school, and all the pupils who had walked out got a detention. Apparently, ours was the first school in the country to stage a strike. Not to be deterred, we then found out which institution Nigel had been taken to and a few of us went down there at the weekend in the hope of kidnapping him and bringing him back to school. We were caught by staff before we found him, though, and promptly shooed off the premises. I was despondent that our mission had failed to liberate Nigel, but I comforted myself with the fact that at least I had tried my best and hadn't just stood and done nothing. I thought about Nigel often and prayed that he wasn't being treated too badly in the institution.

Despite having been expelled from my last school, I still didn't bother turning up to school very often, though I would generally wander back in for lunch because I was ravenous or wanted to see my friends. Some of them were deaf children who had been placed in a special unit at the school. The teachers tried placing me in that unit, thinking that I might do better there than in the mainstream part of the school. Although this wasn't an appropriate place for a hearing child, they didn't know what else to do with me. While there, I became friends with the children in the unit and felt very lucky that I was able to hear and didn't have any disabilities. I watched them struggle to pronounce words and felt for them when only grunts came out. While I was in the deaf unit, I watched out for them in the playground because they sometimes got bullied.

After a few months I was expelled from that school too for truanting, but continued to pop back for lunch and to check up on my friends from the deaf unit whenever I saw them. I wanted to make sure they were surviving the rough and tumble of the playground jungle, and if I saw anyone bullying them, I confronted the bully and made them back off.

At the third school I was placed in, some of the teachers were particularly nasty to me. I pretended not to care, but inside I felt very hurt. Nobody liked me, and although deep down I longed for someone to show me love and kindness, on the surface, I came across as very tough.

The cookery teacher did her best to humiliate me in lessons. I was not a natural cook and she watched me like a hawk so that she could criticise me whenever I messed things up.

'Goodness me, no, no, no, Louise, we certainly don't rub fat into the flour that way. It'll taste like a lump of lead. A light-fingered touch is required, like so.' She demonstrated smugly with her own mixture, then with a floury finger walked back to me and poked me in the chest. 'Do you understand now, Louise?' She was talking to me as if I was a baby, and my classmates were tittering.

I couldn't bear to be humiliated and told I was no good. It had been going on for too long. I'd already broken three eggs into a bowl, ready to add to the fat and flour mixture, so I picked up the bowl and tipped it over the teacher's head. Now the pupils laughed at her instead of me.

I was expelled again, but it was a huge relief. I felt wretched at school. When I spent time in the woods, at least I didn't feel like a complete failure.

By this time I was thirteen and the council had run out of schools to send me to, so officials brought in a series of private tutors for me. Like Michael and my mother, they weren't interested in supporting or encouraging me, just in shutting me up and getting me to behave.

Various educational psychologists were wheeled in alongside the tutors. When they gave me basic tasks suitable for a young child, like pushing different-shaped blocks through the

corresponding holes in the lid of a container, I pretended that
the task was beyond me. I felt totally powerless and it was the
only way I could think of to assert some control. With a stupid
expression on my face I tried and tried to shove the square
brick through the round hole. The educational psychologist
diligently scribbled notes, apparently fascinated by my struggle to perform such a simple task. My behaviour did nothing
to help the professionals work out the real me. All of them
failed miserably to identify the turmoil inside me. I had no
respect for anyone in authority, no intention of confiding in
them, and resisted their attempts to control me.

At the time I didn't understand just how much life in a
violent, loveless household and the terrifying attack by Jim
had affected me. The belief I had developed when I'd been
abandoned by my mother in the children's home at the age of
four – that I was on my own in the world and that nothing
mattered except survival – had been reinforced over the years.
Jim's attack had been the final straw. The more hurts that
were heaped on me, the deeper the real me became buried
under my protective shell. I pretended I was a tortoise, able to
take refuge inside a very robust outer layer whenever I needed
to. But although I gave the impression that I was as tough as
old boots and didn't care about anything, the defensive
coating I had built up was in reality more akin to eggshell
than tortoiseshell. Acting hard didn't stop me from hurting
when my mother or Michael beat me or when a teacher said
something demeaning.

Because of my profound distrust of adults, I felt I couldn't
risk telling anyone what was really going on at home in case
they ran to Michael and my mother and told them what I'd
said. I knew that if Michael and my mother found out I'd been

talking to professionals about all the beatings, they would beat me more, so I kept my mouth shut.

When the more timid tutors failed to make any headway with me, some giving up after a day, a retired policeman with red, mottled skin was wheeled in. His sparse strands of grey hair were combed peculiarly across his head, his bushy moustache twitched constantly, and he bellowed rather than talked, spraying saliva at anyone in the line of fire.

'I don't need a shower,' I said, glowering at him.

'You will do what I say, you bad, wilful child,' he spluttered.

I sat and stared calmly at him and refused to even lift my pen. He thought he could break my spirit and slapped me across the knuckles with an old-fashioned wooden ruler. I was well used to this kind of treatment and began to hum in a long, low monotone. The more he hit me, the louder I hummed.

'Leave me alone, Hitler,' I snapped.

'You are not going to win,' he said, saliva splattering through his teeth.

But I did. After a week he was gone.

What none of the professionals brought in to tame me seemed to understand was that the more they screamed and shouted, the less headway they made. They thought that by shoving a pen into my hand they could force me to write, but it didn't work like that for me. My anger towards adults was mounting, and it was about to make me do something I would regret.

FIGHTING BACK

I had got into a routine of coming home during the day, when I knew Michael would be at work, to grab some food and have a bath. I had just climbed out of the bath and pulled the plug and was wrapping a towel round myself when I heard a key turn in the front-door lock. Somehow I sensed it was Michael, but I couldn't jump out of the window and slide down the drainpipe naked, so I hurriedly dried myself and threw some clothes on in the hope that he would stay downstairs and not realise anyone was at home. I thought that once I was dressed I could escape out of the window. Unfortunately, he heard the sound of the bath-water emptying and knew straight away that I was at home.

The bathroom door burst open and Michael, red with anger, stood in the doorway. I stiffened. It had been a while since I had had a beating from him, because I was so rarely at home when he was.

'I'm not going to let you beat me again. I'm not,' I said defiantly. 'I'm thirteen years old now and I'm getting strong. You can't crush me the way you did when I was a weak little girl,' I added under my breath.

Michael strode triumphantly towards me. 'You, you,' he hissed. 'I've been waiting for you to come back. Using the place as a hotel, are you? After all your mother and I have done for you, you ungrateful girl. What you need is a real beating. I'm going to make sure your backside is so sore that you won't be running away again for a very long time. It's about time you did as you were told.'

'No, Michael, no,' I said.

Just then, from nowhere, every beating I had ever received from him flashed through my mind. It was like my brain was replaying all the times that blood had poured from me. The red was blotting out everything, and I was deafened by the sound of my screams from the countless times he'd hit me. Then an image of Jim came into my head. He was forcing himself on me and splattering his sticky sperm over my stomach. I felt like a volcano that was about to erupt.

Now, Michael advanced towards me and began kicking and hitting me violently, but as he did so, I was suddenly filled with an almost superhuman strength. It was time to pay him back for all the pain and suffering he had inflicted on me.

'Not this time, Michael,' I said determinedly. 'I'm never going to let you beat me again.'

I had never retaliated before and it took him by surprise. Like a coward, he started edging backwards out of the bathroom. I kept advancing towards him and he kept on taking steps backwards. He looked small and pathetic. He was standing uncertainly at the top of the stairs, facing me but hardly daring to look me in the eye. Determined to teach him a lesson, I started kicking him forcefully in the legs and stomach. Neither of us realised how close to the top of the stairs he was standing. Suddenly he lost his balance and tumbled all the way down to the hall below. I was horrified – it hadn't been my intention to make him fall.

At the bottom, he clutched his back, screaming, 'What have you done to me, you vicious bitch.'

At that moment my mother returned home from the shops. She raced to Michael's side. 'Oh, my God, what's happened to you?' she said, rubbing his back.

'It's her,' he groaned, waving his finger at me as I came down the stairs. 'Call the police. Look what she's done. I've had enough of this. Either she goes or I do!'

My mother looked nervously from me to Michael and back again.

'She's destroying our lives,' he insisted.

'OK, OK, we'll have to make arrangements for her to go into care,' said my mother, almost in a whisper.

Despite her treatment of me, I couldn't believe that my own mother had chosen her violent, mean-spirited boyfriend over her own daughter. Although I loathed her and knew that she loathed me, her words were like a bullet piercing my brain. Usually I managed to conceal all my tears from my mother and Michael, but now I couldn't help myself. I sank on to the floor and cried so hard I thought I was going to empty out all my insides. At last it was official. My mother didn't love me or want me. I felt broken and didn't even have the strength to run away. I knew that this was the end for me and her. I sat on the floor crying while she phoned the police.

As I waited for the police to arrive, I vowed that I was never going to set foot in the house again and that somehow I would find a way to survive without popping back for baths and food and the comfort of my bed. The police came ten minutes later with two social workers. All of them had sad, serious expressions on their faces as if someone had died.

It was discovered that Michael had slipped a disc. Luckily for me, the police weren't prepared to accept that I'd tried to kill him.

'Something needs to be done to control that girl,' Michael kept saying, pointing his finger menacingly at me.

I sat down with them and tried very hard to transport myself mentally out of the room. Inside my head, I could see the peaceful woods with the ponies tethered to a tree and the overhanging branches, which sheltered every living thing that moved.

The adults decided between them that I should be sent to an assessment centre. It was explained to me that it was a kind of children's home where the most suitable care plan for me would be worked out. It sounded alarming, but I told myself that I could just run away to the woods again.

'OK.' I shrugged and couldn't think of anything else to say.

The social worker made a phone call to the assessment centre, and the person on the other end of the line said they could bring me in right away. My fate was sealed.

The assessment centre was a dreary place. It had a lounge with battered sofas in it and about ten children, who were similar ages to me and looked as miserable as I did. There didn't seem to be much assessment going on. For the first couple of days I was left to my own devices and spent a lot of time playing football with the other kids.

'It's crap here. This is the third time I've been in,' said one boy with short, spiky hair. 'They're so know-it-all, those social workers, but they know nothing. They just keep moving us around the system like parcels nobody wants.'

On my third day there I was on my way out to play football with the other kids when I noticed that some of them had started taunting one of the residents of an old people's home next door. I was furious with them for picking on this vulnerable old lady and called them away. 'Stop taunting her. What harm has she ever done to you?' I shouted over.

I walked towards them and was amazed to see one of my former deputy head teachers, Miss Bander, sitting with the old lady. She had been failing miserably to control the wild children who had surrounded the old lady. I assumed she must be Miss Bander's mother. The children left the old lady alone after I'd intervened, and I walked away and thought nothing of it.

The next day, however, Miss Bander turned up at the assessment centre and asked to see me. Oh, no, here we go again, I thought. She's going to accuse me of being the ringleader and insist that the head punishes me.

Usually children were sent to the main office for punishment, but I was ushered into the lounge, where Miss Bander was waiting for me. She wasn't accompanied by a member of staff from the assessment centre and I couldn't understand what was going on.

'Hello, Louise. I'm here because I wanted to thank you very much for defending my mother against those hoodlums yesterday. I really do appreciate it. I don't know what might have happened to her if you hadn't been there. I was certainly unable to control them. I saw how you stood up to those bullies and I was extremely impressed.'

'No problem.' I shrugged. 'I don't like to see weaker people being bullied.' Relief flooded through my veins that I wasn't about to get a big telling-off. Miss Bander sounded very genuine, and despite my vow never to trust an adult, I couldn't help getting a very unfamiliar, warm feeling inside.

She hesitated for a moment and then handed me a beautiful picture of a horse and some books on equestrianism. 'I know you were always running off to spend time with the ponies in the woods at school, Louise, and I thought you might like these.'

She had obviously put a lot of thought into choosing these things for me and I really appreciated it. 'Thanks, Miss Bander,' I said awkwardly. 'These are great.'

She smiled. 'Louise, I know you've had a bad childhood, but you've proved to me that you are not a bad girl. I really do hope you can sort yourself out.' She gave me a quick hug and left.

I was very touched. It was the first time I had ever heard a teacher say anything positive about me. Every human being loves to be praised, and I was no exception.

A couple of weeks later, when the gate to the assessment centre was left open, I ran away and slept in the woods near my home. I found myself a job strawberry-picking on a nearby farm and earned enough money to buy some food. Nobody seemed to be looking for me. I think the staff and the police expected assessment-centre children to run away. I was over-joyed to be free and didn't mind if I got caught again because I knew that wherever they put me I would find a way to escape.

My desire to rebel had not diminished now that I had been excluded from school and shunned by my mother. One time I found a pony tethered on a chain. I decided, impulsively, to unchain him and put together a makeshift halter from a rope. Once I'd climbed on to his back, I rode him through the field and, soon becoming restless, thought I'd pop in on one of my friends, who was at one of my old schools. When I arrived there, I galloped him round the school playing field in full view of the children in their classrooms. I could see through the windows children getting up off their chairs and craning their necks to see what was going on. When the pupils realised it was me up to my usual wild tricks, they all started cheering. I had certainly succeeded in livening up their lessons.

I could see the teachers trying, and failing, to restore order. One of them screamed at me through the open window, and then three teachers and the headmaster, Mr Bromley, came out on to the playing field. I disliked this head teacher even more than the previous one whose chair legs I'd sawed through.

I said coolly, 'I thought the children would like to see some living nature, instead of being stuck with all the dead words and pictures in their science textbooks.'

The headmaster spluttered but was unable to come up with a suitable putdown. 'Get out, get out. I'm calling the police,' he said. His face was getting redder and redder, and his already rotund belly seemed to be swelling. I wondered if he was going to pop.

'Come and get me,' I taunted them.

I was sat still on the pony. As they approached me, I galloped off and jumped the fence. But once again my freedom was short-lived.

ROCK AROUND THE CLOCK

By now the police usually knew where to find me when I ran away. Sometimes they spotted me when I was walking through the streets of Southampton, sometimes sheltering under my favourite tree in the woods, and sometimes curled up on a doorstep of a council flat late at night, where I'd be sandwiched between two prickly doormats. Whenever they found me, I was sent off to a children's home, as it had been agreed that the relationship between me and my mother had broken down to such an extent that we could no longer live under the same roof. I thought often of my mother's decision to choose Michael over me. Every time I thought of it I got a sharp pain in my stomach, so I tried to push it out of my thoughts whenever it presented itself. Even though I tried to pretend that I didn't care what my mother did or said to me, I was desperately hurt.

My spells in children's homes were generally short, and in my memory they have become one extended event. I recall some of the children who were in the homes far better than the homes themselves. I will never forget a fourteen-year-old girl called Melanie, who had been repeatedly raped by every male member of her family from the age of six. She had lost all sense of fight, and when boys from the children's home and sometimes male members of staff led her off into a quiet room to abuse her further, she acquiesced without a murmur. She reminded me of a doll rather than a human being.

My natural reaction to being used was to fight back, and I begged her to do the same. 'Don't let them do that to you, Melanie. Say no and run away,' I urged.

She just looked at me blankly and allowed her abusers to continue leading her away.

'You don't understand how much damage they're doing to you,' I said urgently on another occasion. I would have been quite happy to give all these predatory men a good punch on the nose on her behalf.

As usual, she met my intense gaze with an empty stare. Perhaps she understood perfectly what was going on and it was me who couldn't grasp the essential truth of this situation.

I could hardly bear to see the terrible state this girl was in, and watching the staff who were paid to protect her causing her yet more pain was torture. I didn't cry very often any more, but being near her broke my heart, and when nobody could see, I cried for her. I had never seen a human being in so much pain. Her spirit had been killed and her body was all that remained.

At the same home, I met a boy called Joey, who was a few years younger than me. His mother had stubbed out cigarettes all over his skin and locked him in a dark cupboard. He was a beautiful child, crying out for love, but he was terribly damaged and screamed when staff turned out the lights and he was left in the dark. My heart went out to him too. Sometimes he let me cuddle him and I'd stroke his hair, whispering, 'Don't worry, Joey. Be a strong boy. Things will turn out OK.' He was moved a week after I arrived, and I never got to find out what happened to him next.

In another home, a black boy called Mark was forced to walk backwards and forwards across the lounge wearing a placard a manager had made for him, which said, 'I'm a stupid nigger.' He would hang his head in shame. None of the staff challenged the colleague who had made the placard. It was extraordinary how much staff in children's homes got away with in the mid-1970s when I was there.

A priest was sometimes brought into the children's home to counsel us. I asked him to explain why God let so many unfair things happen. He failed to offer any sort of satisfactory explanation. Later he was convicted of sexually abusing choirboys at Sunday school. Once again this proved to me that adults were not to be trusted.

My heart went out to Melanie, Joey, Mark and all the other damaged children I came across. All of them had had their lives ruined by cruel adults. Seeing that so many children had suffered at the hands of adults simply made me hate them more.

Each of us who had been dumped in institutions had suffered in one way or another, and it seemed very unjust that our parents punished us once because of their own shortcomings and then a second time by depositing us in what was in effect a rubbish bin for unloved children. We needed to heal, and in order to do so, we needed someone who would love us unconditionally, someone who would positively smother us with the kindness, attention and consistency we'd been starved of. We were given the opposite. I'm sure that if such a person had intervened and rescued me from my childhood, my life would have taken a very different course. At the time I didn't understand any of this. I didn't consider myself to be damaged and prided myself on my tough, feisty approach to life. All that mattered to me was running away and being free and finding ways to earn enough money to survive from one day to the next.

You had to be very tough to survive in the children's homes. Newcomers were often initiated by having their heads shoved down the toilets. A system of forfeits was devised too, which involved dares like playing chicken on the nearby motorway. Those who had the courage to refuse these forfeits were subjected to walking down what was misleadingly named 'the tunnel of love'. I had been subjected to this when I first arrived and then I joined in and did it to other new children. Five or six children stood on each side, and the person who had refused to carry out the forfeit had to walk down the centre. Then kicks and punches would be rained down on them. I never took part in the attacks on newcomers, as I thought they were very cruel. Usually, though, the new arrivals coped well with this 'welcome'. Most of them were used to being kicked and punched.

We also used to play war games with pellet guns. One of the attractions was that quite serious injuries could be inflicted with the guns. I still have a mark on the bottom of my right cheek just below my ear where I was wounded by a pellet.

Another dangerous game was making bicycles from bits of scrap metal and old wheels, and whizzing down a very steep hill on them onto a dual carriageway. We would shoot out, forcing motorists to slam on their brakes. I heard that one boy got killed doing it, another had all his teeth knocked out when he collided with a car, and a third was blinded. But the danger was part of the appeal. All of us were thrill-seekers, and because we'd had such miserable lives with our families, we didn't have the same sense of self-preservation as children from happy homes. To us, life was very cheap.

One day a few of us escaped from the children's home and walked more than twenty miles to the River Hamble. It opened out to the sea. We were exhausted when we arrived, and evening was drawing in, but we were delighted to find a small, battered rowing boat moored at the edge of the water. We untied it and jumped in, even though none of us knew how to row. We lay down in the boat and let it carry us out to sea. The water was very dark and calm, and the full moon made it look as if thousands of candles had been lit beneath it. It was very peaceful and we fell asleep under the stars. It never occurred to us that we might drown. It all seemed like a huge adventure. When we woke up the next morning, the tide had washed us back to shore. We'd been very lucky. A couple of hours later the police caught us and took us back to the children's home.

One of my favourite forms of entertainment was dancing on top of lorries just before they pulled out of the lorry park on to the motorway. When the lorry got to the slip road and slowed down, we jumped off. Our favourite lorry-dance tune was 'Rock Around the Clock'. We used to do rock 'n' roll dancing in twos. One time my dance partner was a particularly daredevil boy called Tom. He was about fourteen, a year older than me, and seemed to have absolutely no fear of death. As the lorry we were dancing on top of started to gather speed, I was keen to jump off, but Tom wasn't ready to stop dancing and clung on to my hands tightly. Although I was a

brave child, hurtling down the motorway on top of a huge
lorry was a thrill too far for me. After a few moments a
passing police car spotted us and flagged down the lorry. The
lorry driver had no idea that there was anything on his roof
and his mouth fell open when he got out of his cab and saw us.

'Get down here at once,' ordered the police officer, ablaze
with anger.

At first Tom and I refused, taunting him with, 'Why
don't you come and get us?' But when the policeman turned
away from us for a split second, Tom and I grabbed our
chance; monkey-style, we swung down the other side of the
lorry from where the police officer and driver were standing, and sprinted over the embankment. We were out of
sight before the policeman could even think about chasing
us. It was thrilling to have got away with such a daring
stunt.

Tom persuaded me to get involved in other mad deeds. He
encouraged me to steal cars and go joyriding with him. Cars
were much easier to steal then. If you had a Cortina key, it
opened all Cortina doors. We always tried to steal cars that
looked as if they belonged to rich people rather than poor
ones, and we made sure the stealing was done after dark,
when we were less likely to get noticed.

The boys were in charge of the break-ins, but all of us took
turns at driving. None of us had been taught, but we just tried
to pick it up as we went along. We drove the cars on waste
ground in the woods, where we wouldn't be spotted by the
police. The boys showed me how to change into fourth gear as
fast as possible and then to ram my foot down hard on the
accelerator pedal. I loved driving fast. It made my heart pound
against my chest with excitement.

We ran away to a fairground once and Tom led me onto the big wheel. When we reached the top, he climbed out of his seat and started rocking the wheel. He was trying to get it to flip right over. I was absolutely terrified and was relieved when we got back on to the ground.

One evening a new girl arrived. She looked tough like the rest of us. Her brown hair was scrunched into an untidy ponytail, her jeans were full of holes, and her trainers were scuffed. Billy, one of the oldest boys, who usually took the lead with any pranks, told her that we were all going to run away and that as the new arrival she had to be the first one to clamber up on to the roof from where we would make our escape. She didn't know that there was no way down from the roof. Generally when we escaped we left by jumping over the garden wall.

'Great idea,' she said, and climbed through the window of the dormitory on to the roof. It was dangerous climbing up there, but she managed it. Then she kept calling to us, 'Come on, come on.'

The noise attracted the night-duty staff, who looked out of the window and saw her sitting on the roof. It was a four-storey building, and if she put a foot wrong, she could fall to her death. 'Don't move,' yelled the member of staff.

They had to call the fire brigade to get her down. Billy laughed and laughed, but I could see the new girl looked hurt because she'd been tricked.

After I'd been stuck in the children's home for a couple of months, my father turned up unexpectedly and said I could move in with him for a while. I had seen him very infrequently because the original arrangement that Jay and I would see him at weekends had fallen apart. Neither he nor my mother had pursued the plan and things had drifted, with Jay and me making just occasional visits to him.

I was overjoyed to see him and of course I remembered how he had rescued me once before, from the children's home I had been placed in at the age of four. And now, just when I really needed him, he had turned up again. I saw him once every few months and was always delighted to be with him. I hugged him tightly. 'I'm so glad to see you,' I said.

'Me too.' He smiled. 'Come on – get your things and we can go. We're going to work this out.'

My father had had a meeting with some of the social workers, and between them they had agreed that because I was staying with him, they'd try me in a school not too far from where he lived, which was specially designed for children who played truant.

Before I started there, my father sat me down for a 'serious' talk. 'Look, Louise, I know you've had a lot of problems, and I do understand why you don't like going to school. I didn't like going very much when I was your age. But you can't win this one. If you keep on playing truant, you will be put into a secure children's home, one which will be very hard for you to run away from and where I'm sure you'll be really miserable. Just play the game for a while and go to school. The social worker said it's not like other schools – you should be able to pick and choose what you do.'

I nodded my head. Although the thought of settling down and going to school didn't please me, I knew that what my father was saying made sense. I also liked the way he was talking to me like an adult, not like a stupid little girl, the way my mother spoke to me.

To my amazement, I really enjoyed my time in the new school. Instead of being squeezed into the straitjacket of the curriculum, we were allowed to do whatever interested us. I loved painting, and as it was getting close to Christmas, I was allowed to paint the backdrop for the school's nativity play. I had the art room all to myself and I felt very contented sitting among the brightly coloured canvases propped against the walls and breathing in the smell of oil paint and turpentine.

The art teacher was extremely supportive. She popped in now and again, uttered unqualified words of encouragement and offered me little chunks of the cheese that she carried around in her bag and perpetually nibbled on. 'Take some cheese – it's excellent for your teeth,' she urged. She was a small woman with long, thick hair. She often wore sandals, even though it was December, and long, flowing skirts with sparkly sequins sewed round the hem.

After I'd painted Jesus, Mary and Joseph, I decided to paint a huge flock of geese moving across the sky so that they could take a peek at the new arrival in Bethlehem. I worked very hard on my paintings and didn't miss a single day of school until my mission was complete. Other teachers kept coming in to have a look, and like the art teacher, they all praised me for my hard work and artistic flair. I decided that if other schools could be like this one, I would actually be prepared to stay around long enough to learn something.

My home life also improved drastically when my father took me in. He was living with a woman called Pam. She seemed very kind and had three daughters of her own, all younger than me. She moved them into one room so that I could have a bedroom to myself, and she helped me paint the walls lilac. Her eldest daughter, who was a few years younger than me, protested about being moved out of her bedroom, but after a day or two things settled down between us and I got along well with all Pam's children. For the first time I was leading a tranquil and almost normal life. I went to school every day and came home to a reasonably happy family environment.

Sadly the flimsy bubble of peace was punctured after I'd been living with my father for seven or eight months. I got into a stupid argument with my father and decided that it was time to run again, even though it meant leaving the first school I'd ever been happy at, and the first place that had felt like home. I picked up my things and ran out of the house. In a few seconds I'd destroyed the first taste of tranquillity I'd had. Tears stung my eyes as I made my way back to the woods. Once again things had gone wrong. I wondered if I'd ever be able to live a normal family life. There was certainly no sign of it at the moment. I was on the run again.

'QUEEN BEE? NO THANKS'

I spent a few days sleeping in the woods, but hunger soon drove me back into the town. I had saved some money from strawberry-picking and other odd jobs, so headed for a corner shop to buy some bread and cheese. Unfortunately, a police officer who had dealt with me before recognised me and grabbed me by the collar. 'Where do you think you're off to, young lady?' he said, before roughly bundling me into his patrol car and taking me down to the police station.

A social worker and my mother were duly summoned to discuss what was to be done with me. The social worker was middle-aged and balding with thick glasses. He looked extremely bored and irritated that he had been called to a meeting at the last minute to deal with a 'difficult' child whom he didn't know and, from what I could see, didn't care about.

I remained silent while discussions about what was to be done went on around me. My mother kept on shaking her head and tutting at my behaviour, but still I said nothing. Finally it was agreed that I would be sent to yet another children's home.

The social worker took me to an old, slightly neglected building, which staff had made rather feeble efforts to pretend was a family home. The hallway smelt of musty neglect overlaid with cheap disinfectant. The only colours I could see were sludgy greys and browns. I longed to slip out of the front door and get back to the clear bright greens and fresh smells of the woods, but the social worker who had brought me had clanged the heavy front door shut and was standing in front of it, just in case I had hatched a plan to abscond.

Inside, I was led into a room where battered chairs pocked with cigarette burns were arranged in a semicircle round a TV.

'Have a seat in here, Louise, while we go into the office and sort out your files,' said the social worker, whom I'd nicknamed Mr Couldn't Give a Damn because he looked bored and weary, and was obviously anxious to get me signed over to anyone but him as soon as possible.

I sat on one of the hard wooden chairs and turned on the TV. I knew that the social worker was likely to be about ten minutes and that he'd return with a nondescript member of staff. This person would reel off the regulations to me, warn me of the penalties of breaching the rules and then show me upstairs to my shared room, which would have the same shabby décor and curious smells as the lounge, plus the unappealing addition of a bed covered in pink nylon sheets and an ugly bedspread. I also knew that in their meeting about me the terms 'serial runaway' and 'problem child who nobody knows what to do with' were likely to be used.

While I was waiting for this to happen, the residents of the children's home returned from school. An enormous girl of fifteen lumbered into the room with a thunderous expression on her face. 'Oi, you, get out of my chair!' she bellowed.

I had guessed even before she opened her mouth that she was a bully. Bullies didn't scare me, and I was furious that I was being greeted with such hostility when as far as I could see I'd done nothing wrong.

'Oh, has it got your name on it?' I said sarcastically. 'Well, you can get lost, because I'm not moving.'

The girl, whose name was Angela, obviously wasn't used to people standing up to her. Her cheeks swelled, and her breathing became heavy. She turned round, swiftly grabbed another chair from behind me, lifted it up high and smashed it forcefully over the back of my head. The pain of the impact on my head was unbearable. I fell to the floor, blood pouring from my forehead. I felt as if I was going to pass out, but driven on by rage, I managed to stand up. I was determined to retaliate, but at that moment a few members of staff rushed in to see what all the commotion was about.

'Oh, no, what on earth has happened to you, Louise? Looks like Angela has been causing more trouble.'

'I . . . I . . .' I spluttered, salty blood dripping into my mouth '. . . I was sitting watching TV when someone decided to smash a chair over my head.'

A couple of members of staff examined my wound.

'Looks like she's going to need stitches. Better get her down to the local hospital,' said one of the staff, looking worried at the amount of blood pouring down my face.

Usually I was formulating my escape plan as soon as I arrived in a children's home, but I first wanted to show Angela that she couldn't get away with battering anyone and everyone. I knew how tough it was in children's homes. I could look after myself, but I hated the thought of Angela attacking someone who couldn't fight back.

My opportunity came the very next day. A game of rounders was arranged on the field outside the children's home. Angela was fielding at first base. When it was my turn to bat, I hit the ball and sprinted to first base, hanging on tightly to the bat instead of dropping it, as dictated by the rules of the game. My plan worked like clockwork. At first base, I stopped and, to Angela's amazement, started beating her up with the bat. There was more shock than pain in her face when I launched my attack. It was obviously a long time since anyone had dared to take her on. For years she had been doling out beatings to others, but had never received the same in return because everyone was so scared of her.

Once again it was down to the staff to intervene. I had struck her at least ten times by the time the staff pulled me off her. I was severely reprimanded, but the telling-off meant nothing to me. As far as I was concerned, I'd managed to show her that she couldn't go around behaving like that, which was all that mattered to me.

The staff placed me in the detention room, a damp, gloomy place in the basement, where the most problematic of the problem children were dumped to cool off. They released me several hours later and told me I'd better behave myself or I'd be out.

Don't you worry, I thought to myself. I'll be gone sooner than you think.

A little later, I went back into the TV room, expecting Angela to be waiting to give me a good punch. To my amazement, she beamed at me and then took me to one side. 'Hey, Louise, you're an impressive little fighter, aren't you? What do you say to you and me teaming up? Between us we could be queen bees of this children's home and have everyone under our thumb.'

I think she assumed that I would gratefully fall in with her plan, and that I would be relieved to have her patronage and protection. Once again my reaction shocked her.

'No way, Angela. Bullying isn't my style. If someone attacks me, I will defend myself, but I'm not one to go looking for trouble. I don't want to have you as my friend because I don't like bullies. And while I'm here, I don't want to see you attacking the little ones any more. If I catch you doing that, you'll certainly be getting a few more punches from me. Got that?'

Angela nodded almost timidly and walked off sulking.

That night, I lay in my bed wondering why it was that whenever I did anything kind or soft I suffered for it and wasn't respected, while the language of force seemed to be the only thing that could protect me from harm.

SOHO LIVES

Now that things had been sorted out with Angela, I decided that the time had come to run away. I had started talking to a girl called Meera, who was also keen to get out of the children's home, and together we devised a plan to sneak out of the front gates, which unbelievably were unlocked, head for the railway station and jump on a train to London, where Meera was originally from.

Meera told me she came from a large East End family. Her mother had fourteen different children by different men, and both her elder sister and their mother had a child by the same man. The family had moved from Bethnal Green to Southampton, but had recently drifted back to London. I'd never been to the capital before, and the thought of going was very thrilling.

Meera seemed bolder than me. 'Our family is very poor, and our mum's taught us all kinds of ways to steal and con things out of people. Stick with me and I'll show you the ropes,' she said.

Among the skills her mother had taught her was to walk into shops selling fur coats on Oxford Street with a pair of pliers discreetly tucked up her sleeve, snip the chain from one of the coats and calmly walk out of the shop with it. I couldn't understand why the staff failed to spot her doing this, but she said they never suspected a child of doing such a thing. Meera was skinny and wiry like me, and was small for her age, so probably didn't arouse suspicion.

As planned, the next day we slipped out of the children's home while the staff were having a meeting in the office. We headed for the railway station and managed to avoid the ticket inspector by hiding in the toilets. We ambled off the train, extremely pleased with ourselves for not having got caught, but as we left the platform at Waterloo Station, two rough, thick hands clamped themselves to our shoulders. We turned round to see two police officers. Our bravado deflated as quickly as a popped balloon.

'And where do you think you two young ladies are off to, then?' asked the taller of the two, an officious-looking man with a red, bulbous nose.

'Er, nowhere, Officer,' stammered Meera.

In the end the policemen got it out of us that we had come from a children's home in Southampton and they delivered us straight back there. The staff seemed unsurprised that we had run away. I think it was something they presumed most of the children would try to do. We kept our heads down and said little to the other children. I thought Angela seemed envious of our friendship, but she said nothing.

Undeterred by the police spoiling our dash for freedom, we decided to try to escape again the next day. At 6 a.m., while everybody was still asleep, we left via the back door of the children's home. Again we got the train without any problem. This time, when it arrived in London, we waited until all the passengers had left the platform and any police and station staff had wandered off, and then we left the train separately. Nobody stopped us at the station, and once we got out into the street, we gave each other a victorious wink.

'Come on, let's find a bus to Bethnal Green and we'll go and find my mum,' said Meera.

Both of us felt euphoric as we sat on the top deck of the red London bus, which I'd seen pictures of so often on TV. London didn't look too different from Southampton to me, just much bigger. There were lots of shops and traffic, and people were hurrying around everywhere. I did notice, though, that there was a much richer mix of races than I had ever seen in Southampton – more black people, more Chinese and more Asian women dressed in saris and glittering scarves.

Meera knew her way around London well. 'Here, this is our stop,' she said, sprinting off the bus.

She led me from the main road, which was full of busy market stalls selling everything from fruit and vegetables to battered armchairs, down a warren of back streets filled with grim-looking concrete tower blocks.

'My mum lives in that one over there.' She pointed to a particularly dilapidated building.

We climbed up nineteen flights of stairs because the lift was out of order – 'It's always out of order,' shrugged Meera – and arrived panting at her mother's battered front door. Meera walked straight in and introduced me to her mother, who was a typical East Ender, plump with mousey hair scraped off her face into a messy ponytail.

'Hello, Meera. You're back, are you?' she said, smiling and showing no trace of surprise. 'Run away again?' She gave her a quick hug.

'Yes. It was rubbish in that home they put me in – no point in hanging about there.'

I looked around the small living room. There were children of varying ages and skin colours draped over every surface.

'We're both absolutely starving, Mum. Have you got any food in?' said Meera.

'No, love. Nip out to the Indian takeaway on the corner, order a nice big meal, then do a runner.'

Meera nodded. 'OK. Come on, Louise, let's go.'

I'd never done a runner from a takeaway before and was curious to know how to get away with it. Meera managed to look very angelic as she placed her order. I could see that the man behind the counter didn't suspect a thing. She had told me to wait by the door and hold it open. While I did so, I pretended to be reading adverts for taxis and second-hand cars, which were pinned to a nearby notice board. When the bags full of steaming food arrived, Meera at first began fumbling in her handbag for her purse, then like lightning grabbed the takeaway and ran. The man behind the counter was furious and called to a group of men standing in the kitchen to give chase.

We hurtled down the street like wildfire. I'd never run so fast in my life. My heart was banging against my chest and I was sure it was going to fly out. In the end we managed to lose them and clambered on to a rooftop, still clutching our bags of curry. When we opened them, a lot of the curry had spilt. It looked pretty revolting, but we were ravenous and sat on the roof shovelling handfuls of the spicy food into our mouths with our dirty fingers. When you're very hungry and you finally eat, the food has a completely different quality to it.

We took the leftovers home to Meera's mum to divide up between the children. She smiled when she opened the bags. She knew without asking why we'd delivered the takeaway to her in such a mess. 'You must have built up quite an appetite,' she said, smiling.

My time in Bethnal Green was short-lived. The very next day I went out with Meera, and when we returned, her mother told us we had to leave and quickly. 'I've had a couple of social workers knocking on the door spying on me. You and Louise are classified as runaways and they wanted to know if you've been here. I told them I hadn't seen either of you but I can't be doing with trouble from the social. You'll have to get out of here before they come round again.'

Meera's mother was as keen for her daughter to keep out of the way of the authorities as she was. The last thing she wanted was to have social workers snooping around accusing her of being a terrible mother. Both Meera and her mother were very matter-of-fact about the whole thing. It was something that had obviously happened before.

Meera and I picked up our rucksacks, which had a few essentials in, bade Meera's mother a hasty farewell and left.

'Don't worry,' said Meera, seeing that I looked rather dejected as we descended the nineteen flights of stairs once again. 'We'll go up to Soho. There are lots of young runaways around there, and it's easy to find ways to earn money.'

Like me, Meera had no particular plan for the future. Our aims were short term – to get enough food to fill our stomachs and to avoid being caught by police and social workers and sent back to a children's home. I had learnt to survive in the rural setting of Southampton and the New Forest, but Meera had a lot to teach me about getting by in a capital city.

She introduced me to her friends, who survived by doing odd jobs for some of the shady characters who 'ran' Soho. They were also runaways who had decided they preferred making their own way on the streets to their unhappy lives at home. Meera and I didn't speak much. We'd both had a very tough time, and without telling each other our life story, we knew that our priorities were the same. Like me, she knew that for the foreseeable future her life was going to be a constant series of ducks and dives to keep out of the way of the authorities, and like me, she would do whatever she needed to do in order to survive.

Next, Meera showed me the lock-up garages near Berwick Street Market, which runaways often crept into at the end of the day and bedded down on wheelbarrows and sacking. That night we slept there with them. It was far safer than on the streets, but the sheds were alive with rats, which ran back and forth over our bodies all night long in pursuit of scraps of fruit and vegetables. I had no fear of the occasional lone rat, having kept them as pets when I was little, but there really were too many in one small space for any human to stomach. I could see that the others hated the rats too, but we all managed to muster up enough bravado to make it through the night.

Meera showed me which market stalls would give me left-over fruit and vegetables to eat. To begin with, I took a bag of apples and carrots into the shed with me, but the rats devoured it, and I quickly learnt to do all my eating in the open air.

After a few days of acclimatisation I decided that Soho was somewhere I'd be able to scrape by. I was dazzled by the sights, smells and sounds of the area. There was nothing to compare it with in Southampton, and it was a different universe from the woods. There were no tranquil trees or birds or ponies; everything was fake and neon and never appeared to sleep. Yet both these contrasting environments offered similar scope to hide, and for me, that was the most important thing.

In the next few days I got used to seeing the women of Soho, dressed in their scarlet basques and flimsy black stockings with a cardigan thrown casually over the top, nipping out of their walk-up flats to buy a packet of cigarettes. Male tourists prowled with slightly dazed expressions on their faces, over-whelmed with sexual choices.

Instinctively I knew that as a teenage girl I would be at risk from the greasy pimps who controlled some of the prostitutes, and so decided it was more important than ever for people to think I was a boy. I was haunted by the attack by Jim, the milkman. I still had nightmares of him chasing me through the woods, but they were less frequent now. Protecting myself from men like him was almost as big a priority as finding enough food to eat each day and keeping away from the authorities. I had always been a tomboy, living in jeans and T-shirts, but now I seldom removed my cap, and had perfected my masculine look. I asked Meera to introduce me to her friends as a boy. She agreed, giggling at the sight of me in my flat cap and macho leather jacket, though she also dressed like a boy. It just wasn't practical when sleeping rough to look feminine. Besides, the children's home had alerted the police that two girls had gone missing; because we looked like boys, we never aroused the suspicion of passing police officers. If we caught sight of a police officer, we moved so fast that nobody could catch us.

My disguise was the equivalent of donning a magical coat of protection, and I now felt safe as I walked around Soho, working out which odd jobs or scams I could involve myself in to fill my stomach and yet still keep me below the radar of the authorities.

Meera introduced me to some boys who were around our age. She announced that we were going out 'tea-leafing' in Oxford Street to earn some money. We headed over to Oxford Street and started shoplifting, but somehow I became separated from Meera. I don't know if she got picked up by the police or if she decided to risk going back to her mother, but she wasn't anywhere to be found when I returned to Soho. Relationships on the street were often transient. None of us living this hand-to-mouth existence expected that our friends would always be there. The teenagers who lived on the streets were constantly disappearing and reappearing.

Rather than staying on my own, I decided that I better start hanging around with the boys I'd been shoplifting with, as they knew Soho and London's West End much better than I did. There was a law among runaways, a kind of honour among thieves, that everyone looked out for each other. The boys seemed to like me. They sensed that I had no fear of anything – more than half the battle when it came to making a success of living on the streets.

The Maltese Mafia controlled Soho in the mid-1970s, and it was a very sleazy place, not the tourist magnet it is now, with nice restaurants and fancy shops alongside the brothels. I was very naïve about what went on in Soho, although I did understand that it was a place where women sold their bodies. Because it seemed such a shady place, with everyone trying to dodge the law, I was sure I could make money here.

The blue-movie cinemas, which were illegal, were forever being raided by the police, who would confiscate the film reels. The gangsters who ran the cinemas tried to get round this by having as few film reels in each cinema as possible. The idea was to keep the films moving and off the premises. As soon as one cinema finished showing a film, a runner raced to pick up the film and take it to another cinema so they could screen it. They recruited some of the homeless boys as runners, including one of the boys I had started hanging out with. His job was quite literally to run from one cinema to the next with the film.

Soon I too became a runner and was paid well for it. With the money I earned, I no longer needed to worry about where my next meal was coming from. I had more than enough money to buy food from the nearby down-at-heel cafés and even some new clothes. I bought the most masculine clothes that I could find and nobody guessed that I was a girl.

Sometimes when the rats in the lock-up sheds seemed too lively and the wheelbarrows were too cold, I would look for warmer places to lay my head. Occasionally, if the back door was open, I managed to sneak into the ladies' toilet of a Soho club frequented by drag queens and clippers. One evening I had tucked myself into my favourite corner underneath the mirrors when a very attractive, heavily made-up woman with large breasts walked in, peered into the mirror and began applying a fresh layer of lipstick. I watched her, fascinated.

Suddenly she looked down at me huddled in the corner in my thick sweater and cap. 'What are you looking at?' she said. 'I'll give you something to look at.' She lifted up her skirt to reveal no knickers – and a penis!

I was so shocked that no words came out. She let her skirt drop back into position and flounced out, blowing me an exaggerated kiss. 'The more I see of grown-ups, the less I understand them,' I thought to myself.

When the winter wind bit through our clothes, the boys and I sought refuge in one of the Soho launderettes. An attendant came every evening to collect the money from the machines and lock up but the rest of the time we were left to our own devices. The combination of warm air from the dryers and the scent of washing powder made me feel very safe and comforted. We managed to find unusual ways to occupy ourselves while we kept warm, such as climbing inside the tumble-dryers and seeing who could cling on for the longest when it started turning. Eager to prove myself to my male peers, I was always the first to dive in, even though spinning in the hot dryer wasn't much fun. If you made your body rigid and hung on, you wouldn't actually tumble, but it did make me feel nauseated. Often I won the tumbling competitions; it was down to a combination of gritted-teeth determination and my light, wiry frame.

During one of those cold days at the launderette, I expanded my knowledge of Soho's sexual proclivities. I was clinging leech-like to the innards of the spinning dryer when a blowsy woman of about thirty-five with dyed blonde hair bouffed into a 1960s-style beehive walked in, laden with bags of dirty washing. Her make-up was so thick and false that I wondered if she was on her way to a fancy-dress party. Both her lipstick and foundation sat, almost three-dimensionally, on top of her features, and her false eyelashes looked as if they were about to claw her eyes out. I jumped out of the dryer and swayed giddily.

The woman shook rainwater off her umbrella and didn't seem to notice or care that it splashed all over me. 'Have you finished in there?' she said dryly. She strode past me and tipped her dirty clothes into two of the washing machines. I was overpowered by her cheap scent. It clogged my nostrils and my throat.

One of the other runaways, Colin, bounded over, grinned confidently and looked her in the eye. 'Have you by any chance got a couple of fags to spare?' he wheedled.

She looked at all of us and decided that we were probably harmless. 'Oh, go on, then. I expect you'll all be wanting a fag.' She smiled and offered her packet of John Player Specials around. For some reason her gaze fastened on me. Maybe she thought I was more trustworthy than the others. 'I'll tell you what, love,' she said, pinching my cheek. 'If you keep an eye on my washing and pop it in the dryer when the wash has finished, I'll slip you a couple of bob when I get back.' She left me a few shillings for the dryer.

I happily agreed. I was going to be earning some money and could carry on playing the spinning game. As soon as she left, the other boys crowded around me and tried to get me to share the money with them, but I refused. Although the boys were older than me, I had learnt to stand up for myself and they all backed off.

I was diligently folding the woman's dry laundry when she returned, with bags from the market in one hand and her umbrella in the other. She obviously had no free hands to carry her washing.

'If you help me carry my laundry back to my flat in Dean Street, I'll give you a bigger tip.'

I nodded eagerly and picked up her bags of washing.

When we arrived at her flat, she asked me to ring her doorbell in the hope that her maid would answer. I saw the word 'Model' under her bell.

'Are you a real model?' I asked, wide-eyed, thinking that she looked too old and too rough to be one.

She shook her head and smiled. 'Damn that bloody maid,' said the woman when nobody answered the door. 'She's forever not turning up when she's supposed to.'

She led the way to her flat upstairs. The door was open and we went straight into the kitchen. I put the washing down and she gave me a generous tip. Just then the doorbell rang.

The woman spoke into the intercom. 'Hello?'

I heard a muffled voice ask a question.

'Yes, I'm free. Come on up,' she responded. Then she turned to me and said, 'I've got a male visitor. You stay in the kitchen until I've taken him into the other room. All right, love?'

I nodded and tried to peek at the man who walked into the flat. He was wearing a freshly pressed pinstripe suit, a crisp white shirt and a red tie, and was carrying an expensive leather briefcase. The man had a pale, pasty face as if he never ventured out into daylight, and greased-back hair. Very strange, I thought to myself. They don't seem the type to be friends.

The woman reappeared in the kitchen. 'Off you go now. You can let yourself out,' she said.

The door wouldn't close properly, so I left it ajar and sat on the landing outside, smoking a cigarette she had just given me. I was in no hurry to go back outside in the pouring rain, nor did I particularly want to return to the launderette to play the boys' stupid games.

Suddenly I heard horrible sounds coming out of the woman's flat. The man was yowling in pain and I became convinced that he was being murdered. I peeped through the front door and saw a very curious sight – the man was dressed in a frilly apron and suspenders, and the woman was standing over him whipping him.

I clapped my hand over my mouth. Oh, my God, I thought, she really is about to murder him!

I raced back through the pouring rain to the boys, who were still spinning themselves aimlessly in the dryers.

'Come quick – that woman whose washing I took home is murdering some city gent in her flat. Hurry up before she kills him.'

The boys were glad of a new diversion and followed me as I raced down the street. When we arrived, the terrible sounds were still emanating from the flat.

One of the older boys looked inside and roared with laughter at my mistake. 'She's not murdering him. That's some kind of kinky sexual thing. It's called S&M. He won't thank you for disturbing him. Come on, let's go,' he said, still laughing.

I walked off down the street by myself. I didn't want to go back to the launderette to be mocked, and I didn't want to stay around the woman's flat to hear her customer's peculiar yelps.

For a thirteen-year-old girl, this all came as a big shock to me. Jim had taught me about the way men could force themselves on vulnerable girls, but the idea of something connected with sex involving a woman hurting a man was very alien to me. I had assumed that as far as sex went, it was always men who hurt women. Was this a part of normal life in Soho? I wondered to myself, feeling very confused.

The more I discovered about adults, the less I liked them and the less I understood. I decided to redouble my efforts to keep out of their way. Adults meant trouble, and more than anything I wanted to keep my head down and hang on to my freedom.

I started to think more and more of my beloved horse, Starlight Bourbon. I knew he would be well looked after in my absence at the stables, but I longed to climb on his back once again. I began thinking that maybe the sleazy world of Soho wasn't for me and that I should consider going home.

A GYPSY CARAVAN OF MY OWN

In the end the decision was taken out of my hands. All of us runaways tried very hard to make ourselves invisible on the streets of Soho, but one day the police must have received a tip-off that a small group of us were sleeping under some railway arches. I had no longer been able to bear spending my nights with the rats in the stallholders' lock-ups and had managed to get a better, if colder, night's sleep out in the open.

We were all fast asleep under the arches when the police arrived, shining their torches in our eyes. Within seconds we were on our feet and had abandoned our dirty blankets on the floor and sprinted away. A few people got caught, but I managed to outrun the officer who was chasing me and hide myself in one of the lock-ups until the coast was clear. My heart was pounding with the exertion and fear.

I was determined that nobody was going to put me back in a children's home, where I had seen so much cruelty and indifference from the staff, and nor was I going to return to the daily beatings from Michael and my mother. No child will run back to a home where they are constantly beaten. I decided I would go back to Southampton and live in the woods for a while. Even if the police hadn't been chasing me, after a few months in the grime of Soho I longed to get back to the clean air and familiar surroundings of the forest. I was still only thirteen years old and had already been running from place to place for more than four years. Existing in this hand-to-mouth way was preferable to life with my mother and Michael, but I was beginning to wonder if I would end up spending the rest of my life on the run.

Since I had run away from the last children's home, I had had no contact with my mother, my father or Michael. I had no idea if they were making efforts to find me or if they were just relieved that I had disappeared.

I jumped on a train and travelled back to Southampton in the usual way. I wondered why I always felt the need to be in transit. I felt much happier when I was travelling than when I actually reached my destination. Staying in one place gave me a persistent itch under my skin, and the only way to relieve it was to run again.

When I had spent time in the woods before, I had often seen groups of gypsies living there in their brightly coloured caravans. I had watched them from a distance as they hunted rabbits and pigeons. I noticed that they didn't run for cover as soon as it rained, and that they knew which roots, leaves and berries could be eaten and which had to be left well alone. I had always felt they were far more in tune with nature than the people who lived on my estate. Although I had sometimes chatted to them, I had never got to know them well. All that changed when I returned to the woods from Soho.

I was walking near the gypsies' camp one day when they suddenly started pointing and shouting at me. Someone had let one of their ponies loose and they were convinced it was me. In their anger, they began throwing stones. I ducked and managed to avoid serious injury, throwing back every stone that landed at my feet. Ever since I was young and Michael had started to hit me, I had developed a conditioned response to retaliate as soon as I was attacked. It was like an animal instinct. I didn't take time to process what was going on or to negotiate with my assailant; all that mattered was protecting myself against further onslaughts.

'You gorgies should stop going around messing with our animals,' one of the men shouted. His skin had turned the shade of dark leather from a lifetime in the sun and the wind. He had curly, chestnut-coloured hair and was wearing a white shirt with rolled-up sleeves, a waistcoat and a little neck scarf.

'Look, it wasn't me. I love animals and I would never do a thing like that,' I said, trying to sound as strong and brave as I could. 'If you stop throwing stones at me, I'll help you find your pony.'

They looked at me suspiciously, but then decided I sounded sincere. A group of teenage boys gestured for me to follow. I set off through the trees with them, and after about twenty minutes of searching we found the pony grazing in a clearing. One of the boys led him back to the camp, and the rest of us started laughing and joking and showing off how quickly and nimbly we could climb the stocky trees. All of them were dressed in scruffy trousers and shirts, and some of them had splodges of mud on their faces. A lot of them had beautiful, greeny-blue eyes and tousled hair. In my scruffy jeans and T-shirt, with my nut-brown skin and unbrushed hair, I didn't look very different from them. By the time we had got back to the gypsy camp, I had firmly bonded with them and we soon became good friends.

From then on I spent more and more time with the gypsies. They were very resourceful and taught me lots of different ways to make money. I helped them collect horse manure to sell to farmers. Strawberry picking was another way to earn money. Because I was young and lithe with nimble fingers, I could pick quickly and my back ached less than some of the adults who crouched over the plants hour after hour. I could also eat strawberries to my heart's content, and my mouth and chin were perpetually stained with the sweet juice.

They knew of an old dumping ground for machinery that had been there since the Second World War. We managed to extract lots of copper coils and sold them to scrap-metal merchants. A less honest, but more lucrative, way of earning money involved going to church, not to sit in the pews and pray but to climb on to the roof and strip off the lead. That also found its way to the scrap-metal merchants.

With cash in my pocket I was a free agent and could spend my days in any way that I wished. Increasingly, I chose to spend them with the gypsies, learning their ways and customs, though I still slept in the woods. The more I got to know the gypsies, the more entranced I was by their lifestyle, which could not have been more different from the life I had led with my mother and Michael.

They lived as a community, always arranging their brightly painted caravans in a circle and making a fire in the clearing in the centre. People had private space at the back of their caravans, but anything that went on in front of the caravans was public knowledge. They were more generous than the people I had come across on our council estate. Although they didn't have much, they always shared food with anyone who was hungry.

'I've never been able to understand how you gorgies can live your lives cooped up in chicken huts,' said Gideon, one of the gypsy men, to me.

'Although that's how I was brought up, I've always hated living like that,' I confided. 'I love the way all of you live. It feels right to me.'

Ever since I was a little girl, when I'd daydreamed that my parents weren't really my parents, I'd felt that I didn't belong. After a few weeks of spending time with the gypsies, I began to feel that they were my real family and their community was my real home. I felt that my wandering spirit was in tune with theirs. I loved the sense of freedom they had, the knowledge that no one was tying them down to a particular place and that whenever the fancy took them they could simply pack their things and take to the open road. I also loved the idea of living in harmony with the natural world and earning just enough money not to go hungry.

I had my first proper relationship with one of the gypsies, a boy of seventeen called Will. He was kind and gentle, with dark, curly hair and twinkling blue eyes. Sometimes we sat and drank beer in his family's caravan when they were all out, and after a few weeks together we had sex. Sex was something I had kept away from since the assault by Jim. I was terrified of letting a man anywhere near my body. But somehow Will's kindness took away my fear. I was very grateful to him for showing me that not all men were the same and not all sex had to be violent. Our relationship wasn't a serious one and fizzled out after a while, but I was very glad to have met him.

The gypsy women, in their headscarves and brightly coloured skirts, were responsible for the maintenance of domes-
tic life. Settled people sometimes accuse gypsies of being dirty,
but their caravans were absolutely immaculate. All day long
the women washed and scrubbed and polished, while the men
made money in various legal and not so legal ways and hunted
rabbits in the woods for their wives to cook. Sometimes they
roasted hedgehogs on a spit or made a kind of bread that
could be cooked over an open fire.

I wasn't interested in spending time with the girls and
women because they spent their days doing chores and I felt
we had nothing in common. I had never been interested in the
things that other girls of my age enjoyed, like daydreaming
about impossible relationships with David Cassidy or Donny
Osmond. I wanted to do the kind of real, non-dreamy things
that boys did. Because I was even more of a tomboy than the
gypsy boys and men, they accepted me as one of them.

I never had any unwanted sexual attention from them. I
noticed that the young gypsies were always deeply respectful
to the young women, and rape was unheard of in their
community. With the gypsies I attained a status beyond
gender. I wasn't a girl and I wasn't a boy; I was simply a
fellow adventurer. Our escapades bound us more closely
together than our respective sexes. I had a knack of fitting
in with whichever group I was with, and because I quickly
picked up the gypsy language and looked similar to them,
many gypsies assumed I had come from another campsite and
never questioned my Romany credentials.

I became so much 'one of the lads' with the gypsy boys that,
with the obvious exception of Will, they seemed to genuinely
forget that I was female. 'Oh, I really fancy that girl,' they

confided every now and again. I could do everything the boys could do, except pee standing up, and constantly tried to show myself to be tougher than they were to ensure my continued place in the boys' club.

Many people were terrified of the gypsies. They could be very hostile to those they didn't like, particularly the police. I got on well with their dogs, but whenever the police showed up, the gypsies ordered their dogs to attack. One time a terrified constable leapt on top of his Panda car to escape the dogs' snapping jaws. I couldn't help but giggle at the sight of the police officer quaking on top of his car. This may sound mean, but as far as I was concerned, adults and particularly people in authority had never done anything to help me, and so any kind of victory by the weak over the strong was something to celebrate.

In time I got to know the gypsy customs and the rhythm of their days. One of the gypsies' traditions was that when someone died, they burnt down that person's caravan with all their possessions inside. They didn't believe in passing on material goods. The first time I witnessed this ritual was when a young gypsy had been knocked down and killed by a lorry driver. I was dumbfounded when they set his caravan alight. It burnt very quickly, releasing a noxious smoke.

'This is our way,' said Johnny, one of the young gypsies, when he saw me gasping as the caravan melted into gnarled black lumps of molten plastic.

Another custom was that everybody removed their shoes before setting foot inside the spotless caravans, and to this day I remove my shoes before I enter someone's home.

I also loved it when there was a gypsy wedding. Members of extended families came from miles around and pinned money on the bride's dress. Then the young couple's fingers would be pricked by a needle and their blood would be mingled. I thought it was a very romantic gesture.

The gypsies often stole cars and stripped out the saleable parts, but first the teenage boys took the cars on joyrides on rough ground in the woods. I had learnt how to drive while in the children's home, but it was the gypsies who taught me how to do daredevil handbrake turns, how to spin cars round and perform all manner of stunts not mentioned in the highway code.

Another thing the gypsies taught me was how to break in the wild ponies. We would dig a trench in one of the shallow ponds so that the water went up to the tops of the ponies' legs. We put rocks in the bottom of the pond so that it was uncomfortable for the ponies to buck. First of all we threw sandbags on their backs, and after they had stopped tossing them off, we jumped on ourselves. The gypsies really knew what they were doing, and the technique always seemed to work. I loved the challenge of taming these wild spirits and was praised by the gypsies for my skill and daring.

I started going to the livestock auctions in the New Forest every other Thursday with some of the gypsy men. The auction was a crowded, bustling affair. The smells and sounds of horses, ponies, cows and pigs filled the air. Ever the entrepreneur, I bought a wild pony for £25, broke him in and sold him to a local family for £150. Then I bought three more wild ponies at the next auction and earned myself good money. I saved my earnings and after a few months I spent £80 on buying a car and a caravan from the gypsies. It was certainly something a bit different for a thirteen-year-old! The caravan had become vacant when one of the young gypsy men had got married and moved into a new caravan with his wife. The car was a battered Mini.

Now I was completely independent. Although most children of my age would have missed home and felt nervous about living by themselves, I just felt incredibly happy that I would never again need to be dependent on my mother and Michael. I had had no contact at all with my mother, my father or Michael since running away to London, so I had no idea if they were upset about my absence, though I doubted it.

The gypsies placed my caravan deep in the woods, deliberately setting it apart from their circle of caravans so that if the police did come calling, I wouldn't be found easily. When I moved in, I scrubbed the caravan from floor to ceiling with a coarse brush and water boiled over an open fire. I removed dust and grease deposits and other unidentified stains, and when I'd finished, everything gleamed. Then I decorated the walls with pictures I'd drawn of horses.

There was a tap in the middle of the site that contained drinking water. Gas lights and a gas heater made the place cosy on chilly evenings, and there was a little stove to cook on. When I brewed a cup of tea for myself in my new home and tipped a fried egg out of a pan on to one of the chipped blue plates the previous owner had left for me, I felt like I'd never been so happy.

Because I'd spent so many years surviving at least partly on my own resources, moving into my own home seemed like a natural progression. On the whole, I managed very well, and to have a place that was as secure as a castle compared with my days of sleeping in tower-block corridors, lock-ups and undergrowth made me feel very contented.

A particular joy was being able to step outside my front door in the morning, smell the pungent ferns, listen to the sound of the trees and birds, and see the exquisite patterns the sunlight made on the ground when it filtered through the branches.

In the springtime, I befriended a few lambs who had become separated from their mother, either because she had been killed by a fox or because they had lost their bearings and couldn't find their way back to her. I loved touching their soft, curly fur and watching them skip unsteadily. They began to follow me around. I got hold of a baby's bottle and let them suck milk from it because they didn't have their mother's milk to sustain them. As they grew older, I fed them potatoes and apples.

I also became acquainted with grass snakes, lizards and some of the birds, in particular a little thrush with a broken wing who couldn't fly very far or high, but flitted just above me and landed on my shoulder when he was tired. Like humans, animals respond to kindness. This kindness was shown by all the humans I knew who inhabited the woods. The creatures, whether two-legged, four-legged or winged, lived in true harmony with each other.

I adored my caravan. I had always taken pleasure in my own company, and being inside my own little world in the woods made me very happy. The house I lived in with my mother and Michael had never felt like a home to me. It was a house where I was sometimes forced to be but as often as possible managed to avoid. For the first time in my life, I truly had a home, and it felt like heaven.

NEWS AT TEN

Earning enough money to survive was very important to both me and the gypsies. Consequently we became partners in various schemes to earn cash. As well as picking strawberries and foraging for scrap metal to sell, one of our main sources of income was stealing valuable saddles. We had a rule that we would never steal a saddle from a modest-looking house. Our targets were the wealthy commercial stables, which had more than fifty saddles hanging on the stable walls. We reasoned that people with that much money wouldn't miss a saddle or two.

As I knew only too well, stable workers were used to having horse-mad youngsters hanging around offering to help groom the horses. My job was to wander into the big stables and coo over the horses, while surreptitiously casting my eyes around to see how many saddles there were. Then we would return that evening when all the workers had left for the day. As the youngest and slimmest, it fell to me to squeeze myself through small windows high up in the stables and pass saddles out to the gypsy boys below.

One night we raided a big stud farm with more than thirty saddles hanging tantalisingly on the wall. The scent of well-

worn leather and horse mingled in our nostrils. I was given
two saddles to carry, but they were so heavy that I could
barely carry one. Somehow I struggled across the field in the
black night, unable to see anything. All of a sudden a horse
galloped towards me and knocked me flying. Not knowing
what had hit me, I screamed and suddenly lights went on
across the estate.

'Drop the saddles and run,' hissed one of the gypsy boys
ahead of me.

Somehow I managed to keep hold of one of the saddles and
clambered inside the waiting car, which roared off. I was
shocked that we had nearly been caught and was so exhausted
from running with the heavy saddle that I felt like I was going
to collapse.

Another money-making scheme was to steal peacocks to
order for nouveaux riches clients. They considered that having these magnificently plumed creatures parading across
their expansive lawns would add some class. One such
man promised us £100 if we could deliver a few of the birds
to him. The gypsy boys knew of an estate where the owners
kept peacocks. The plan was to scale the security fence, grab
the birds, stuff them into a sack and get out as fast as we
could. We managed to shin over the high-security fence
without too many problems. All of us were nimble and
had learnt how to avoid barbed-wire grazes. Grabbing the
peacocks, however, was no easy task. Their feathers are not
securely attached, and each time we made a grab for one of the
birds another handful of feathers came away. In the end we
only succeeded in stuffing two of them into a sack, both of
which were by now as bald as plucked chickens. They were
making a terrible racket, as were some guinea fowl in the

grounds, and we were convinced we were going to get caught before we could scramble back over the fence. Adrenaline speeded us up and somehow we escaped with the two protesting peacocks.

When we presented them, rather shamefacedly, to the man who had ordered them, we weren't sure how he was going to react.

'You can't expect me to take those ugly things,' he said eventually, gazing in astonishment at the bald, pathetic creatures in front of him. He was trying to sound cross but looked as if he was struggling not to laugh.

We had little choice but to keep the peacocks ourselves. I fed them chicken maize every day and they soon adapted to their rather less privileged life in the woods. My mother, Michael and the various schools and officials had done their best to destroy my spirit, but one thing they had never managed to snatch from me was the soft feelings in my heart for animals.

Most of the time I drove the Mini I had bought from the gypsies on waste ground in the woods, where I'd perfect my handbrake turns and other tricks, but occasionally I ventured on to a quiet country road. One time I did this, a policeman in a patrol car spotted me, and as his blue lights went on immediately, I knew that he seen I was under age – I was only just fourteen. The gypsies had told me that the police can only arrest you for a driving offence on public land, not private, so I steered the car on to a dirt track.

Unfortunately, I came up against a locked gate and had to stop. Two police officers raced to my car, and one of them hauled me from it. One of the ponies had bitten a chunk of flesh out of my arm the day before, and the painful wound had barely closed. A police officer grabbed me and threw me to the ground, breaking open my wound. Fresh blood spurted out and just then a local doctor happened to pass by, walking his dog. He looked at the police in horror and rushed to my aid.

'What have you done to that poor child?' he said, aghast, gaping at the blood pouring from my arm. 'This looks like a serious wound. I insist that she comes back to my house so that I can clean the wound properly and bandage it. I only live a few minutes away.'

The two cowed officers could do nothing but agree, and they tagged along with me to the doctor's house.

Once there, he treated the wound and said sternly to the officers, 'I'm going to report you to your superiors for manhandling this child.'

Needless to say, the police didn't press charges against me. The doctor and the pony bite had saved the day.

Back at the gypsy camp, Reuben, one of the gypsies I was particularly friendly with, hugged me warmly when I told him how I had escaped being charged with driving underage by the police. He was a kind man and was married with four children, although he was probably no more than twenty-five.

'That was a real stroke of luck,' he said, genuinely pleased for me.

The next day Reuben and I, along with three others, set off as usual to the livestock auction in the New Forest. When we arrived there, we saw to our horror some Frenchmen from an abattoir beating a group of pregnant mares and foals, which they were transporting to France for slaughter. The animals were whinnying and crying. They were picking the foals up and throwing them roughly in the cattle trucks. I felt as if I was going to be sick. I couldn't believe that human beings could behave like that towards animals. I began screaming at them to stop, and all of us started trying to pull the abattoir workers off the horses. One of the older gypsies managed to unlock a truck and release fifteen horses. I was overjoyed that some of them were able to run free again. Suddenly I knew what we had to do.

'Quick, into the ring,' I whispered. I thought that if we disrupted the auction, the abattoir workers wouldn't be able to buy any more horses for slaughter.

I knew we might get a punch in the mouth, but it would be worth it to save some horses. We leapt into the ring as one, shouting that the abattoir workers shouldn't be allowed to buy horses. To my disbelief, the officials released more than ten wild ponies into the ring, clearly hoping that they'd trample us and that we'd leave the ring. Two of the boys ran off, but three of us stayed put, determined to continue our protest. The ponies galloped towards us. I raced to the edge of the ring and pinned myself to the wooden fence, trying to keep as much of my body off the ground as possible. The other two did the same. Because of the work I had done breaking in wild ponies, I was used to seeing these beautiful creatures bucking and kicking, and knew what damage they could do. As the ponies kicked and trampled us, I willed my mind to separate itself from my body, a technique I had learnt to cope with the beatings from my mother and Michael. My left leg was badly trampled by the ponies, and all of us were bruised. We stuck it out for twenty-five minutes, before we were dragged out by some of the auction officials.

Some of the traders were horrified at what had happened, but others saw us a huge nuisance who needed be removed whatever it took to do it. They were saying that they'd called the police because we had disrupted the auction, so we fled. A group of gypsies who lived in the New Forest and were also regular attendees at the horse fair hid us. They were very protective towards their own, and the police didn't manage to track us down.

The next day our impromptu protest made it into the local paper. I was delighted that our cause had been put on the map, locally at least. I realised that if we could get more publicity, then we might be able to stop the abattoir workers from buying any more ponies for slaughter, or at least treating them so cruelly. I was enraged about the way the animals were being treated and was determined to put an end to it.

We continued trying to disrupt the auctions as much as possible. Lots of country folk who went along to the auctions came up to us and said they thought we were doing a wonderful job. 'Keep up the good work,' they said encouragingly. Some even gave us donations. One of the local animal welfare groups saw the article in the local paper and got involved. It helped our cause, but the animals were still suffering.

One day when I was in a local newsagent's, I saw an advert which said, 'Got a story? Call us and we'll make sure it gets told.' I called the number out of curiosity and it turned out to posted by a regional news agency for the south-west of England. I asked the woman on the other end of the phone what kind of stories her news agency was interested in.'

'All kinds,' she said. 'Anything that it is the topic of conversation between you and your friends.'

'Are you interested in stories about young people trying to save horses from the slaughterhouse?' I asked.

'Yes, we may be interested in that sort of thing,' she said.

That evening, when we were sitting round the fire, racking our brains about what more we could do to help the ponies, I suddenly came up with an idea. 'I know what we can do. Stonehenge is the most famous thing around here. Why don't we graffiti a message about the ponies on the stones? That will really get into the news.'

The response was enthusiastic.

'Great idea. What are we waiting for?' said Reuben.

It was agreed that he and I would go because we felt so strongly about protecting the horses and we could both run extremely fast.

Georgie, an older gypsy from an encampment in the New Forest, was visiting. He too was very supportive of the idea. 'I'll drive you there when it's dark, if you like. It'll probably take a couple of hours from here to Salisbury.'

We went to a local hardware shop and bought a couple of cans of luminous spray paint and some gardening gloves so that we didn't leave any fingerprints on the cans of paint, which we would discard as soon as we'd finished with them.

I had never been to Stonehenge, but had heard a lot about it. We knew that the place would be heavily guarded, but were sure we'd find a way to evade the security.

As we approached Stonehenge in the car, the size of the stones took my breath away. I suddenly felt like a very tiny speck on the earth. I wondered why the stones had been brought to this particular place and how men had managed to transport them. I liked the idea of this ancient monument, which seemed so much a part of the environment, helping creatures who were also part of it.

We saw that there were guards patrolling the front entrance with Alsatians and decided that we'd have a much better chance of getting in through the back way. We had to go a long way round along a narrow road, then come back on ourselves and cross muddy fields. There were lasers surrounding the site, but Reuben and I managed to wriggle under the fence and avoid detection by these bright, sweeping lights. Then we heard one of the guard dogs barking. We hid behind the gigantic obelisks. The rock was surprisingly smooth. My heart was banging so vigorously I almost thought it was going to leap out of my chest. Excitement and fear rippled through me in equal measure. I had always loved adventures, and this was certainly that.

The dogs were patrolling the perimeter with the guards and couldn't pick up our scent in the vast site. Having escaped detection, Reuben and I whipped out our cans of red and black spray paint. As agreed beforehand, I sprayed 'Save the' on the first two stones and Reuben sprayed 'Ponies' on the third one. My faithful friend the moon was almost full and helpfully lit our handiwork. The sheer scale of the stones and the light of the moon filled me with a sense of spiritual calm.

I'm sure the stones will understand why we've done this, I told myself, stepping back to admire our labours for a second before we sprinted away. Equal feelings of terror and exhilaration pulsed through my body – the greater the fear, the greater the thrill. We ran back across the fields, barely able to see a foot in front of us, and got back on to the road.

'We did it! We did it!' Reuben and I punched the air with our fists.

We almost danced down the lane running down the back of Stonehenge. As far as we knew, nobody had ever pulled off such an audacious stunt before, let alone a spirited teenager and an impassioned gypsy.

'I'm going to call the news agency, Reuben,' I said. 'We want as many people as possible to hear our message. If enough people know what's going on, the ponies will be saved.'

I found a phone box, and still wearing my gloves so I wouldn't leave any fingerprints, I pulled a scrap of paper out of my jeans pocket that had the news agency's phone number on and dialled the number. I decided that I had better disguise my voice. I pinched my nose and tried to speak like the Queen.

'Oh, good evening to you,' I said in a cut-glass accent. 'You might like to know that there's some very interesting graffiti on Stonehenge. Some people have spray-painted on the stones "Save the Ponies" right under the noses of the guards. As far as I know, the guards haven't even noticed this yet.'

The journalist seemed very interested indeed. He kept asking if it was me who had graffitied the historic monument. I denied that I was one of the perpetrators, but said I was an animal lover and a supporter of the people who had daubed the stones. He said he was going to send a reporter and photographer down right away.

I put the phone down and once again Reuben and I cheered. We headed back to the side road where Georgie was waiting for us in his car. He said he would take us to his camp in the New Forest so that we could lie low and keep out of the police's way.

We arrived back at the gypsy camp in the early hours of the morning. Everyone was asleep, so we couldn't celebrate our successful adventure.

The next morning I was woken to an urgent banging on the door. It was Reuben and a couple of the older male gypsies. Reuben's eyes were shining.

'What we did is all over the radio news. It will be in the evening papers too,' he said excitedly. 'The radio is talking about nothing else. I'm sure the ponies will be saved now.'

As the day went on, the story gathered pace. Some of the gypsies gave interviews to journalists about the plight of the New Forest ponies, which were then highlighted in the media. TV cameramen and newspaper photographers took pictures of our graffiti, and the story was the lead item on the ten o'clock news. When I saw pictures of one of England's most famous historic monuments daubed with our words, I felt a sudden pang of guilt, but I knew that the spray we had used could quite easily be cleaned off and that our message was being relayed to thousands, if not millions of people, so it would have all been worthwhile.

The gypsies hailed Reuben and me as heroes. Meanwhile, I became the most wanted person in the south of England; it didn't take the authorities long to work out that I was behind the graffiti. I should have been locked up in a children's home, not performing high-profile stunts like spraying Stonehenge. It made the authorities look very bad. They were also worried in case I began talking to journalists about some of the unsavoury things that went on in children's homes, such as when weaker children like Melanie had been led off by male members of staff for what I was convinced was sexual abuse.

None of the staff had ever tried that kind of thing with me; presumably they knew I would kick and scream and fight back. In those days children's homes were less regulated than they are now, and many of them were a paedophile's paradise.

It would have made me very happy if investigations started into this cruelty.

I stayed in the New Forest camp for eight or nine days. They assumed that I was a gypsy and made me feel very welcome. Then one of the journalists found me and sent a message that he would like to meet me. I agreed to meet up with him back at the camp where my caravan was and got a lift there with one of the gypsies. As we approached the camp, to my horror I saw a police patrol car; it had been a trap. There was nowhere to run. The officers in the police car radioed for back-up and suddenly there were four police cars surrounding me. Some of the officers grabbed me, but I kicked and screamed in a bid to get away. For them, it was like trying to subdue a wild animal. I was determined not to let them deprive me of my liberty, but they won in the end and forced me into a patrol car. I was distraught to have been caught and was furious that I had been stopped in my tracks just when our campaign had been taking off.

'You're in serious, serious trouble now. You're going to get banged up for a good long time,' said one of the officers smugly.

I had made the police look like fools. Both Hampshire and Salisbury Constabularies had been trying to track me down, and it was hugely embarrassing for them that it had taken so long to catch a runaway teenager.

I was taken to a high-security unit. To this day I have no idea where it was and I never saw any other prisoners there. I was shoved into a cell-like room with a bed, a toilet, a table and not much else. I denied that I'd had any involvement with the Stonehenge incident, and after trying and failing with various 'good cop, bad cop' techniques in a bid to make me

confess, I was left alone. I couldn't stand being locked up and
started screaming and kicking at the heavy metal door. I
sincerely believed that I didn't deserve to be locked up.

'Let me out! I've done nothing wrong,' I screamed.

I had always managed to wriggle out of difficult situations
before and was sure that somehow I would find a way to
escape. There was no chance of getting through the heavy cell
door, and the bars on the window were so thick that I would
never be able to squeeze through. There was also a small
frosted-glass window above the toilet, but the glass was very
thick and the opening was tiny. I thought about films I'd
watched on TV about prisoners escaping, and tried to remember what they'd done. I didn't have anything with which
to dig a tunnel under the cell and couldn't think what else I
could do.

By the evening of my third day in captivity, I could stand it
no longer. I had been banging on my cell door on and off for
three days. Meals were brought to me on a tray, but there was
no sign from the staff that they were going to let me out. I
sank into a corner of the bare room and burst into tears. No
child of fourteen wants to be locked up, but after the months
I'd spent running wild in the woods and living among the
animals, it was doubly hard.

I gazed up to the ceiling for inspiration. I'd looked up there
hundreds of times before and knew that no trapdoor was
going to magically appear. But suddenly I saw the toilet
window and an idea came into my head. It probably won't
work, but anything is worth a try, I thought.

I picked up the little table and banged it against the small
glass window. Because the staff were used to hearing me
hammering on the door, they didn't notice anything unusual.

After a while the glass cracked, leaving a small hole, and gradually I managed to knock out the rest of it. The window was just about big enough for me to squeeze through. I'd jumped out of the window and landed in a walled courtyard. Within seconds I'd scaled the wall. Once again I was free. I swallowed big gulps of fresh air. I was overjoyed, but I was still in great danger. The guards had taken my clothes away and given me an ugly pink nylon nightdress and matching slippers. I knew that it wouldn't take the police long to find me if I didn't find something different to wear. I found a washing line, grabbed the first thing I saw – a huge pair of men's jeans and a T-shirt – threw the nightdress away and stepped into my new clothes.

Now I needed to work out where to go. I couldn't decide where would be safest. The police would undoubtedly be looking for me everywhere, so going into town was out of the question. The gypsies were good at hiding people and had hidden me after the Stonehenge incident, so I decided that if I could make it back to the gypsy camp in the woods, I could lie low for a while. Besides, I was desperate to see Starlight Bourbon again who I'd left with the gypsies and thought it was worth taking the risk just for that.

I managed to hitch back to the woods where my caravan was. As I walked up to the gypsy caravans, my heart lurched when I saw that three police cars were waiting for me. They had guessed that I would come straight back here. I felt paralysed with horror at the thought of being locked up once again. I looked around, frantically wondering if I could make a run for it. I saw Reuben looking at me sadly. He had read my mind and was shaking his head resignedly. There was no point in running.

Wherever they take me I'll escape again, and this time I'll find a way of getting out of the country so they can never catch me again, I told myself.

The police walked towards me and I didn't resist as they bundled me into a patrol car once again.

'We're taking you to the Blue Door Centre,' said one of the police officers grimly. 'There's no way you can escape from there.'

As I sat in the back of the police car staring out of the window, I saw a blur of trees and a couple of wild ponies. I would have given anything to be out in the open air. The worst thing of all was that I hadn't even been able to see my beloved horse.

I'd never heard of the Blue Door Centre, but I didn't like the sound of it. I felt utterly miserable. I didn't believe in God, but I prayed to some higher power to create a miracle and set me free from the prison I was on my way to.

PASSAGE TO FRANCE

Escaping the Blue Door Centre wasn't as troublesome as I'd feared, but I knew that if I didn't act quickly, it wouldn't be long before I was once again confined. Clutching my temporary passport at Southampton docks, I was more nervous than I had ever been. It had been two days since I'd run away from the Blue Door Centre. I had come this far without anyone noticing me and I held my breath that my luck would hold out until I had left UK soil.

Just another hour or two until I get on to one of the boats and then I'll be free, I kept saying to myself over and over again.

I had to decide where in the world I was going to go. The *QEII* was in harbour, and I was sure that I could tuck myself away in this huge ship. It was painted shiny white and had a black underside. I was aware that it sailed to America, though I knew precious little about the country, except that it was a very long way away and that people referred to it as 'the land of the free'. New York was the only city I'd heard of, so I decided I'd go there. I'd also read a book about the horses on the ranches in the middle of America, so I decided that if I couldn't survive in New York, I would go to a ranch and help the cowboys to break in and sell horses, just as I'd done with the gypsies.

How would I cope in a new country? I wondered. I tried to push the risks and dangers of taking such a huge step out of my mind. Right now I was more terrified of getting caught and bundled back into a children's home than I was of travelling to America by myself. First get yourself on the ship, then worry about everything else, I thought.

I couldn't see any passengers boarding the ship, though there were a few deckhands around. Amazingly I managed to simply walk aboard, shaking with nerves but trying to look carefree because I knew that I'd attract less attention to myself that way. No one stopped me and asked what I was doing. I began to relax when I found a cupboard to hide in without too much trouble.

After what seemed like an eternity, the ship finally pulled out of the harbour. All too soon, though, it docked again.

Surely we can't have arrived in America already, I said to myself.

I crept out of my dusty hideaway and saw a sign on the shore that read, 'Welcome to Cowes.' Underneath in smaller letters, I read with my horror the words 'Isle of Wight'. I couldn't believe that after all my plans to go to one of the biggest nations in the world, I'd ended up on a tiny island virtually round the corner!

For a minute I considered getting off the ship in the Isle of Wight, but as it was so tiny and close to home, I knew I'd probably get caught if I stayed. I climbed back inside the cupboard.

After a couple of hours the ship set sail again, and by dusk I discovered I was back in Southampton. So ended my first attempt to leave England. The ship had simply been on her way to a maintenance check, which explains why I had found it so easy to board without a ticket. I decided that getting all the way to America at the age of fourteen had been a bit ambitious!

There were lots of ferries sailing to France and I thought I'd have more chance of leaving the country if I jumped on to one of those. I suddenly remembered that it was France where the ponies were being transported to abattoirs and realised that by going to France I could achieve two things at once: escape from the authorities, and try and rescue some of the ponies from the abattoirs. Images flashed through my mind of creeping up to where the ponies were being held, unlocking the door and letting them all escape.

I watched people boarding a ferry that had a sign painted on the side saying, 'Southampton to Le Havre.' It was Easter time and there were lots of noisy, happy families starting their holidays. I decided that I would try to hover as close as I could to them, like a gecko clinging to a tree. Officials never questioned families, I reasoned. I walked a few feet behind a family with three children aged between about five and thirteen. I had to be clever so that it didn't look to the family as if I was with them, but did look that way to any officials.

My plan worked and I slipped on to the huge ferry. Once there, I began to explore the various decks. I'd eaten very little since I'd escaped from the Blue Door Centre and was now starving. I had no money with me, and the initial euphoria about being free had worn off and the business of trying to survive had kicked in. So much of my life was about survival. My hunger had become so sharp that I felt as if it was

gobbling up my insides. It was too risky to steal food from one
of the restaurants on the ferry, so I surreptitiously swiped a
few sandwich crusts and crisps crumbs people had left. It was
better than nothing, but nowhere near enough to fill up the
huge hole in my belly. I comforted myself that once we arrived
in France, there would be more scope to steal a loaf of bread
or find some odd jobs to earn a little money.

Ten minutes before we arrived, an announcer came on to
the ferry's tannoy and said, 'Ladies and gentlemen, we will
shortly be arriving in Le Havre. Please make sure you take all
your belongings with you. I hope you have had a pleasant
journey.'

I walked off the ferry, once again unwittingly shielded by a
family with three boisterous children. When I came across
passport control, my stomach lurched. I was clutching my
temporary passport in my pocket, but I knew that if I mine
was checked, I might be asked questions. It would be much
less risky to sneak past the men while they were checking a
family's passports. I hovered behind the family while their
passports were being checked, then melted away into the
public toilets. When I emerged, I managed to sidle behind
another family who had just passed through passport control.
It was a huge relief that none of the officials seemed to notice
me.

Walking out of the harbour, for a few moments I experienced pure joy. I had made it; I had escaped from the people
who wanted to lock me up for trying to save animals' lives and
for escaping from places that locked up troubled children. I
knew that I was tougher than most other children of my age,
and I was proud of myself for successfully smuggling myself
into a foreign country at just fourteen years old.

My euphoria didn't last long. I had had visions of all of France looking like pictures I'd seen of Paris – the Eiffel Tower rising up in the background, graceful buildings, onion sellers with bushy moustaches, striped tops and black berets – but the reality was quite different. When I walked through the rather down-at-heel grey streets, I felt very disappointed. There was no beauty here. I couldn't speak a word of French. I had no money in my pocket and nowhere to go. Suddenly I was scared. I longed to be safe at home with a loving family, not my real mother and Michael, but the perfect parents I had often dreamt of. I considered getting back on to the next boat to Southampton, but the thought of going home filled me with even more terror. There was only one way to go and that was forwards.

The scent of freshly baked bread tortured my nostrils. I had never been so hungry in all my life. In Southampton and London, there had always been ways to steal a loaf of bread if I was hungry or a pint of milk if I was thirsty, but I was far too scared to risk doing that here, in such an unfamiliar place.

After I'd walked for a while, I saw a bus that said, 'Centre,' on the front. Thankfully, nobody asked me to buy a ticket, and I got off in a large square along with lots of other tourists. There was nothing in the centre that made me feel comforted. Everybody was bustling around, knowing exactly what they were doing and where they were going, except for me. I tried to make myself look invisible. I felt very small and scared. The last thing I needed was to be picked up by French police and sent back to England.

I once again pushed my fears to one side and continued wandering around the centre of Le Havre. Looming up out of the gloomy dusk was a cathedral. I walked in and saw that a service was underway. It was, of course, in French, so I didn't understand a word of it. I felt exhausted as well as hungry and sank into one of the pews at the back. Within minutes I had fallen asleep.

I woke up after the service had ended and people had begun to file out. After a few minutes I realised that there was only the priest and me left in the cathedral. He was a tall man with cropped grey hair and a beard like Michael's. Because of Michael, I always distrusted men with beards. He walked towards me looking stern. He began speaking quickly in French. I didn't understand what he was saying, but I could hear that his tone was harsh.

'English,' I kept saying helplessly. 'Can I sleep here to-night?'

The milk of human kindness that men of God like him were supposed to have seemed to have completely dried up. He shook his head, pointed his finger crossly towards the door and frowned at me. I felt more lost and alone than I'd ever felt in my life. Wearily I dragged myself out of the cathedral. If I didn't eat something soon, I would pass out. I lay down in a grassy area at the back of the cathedral. This would have to be my bed for the night, I thought, feeling completely beaten.

As I lay down on the cold, lumpy ground, my thoughts turned to my mother. I blamed her for everything. If it wasn't for her cruelty and the fact that she had never intervened when Michael had beaten me, I wouldn't be here now, I thought to myself. I'd be in a warm, clean, comfortable bed in my own home, hanging out on my estate and chatting to the other girls of fourteen and fifteen. While they were thinking about make-up and boyfriends, the thoughts that filled my head had always been when I was next going to eat and how I could avoid being captured and locked up again by the police.

I knew my mother didn't love me, but I couldn't understand why. I thought that all mothers were supposed to love their children, and although I was determined to be tough and to prove that I could survive without her, the hurt of not being loved never went away. I knew that if I spent time thinking about all the bad things that had happened to me – the beatings at home, the nastiness or indifference of my teachers, the attempted rape by Jim – I would just curl up and die. I didn't want to die, though; I very much wanted to live.

I worried the police would come looking for me, but eventually fell into a fitful, troubled sleep and was woken at first light by a bird that kept flapping its wings in the bush close to where I lay. My hunger had become much more acute, and I stayed dozing on the grass for a few more hours, waking continually. I felt too weak to move, but I knew that if anyone found me lying here, I would be sent back to England.

What am I going to do? I wondered desperately.

I had managed to get all the way to France, but now I was trapped.

MONSIEUR ET MADAME VERT

Eventually hunger forced me to make a decision about what to do next, as I realised

I would simply have to get up, force myself along the street, go into a restaurant, coolly order some food, explain that I was a student if anyone questioned me, then make a run for it before the bill came. With each faltering step, I felt a little more of my strength drain away. I dragged myself past a few bright, bustling eating places, but rejected them because they had too many staff for me to slip away. Then I noticed a small, run-down *pension* with red-and-white checked table-cloths. It was empty apart from an old man who seemed to be in charge. He was small with a kind, wrinkled face.

I knew this place was perfect because there was no way he would be able to chase after me when I bolted out of the door, but I felt guilty that I was about to order a meal I had no way of paying for. Nevertheless, I really believed that if I didn't eat something soon I would die. I'm sure that most people in a similarly desperate situation would have done the same thing.

I walked in with a bright smile in the hope that it would conceal the fact that I was about to faint from hunger. His extremely fast French was incomprehensible to me, so through a mixture of hand and facial gestures I understood that there was only one dish on the menu. I nodded gratefully.

He brought me a basket full of French bread, which I tore into like a wild animal devouring its prey. I could feel my stomach leaping for joy. The bread was followed by a steaming plate of pork and beans. It was without doubt the best food I'd ever tasted. I wanted every hot, spicy mouthful to last for ever. My strength returned, and I felt much more equipped to find ways to survive in France. I was so engrossed with filling my hollow stomach that I didn't notice the old man locking the front door. It was late in the afternoon and he clearly wasn't expecting any more customers.

It was only when I had wiped the last bit of sauce clean off the plate with some bread and was planning my hasty exit that I noticed he had locked the door. The man walked up to my table to clear my plate and was evidently surprised that I'd consumed the entire basket of bread. I suppose most of his customers wouldn't eat more than a piece or two.

With the front door locked, I quickly had to revise my escape plan. I signalled to him that I wanted to go to the toilet and he indicated the direction. Once safely in the ladies', I was devastated to find that there was no window to squeeze myself through. Plans A and B had failed, so I would have to resort to Plan C, which was even more risky. I went back to my table and drained the remains of my glass of Coca-Cola. The man put the bill on the table and seemed to be getting tetchy. Perhaps once he had got rid of me, he planned to pop upstairs for an afternoon nap.

Through a series of melodramatic gestures towards my almost empty plastic bag, shrugs and tearful expressions –

'Money stolen. Money gone' – I was able to make him understand that I wasn't going to pay for my meal. I think he had probably already suspected that to be the case. He gestured for me to follow him. My heart in my mouth, I did so, terrified that he was going to call the police. Instead, he led me into the kitchen, where his elderly wife was washing up. She had a pleasant, plump-cheeked face and wore her grey hair in a plait coiled round her head. The man spoke fast to her and she nodded and pointed to a series of metal shelves. She mimed a scrubbing gesture and got out a bucket, which she filled with hot water. She handed me a scrubbing brush and some scouring powder. They then both pointed towards the upper floor and left the kitchen. I presumed they were going for a rest.

Full of energy thanks to my hearty meal, and grateful that they hadn't called the police, I vigorously scrubbed the dusty, grease-encrusted shelves until they shone. I wanted to prove to them that I was an honest person and wasn't interested in ripping them off. I could have tried to find another way to escape when they went upstairs, but I truly wanted to repay them for the lovely meal.

I was so absorbed in my scrubbing that I didn't hear them coming back into the kitchen a few hours later. When they saw how I'd made their grubby kitchen sparkle, both of them beamed and the woman patted my arm affectionately. She and her husband made it clear that they were so impressed with my work that they would be happy for me to stay on and work for them, and that accommodation would be part of the package. They told me that their names were Monsieur and Madame Vert. They didn't tell me their first names and I never asked.

Madame Vert and her husband spoke a little English and I somehow managed to communicate that I was a student and had been on my way to the south of France to pick up some seasonal farming work before returning to my studies in England. I told them I was happy to spend some time with them and earn some money to support myself.

I spent the first couple of nights sleeping in a dusty storage room in the hotel part of the building. I was delighted that I now had a job and somewhere to stay. When I'd built up their trust by working hard all day long at whatever tasks they put me to, they gave me a proper room of my own. Apart from my beloved caravan, it was the nicest room I'd ever had. There was cream-coloured, rose-sprigged wallpaper and an old-fashioned bedstead with a substantial mattress perched on top of it. I kept the window open most of the time to drive out the musty smell and got used to the sound of noisy pipes and creaking floorboards lulling me to sleep every night.

Things were going very well at the *pension*. The old couple were pleased with my hard work and praised me constantly. I felt like a flower opening itself out in the light. Hardly anyone had told me I was good at anything before, and it was a strange and wonderful sensation. I told them I would spend the whole of the summer with them before I went back to my studies, and for the first time I felt happy and settled.

Since that day at the livestock auction, however, the suffering of the ponies had never been far from my thoughts, and my plan to find the abattoir where they were being taken and set them free was now firmly cemented in my mind. While I was in England, I had asked one of the horse dealers the name of the abattoir. He had reluctantly told me and I had memorised the address. I discovered that the abattoir was a few hours by bus from Le Havre.

Monsieur and Madame Vert gave me a day off every Monday, when the restaurant was closed at lunchtime and didn't open until the evening, and I planned to use my wages to travel by bus to the abattoir once a week throughout the summer to free a group of ponies. I had already asked at the bus station in Le Havre about how to get to the town where the abattoir was.

I decided not to tell the old couple of my plans in case they disapproved. I knew they served horse meat in the restaurant, so I thought they probably wouldn't be too concerned about the fate of the ponies. I didn't hold that against them, though. Horse meat was a common delicacy in France, and I'm sure they hadn't given the issue much thought. Whenever I took customers' orders I used to quietly promote other dishes to them if they ordered horse meat.

'Today's special is a superb vegetable stew,' I half whispered, in case my bosses heard me pushing the animal-free alternative, which was cheaper. They never seemed to hear, though, and would simply nod encouragement to me from the kitchen as I communicated with diners in my halting French, which they had tried to teach me.

The following Monday, after I'd spent two weeks at the *pension*, I set off on my secret mission to rescue the ponies. I felt happy and exited at the prospect of rescuing the animals I loved. The town I was heading for was about an hour away from Paris, and I was going to need to take two buses to reach it. I settled down on the back seat of the bus to Paris and closed my eyes. I filtered out the sounds of young mothers hushing their noisy children and of raucous teenagers. I

guessed that the teenagers were probably about the same age
as me, but somehow they seemed much younger – they might
have been on the earth for the same number of years as me,
but they definitely had some catching up to do in terms of life
experience.

I hadn't really formulated a plan for liberating the ponies.
I had visions of simply slipping the catch off an unattended
door and watching them gallop to freedom, but in reality I
had given no thought to the kind of security measures there
would be at the abattoir, or to the number of employees. I
couldn't even imagine what an abattoir looked like. I had
seen pictures of Auschwitz and wondered if the abattoir
would look similar, with the stench of dead horses filling my
nostrils.

I felt tired when I got off the second bus. The journey had
taken me almost five hours, and I still had a distance to walk
before I reached the abattoir.

Having had the idea of rescuing the ponies in my head for
so long, actually approaching their prison scared me. The
abattoir was a long, low building surrounded by a barbed-
wire fence. A large lorry pulled up outside the building and I
could hear the sound of distressed horses. I think they knew
instinctively that death was approaching. I had brought a
cheap camera with me and planned to get some evidence of the
brutal, barbaric conditions the animals were being held in and
send it to the same journalists I'd talked to when I'd graffitied
Stonehenge.

A couple of broad men in wellingtons, stained white vests
and leather aprons were standing outside the abattoir waiting
for the lorry to unload. When I thought they weren't watching, I darted under the barbed-wire fence and bolted towards

the lorry. Unfortunately, the men had seen me and two of them grabbed me with their strong, coarse hands.

'This is private property. What the hell do you think you're doing here?' one of them said in rough French that I could just about understand.

He dragged me towards a room next to the main building. I was panicking. This certainly wasn't part of the plan. I had no idea what the man and his fellow slaughterer, who had followed us into the room, were going to do to me, but I didn't want to hang around to find out. The first man sat me in a chair and held me forcibly by the shoulders to keep me still. I wriggled and wriggled, then ducked under his arms, sprinted out of the room and ran away from the abattoir as fast as I could.

As I hurtled down the road, the horrible sounds the horses were making filled my ears. My heart was pounding as I thought of what might have happened to me if the men had managed to hang on to me for long enough to hand me over to the police. I had tried my best to free the ponies, but now that I'd seen the layout of the abattoir and the big, strong men who worked there, I realised that it was impossible for me to fulfil my naïve dream. I was heartbroken, but I was also realistic about what I could and couldn't do. Now that I knew there was nothing practical I could do to help the animals, I wanted to get as far away as possible from that place of death. I made my way back to the bus station to travel back to the *pension* in Le Havre.

On the bus back to Paris, I realised that part of me was relieved that I hadn't actually witnessed the gruesome sight of the animals being slaughtered. I had a feeling that if I had, I would be traumatised by it for the rest of my life. I racked my brains trying to think of some other idea to provide salvation, but could think of nothing that I could do to help those poor creatures. I comforted myself by remembering that some of the big animal welfare charities had got involved in the issue of the ponies being exported for slaughter after our graffiti had hit the headlines. I knew that they had much more power to push for change than a lone teenage girl. Maybe their efforts could save the ponies' lives. I hoped they would continue their work and get the evil trade stopped.

By the time I'd been at the *pension* for a few weeks, the old couple were treating me like an adopted daughter. This was one of the happiest times in my life. I wanted to work as hard as I could for them because they were lovely, decent people. They were too old to do much hard, physical work and I tried to do what I could to help them. They were always grateful and I basked in their kindness. It felt like a magic ointment healing some of my pain. Everything I did they praised me for, and craving more and more praise, I worked ever harder and suggested new jobs they might like me to do. After all the years that I had dreamt of my real parents, I wondered if Monsieur and Madame Vert were the ones I was supposed to find.

When I came down with a bad dose of flu, Madame Vert fussed around me and insisted that I stay in bed until my fever had gone. She cooked me chicken soup, which she said was the best possible thing to bring down a fever, and sat mopping my brow. Although I felt really ill, I loved having so much kindness and attention lavished on me. It was a glimpse of what I'd missed during my childhood.

If someone had asked me then, 'Would you rather have a million pounds or be part of a loving family?' I would have answered without hesitation that I would rather a loving family. Now that I had experienced it, I knew that nothing could compare.

As soon as I had recovered from the flu, Madame Vert announced, '*Chérie*, I'm going to teach you how to cook and then you can help me with the meals.'

I'd never taken much interest in cooking up to now, and fried or scrambled eggs on toast were the limit of my culinary skills, but I had always picked things up quickly and was very eager to learn. Madame Vert taught me how to make steak Diane and crêpes Suzettes. She showed me to cook the steak to perfection and make the crêpes wafer-thin. I felt proud of creating something that looked good and tasted even better.

I was also picking up more and more French from Monsieur and Madame Vert, as well as from the customers, and from watching French TV in the evenings, which I did when the restaurant was quiet.

Being with Monsieur and Madame Vert restored my faith in humanity. My childhood had been littered with so many lousy adults, but here were two wonderful human beings who proved to me that if you do good things for people, you are sometimes repaid with kindness.

This was a very tranquil period in my life. Nobody was beating me, nobody was telling me I was a bad girl, and my day-to-day needs were taken care of. I thought little during my time with them of either the past or the future. It was a holiday from the tough business of survival and a chance to recuperate from the rigours of life in England.

The couple had no knowledge of my past and saw me simply as an honest and hard-working student who ably cleaned the nooks and crannies their limbs had seized up too much to get into. I even painted the dingy frontage of the *pension* for them. It was hard, physical work, but I was very proud of the transformation of the exterior from grubby grey to gleaming white. Madame Vert repotted some geraniums that had been sitting in the back yard and placed them on the newly brightened front windowsills.

'It looks so good you could start charging higher prices,' I said to the Verts.

They looked aghast. They were very decent people, and as long as they earned enough money to keep going, they weren't interested in accumulating any surplus.

After a couple of months I had amassed a substantial amount of money in wages and tips from customers. I would have been happy to stay on at the *pension*, but when I had arrived I'd told the old couple I was a student and was planning to spend the summer months fruit picking in the south of France. Because they were such wonderful, trusting people, I couldn't bear to tell them that I'd lied to them and that really I was a runaway who hadn't been to school for years and was wanted by the police.

In order to stick to my story, I knew I had to leave. It was too dangerous to return to England, and at the back of my mind I had a vague fantasy of travelling to a different part of France for a few weeks, then turning up on their doorstep once more and saying, 'I wasn't happy with my course and have decided to take a break from studying for a while. Could I come back to work for you?'

At this point I hoped that Madame Vert would wrap me in her soft, warm arms and say, 'Of course you can, *chérie*. We're overjoyed to have you back.'

When I finally said goodbye to the Verts at the beginningof the summer, I could barely contain the sadness I felt.

'We'll really miss you, *chérie*,' said Madame Vert, smiling fondly. 'You're one of the best and most loyal workers we've ever had here. Come back any time and we'll find some work for you.' She pressed my thin body against her well-padded one and planted a big kiss on both of my cheeks.

Monsieur Vert was a little more restrained. He clasped my hand between his two wrinkled, rough ones. I thought his eyes looked a little more watery than usual, but I couldn't be sure. 'Take care of yourself on your travels,' he said. 'You've been a wonderful help to us.'

I walked off down the road with my new rucksack on my back and tears in my eyes. Monsieur and Madame Vert stood in the doorway waving me off. It was the first time people had ever seemed sad to see me leave. They had no inkling that they had given me so much more than I could ever repay. They had shown me love and how to give of myself to people who gave to me. For so much of my life I had felt as if I'd been trudging through darkness.

I had no idea what I was going to do next or where I was going to go, but as I walked away from the *pension*, for the first time in my life I felt good about myself. I was surrounded by a bright and happy light.

SUMMER ON THE RIVIERA

As I left Monsieur and Madame Vert's *pension*, heading for the bus station, I thought how much things had changed. Two months ago I'd staggered half-starved along this road. Now, I was clean and tidy. My dark, shiny hair was pulled off my face in a neat ponytail, and I'd bought myself some new T-shirts and jeans. The few possessions I'd accumulated were packed into a little red rucksack I'd bought, and Madame Vert had carefully packed some ham sandwiches wrapped in waxed paper, a bag of apples and a generous slice of homemade cheese, which was tied in a cloth.

My thoughts turned to where I should go once I'd reached the bus station. I'd read magazines about the south of France while I was working for Monsieur and Madame Vert, and even though I couldn't understand all the words, I had liked the look of the pictures.

'Go south,' said a little voice in my head. 'You'll be happy by the beach and the sea.'

I recalled the pictures I'd seen and, listening to the little voice, decided to take a bus back to Paris. At the bus station in Paris, there were adverts for cheap train fares from Paris to

Nice. My French had really improved since I'd arrived and I now had a basic understanding of the language. I had never spent much time at school, but I had had a rich education nonetheless – I knew more about the natural world than most schoolchildren and could probably speak French better than those pupils who had begun learning the language at the age of eleven.

I went to the railway station, which was full of smart, bustling people and the delicious aroma of sharp coffee and buttery croissants, and boarded a train to Nice.

When I arrived in Nice several hours later, something about the town set my teeth on edge. I sensed a rough undercurrent and my instincts told me to get out, so I moved on to nearby Cannes, where I felt immediately at ease. I bought myself a baguette, threw off my shoes and sat on a wall overlooking the beach. The sky was an impossibly pure shade of blue, the sand was pale blond, and the droplets of turquoise seawater that bounced off the waves into the air glittered in the sun. At that moment I didn't have a care in the world. I had some money in my pocket, was a long way from Michael and my mother, and had left the police and social workers far behind. I was free and could do absolutely anything I chose. There were no cruel adults dragging me down, I was out in the natural world rather than cooped up in an ugly city, and having worked successfully in the *pension*, I was confident that I could pick up enough casual work to feed and clothe myself. I needed nothing more. It was July and the summer season in Cannes was in full swing. The place was bustling with stylish people swimming, sunbathing and sipping cool drinks.

A couple of boys who looked as if they were a few years older than me were sitting near me on the beach drinking beer. Both were deeply tanned with straight brown hair, which had developed kinks from the salty air, and both had the kind of light-green eyes that reminded me of my gypsy friends. They looked as if they were brothers, although one had more regular, handsome features than the other.

The boys smiled at me and I smiled back. Then they approached me and started chatting in French. Their accent sounded different.

'We're Italian. We're here for the summer season,' they explained.

'We do various odd jobs, cleaning the rich people's boats and serving the rich in other ways.' The boys looked at each other and laughed.

I didn't know what they meant, but it turned out that the more handsome of the two, Leo, worked as a gigolo, lavishing his time and body on a wealthy older American woman, while Marco cleaned boats and did other odd jobs. In Soho, I had only met women selling sex. I had never heard of the arrangement working the other way, but I didn't find it surprising. Although I knew that I would never be able to sell my body, I understood that for both sexes who found themselves living a hand-to-mouth existence, what mattered most was surviving, and sometimes none of us could be too choosy about the way we did it.

'I've come over from England,' I told them. 'I don't really have any plans. I just want to pick up some odd jobs so that I've got enough money to eat.'

Thankfully they didn't ask me any questions about England. It seemed that Cannes was stuffed with people from all over the world who converged while the sun shone.

Leo talked about the American woman he worked for in a very matter-of-fact way. 'She's married to some wealthy guy who works as a doctor in New York, but he seems to leave her to get on with her own life. He's probably traded her in for a younger model. She lives up on California Hill. It's a place for the truly, deeply rich, and she has a boat here.' He gestured with his head towards a pristine white yacht docked in the harbour. 'She likes to spend time with me there.' He grinned. 'Most of the time she doesn't come to the boat, though, and she lets me and Marco sleep on it.'

Marco was less confident than his beautiful brother. His skin was spotty under his tan, and his voice was squeaky, but I liked his quietness. He walked off to the beach café and came back with three cans of Coke.

'I'm sure I could help you find work on one of the boats with me, if you like,' he said kindly. 'There are plenty of jobs here – it's just a question of asking the right people.'

'That would be great,' I said enthusiastically.

The next day Marco introduced me to his boss on one of the yachts. 'This is Louise. She's a very hard worker and I've brought her along to help today. Is that OK? I know you wanted me to scrub the sails and that's a lot of work for one person.'

The man who owned the yacht seemed very easygoing. 'Sure, Marco, no problem – just as long as the job gets done.' He sauntered off the boat and disappeared along the beach.

Marco showed me how to scrub the salt deposits off the deck and the sails with a large nailbrush and some detergent squirted into a bucket of hot water. The sun became hotter and hotter, and we kept shuffling around the deck to find some shade to work in.

After a while I saw a stunningly beautiful and very expensively dressed young woman walk down the pier arm in arm with a rather ugly older man. To me, she looked like a movie star. They walked down the gangplank on to the yacht next to ours. I naïvely wondered what such an attractive young woman was doing with a man like him.

Suddenly emboldened, perhaps by the intense heat or by my joy at being free and happy, I called out in French, 'Hey, do you want your boat cleaned?'

The woman smiled and called back, 'Why don't you come aboard in an hour's time?'

'Great, I'll do that,' I said.

Marco said he could finish scrubbing the sails and deck without me, and so an hour later I climbed on to the neighbouring yacht. I had unoriginally dubbed the couple, whom I soon found out were called Harry and Nicole, Beauty and the Beast.

Nicole and Harry asked me to do some odd jobs for them, including carrying boxes of provisions on to the boat for them, and then told me they were about to set sail for nearby St Tropez and invited me to join them.

I readily accepted, pleased at the prospect of earning some money and having an adventure on a yacht. Nicole had a poodle called Mitzi, and one of my tasks was to look after her and make sure she didn't fall overboard. There was lots of brandy and cigars on the boat, and both Harry and Nicole were smoking them. I had never seen a woman smoking cigars before and thought Nicole looked very cool. I was amazed to

see that when Harry wasn't looking, Nicole discreetly flicked
her cigar ash into his brandy.

She obviously doesn't love him that much, I thought to
myself, still not having realised exactly what the relationship
was between them.

I had never tasted brandy before, and when they had
their backs turned, I tried a couple of sips from Nicole's
glass. It burnt my throat. I had been drunk on cider at one
of the children's homes and hadn't liked feeling of being
out of control. The gypsies didn't use drugs or drink
alcohol, so I hadn't experimented with any substances
there.

Harry kept trying to paw Nicole and she kept fending him
off. 'Not in front of the kid,' she kept saying.

I realised after a while that I was being used as some
kind of bizarre chaperone for her. They had a jet ski, which
they allowed me to try out. The speed of it and the
sensation of being power-showered by the ocean spray
was wonderful. It excited me because it was a completely
new experience. I already felt that I had shed my worries,
but whizzing through the waves gave me a great feeling of
freedom.

Harry and Nicole also took turns on the jet ski, and when
we returned to the boat, they disappeared into the cabin down
below and closed the door firmly behind them. It seemed that
Nicole could fend Harry off no longer. She looked resigned.
Ten minutes later she emerged on deck looking slightly
dishevelled.

'He's asleep,' she said, looking relieved. She slumped down
on a sunlounger and slathered suncream all over her long,
brown, toned body.

We got talking and she asked me lots of questions about myself, which I tried to evade. I shrugged my shoulders when she asked me anything about my life in England. I liked her and didn't want to lie, but equally I didn't trust her enough to confide in her. She smiled knowingly and handed me her card. It was cream-coloured with powder-blue swirls around the edges. It had her name, Nicole Albert, an address in Avenue Foch, Paris, which meant nothing to me, and a phone number. I later found out that Avenue Foch is one of the most expensive streets in the world. It is just off the Champs-Élysées, and only a very elite group of rich people can afford to live there.

Nicole and Harry weren't staying on the yacht; they were staying in one of the best hotels nearby, but were soon going home to Paris, so after we had returned to Cannes, I waved goodbye.

I continued to work on the boats and became very attached to my new lifestyle. I loved spending time with Leo and Marco. The three of us got browner and browner until we were almost mahogany. They told me I could sleep with them on the boat belonging to Leo's 'girlfriend', as she never came to it at night. I jumped at the chance. It was very luxurious, with a large deck and big, comfortable white sofas and sunloungers laid out on it. When Leo didn't need the boat for work, and when Marco and I had finished our daily deck-scrubbing job, we lounged around on deck, only going below to prepare some food or to sleep.

This was the first time in my life that I had lived anywhere luxurious. The council estate, the children's homes, my caravan and Monsieur and Madame Vert's modest *pension* had not been remotely fancy. I had no idea at the time, but I would soon be living in even more luxurious places.

I liked the novelty of being surrounded by beautiful people. I had always tried to conceal my femininity, disguising my breasts under baggy sweatshirts and shoving my long, dark hair into caps. But seeing all the beautiful women awakened an urge in me to look feminine. I had just started my periods and felt much more womanly. I bought myself a couple of skimpy skirts and girlie tops, and I even invested in some eye shadow in a lurid shade of blue, which I plastered over my eyelids as thickly as I spread butter on my toast. Leo, who knew much more about these things than I did, was horrified. He wiped most of it off, leaving a subtle dusting on my eyelids.

'You have to be sparing with make-up, Louise, otherwise you'll end up looking like a clown in the circus!' he laughed.

A couple of weeks after I arrived, a large group of gypsies came to Cannes. There were some magnificent guitarists among them. They sounded very like the Gypsy Kings, and years later I wondered if they were actually the Gypsy Kings in their pre-fame days. When the sun went down, they picked up their guitars and played fast, furious, beautiful melodies. We all sat around in shorts and T-shirts with the warm night air blowing over us. The moon and stars made the water shimmer. We sipped cold beer, made friends with other teenagers who gathered on the beach, and thought that we were the luckiest people in the world.

I felt so secure that I even decided to call home from a phone box near the beach, just to let everyone know I was alive. I had no intention of telling them where I was, but now that I was far away from my mother and Michael, I felt less anger towards them and decided that letting them know I was alive was the responsible thing to do.

'My God, Louise, where the hell have you been?' gasped Jay, when he answered the phone.

'Shh,' I said. 'I don't want Michael hearing.'

'Don't worry – they're out,' he said.

'Listen, I can only talk for a minute because it's very expensive. You OK?'

'Yes,' he said flatly, indicating that nothing had changed at home.

'OK, just tell them that I'm alive, I'm fine, I've got myself some casual jobs and that I won't be coming back.'

I had often wondered what my mother, my father and Michael had been feeling since my disappearance from the Blue Door Centre. Were they relieved to have seen the back of me or worried about my safety? Now that I knew I could survive without them, I was determined never to go back home. I felt pleased that I'd done the responsible thing and called.

As soon as I'd made the call to Jay from Cannes, I forgot about my family and got on with enjoying myself. The whole experience was deliciously alien to me. I woke up happy, I hummed happy songs while I worked at scrubbing decks and sails, I spent many happy evenings relaxing on the beach, and I went to sleep happy. I thought of neither the past nor the future, and inhabited only a pain-free, un-troubled present. I turned fifteen while I was in Cannes, but kept it quiet. I didn't want anyone to know my true age. I told everyone I met that I was eighteen, and nobody ever questioned me.

At the beginning of October the summer season ended.

Almost overnight the place went from being a slice of perfection locked inside a perpetual ray of light into a dog-eared leftover. The tourists retreated to their real lives, far from Cannes, and the sky and the sea became soiled with grey, as if someone had smoked too many cigarettes over their pristine blueness and left an ugly, spreading stain. Leo and Marco announced that they were going home to Italy to see their family. I certainly had no intention of going home to see mine.

'Can I come with you to Italy?' I asked hopefully. They had both been good friends to me, and I had no plans about what to do next.

'Louise, you're welcome to come and join us, but we've been away for months and we need to spend a bit of time on our own with our parents and our two younger sisters first. Take our phone number and come and join us in a few weeks. OK?'

I nodded.

The next day they packed their belongings into rucksacks, embraced me warmly and jumped on the train.

'It's been a great summer, Louise,' said Leo. 'Look forward to seeing you again soon.'

I felt miserable as I waved them off from the platform. The three of us had become very close in just a couple of months and I felt safe with both of them. I also relied on them – it was thanks to Leo and Marco that I had a free and luxurious place to sleep at night, the job scrubbing decks and friends with whom I could enjoy the beach and the sea. I felt very alone and insecure as their train pulled out of the station, and once again I wondered what I was going to do next.

I was determined that however bad things got, I wasn't

going to go back to England and surrender myself to the authorities. I resolved to return to Monsieur and Madame Vert's *pension* with my story about how my studies back in England hadn't worked out, but then I remembered that I had Nicole's address in Paris. I decided to look her up on my way back to Le Havre.

A WRETCHED, GLITTERING LIFE

Now that I was on the train to Paris, I couldn't decide whether to go back to Monsieur and Madame Vert's or not. The little voice inside my head kept whispering, 'Keep on moving forwards.' With most of the events in my life, there had been a very good reason to distance myself from the things that had just happened to me. My time in the *pension* in Le Havre was the first experience that would be worth going back for. But because things had been so perfect there, I was terrified of spoiling them – perhaps they wouldn't have a job for me; perhaps they would no longer like me; perhaps they had found out that I had lied to them and was a runaway, not a student. I decided it was better to hold on to a perfect memory than risk ruining it by going back.

I arrived in Paris late in the evening, but Gare du Nord was still buzzing. The atmosphere was very different from the laid-back vibe at Cannes. I had some money with me, but I knew that if I checked into a hotel, it would be gone very quickly. I decided that even though it was almost midnight, it would be worth calling on Nicole and asking if she could put me up for the night. I was too tired to start walking through the streets of Paris with my bag, so I jumped into a taxi and asked the driver to take me to Avenue Foch.

When the car drew up outside Nicole's apartment, I was amazed. I knew she was wealthy, but I had no idea that she had this kind of money. The road was full of elegant stone apartments with tall, thin windows. I rang Nicole's bell, feeling slightly apprehensive about turning up so late at night and looking so scruffy and out of place in such a smart street.

She opened the door tentatively and gasped when she saw me. Mitzi the poodle was more welcoming and licked my hand enthusiastically.

'Louise, what on earth are you doing here? It's almost midnight. I thought you would have gone back to England by now,' said Nicole irritably.

'Well, the summer season finished in Cannes and I was at a bit of a loose end. I thought I might try and pick up some work in Paris. Could I come in for a few moments?'

Reluctantly Nicole held the door open for me and gestured me through into her living room.

'Wow, what a fantastic place you've got here, Nicole,' I said.

Although the apartment was small, everything in it looked extremely expensive. There were gilt mirrors, antique furniture and a Persian rug on top of highly polished floorboards.

Nicole looked as stunning as she had in Cannes. Her blonde hair was coiled in an elegant chignon, and she was wearing make-up and a black, sparkly cocktail dress. She looked as if she'd just returned from an evening out.

'Can I use your toilet, please?' I asked her as sweetly as I could manage.

She gestured to a door down the hallway. I hoped that once she'd got over the shock of seeing me, she might adjust to the idea of having me around for a while.

Having scrubbed my grimy face and brushed my hair to make myself look like a more appealing house guest, I walked back to the living room.

'Could I just crash on your sofa for tonight?' I asked. 'I'll sort something out for myself in the morning.'

Nicole seemed to have softened a bit. 'Oh, all right, then,' she agreed, smiling. 'I haven't got a spare room, but I'll make up a bed on the sofa for you. Would you mind just taking the dog out for me?'

I agreed eagerly, thinking that maybe the dog could be my ticket to a roof over my head for a few days. I decided to try to behave as I had done with Monsieur and Madame Vert, making myself indispensable in a polite and unobtrusive way.

That night I slept very soundly on Nicole's brocade sofa, swaddled in a soft eiderdown, and awoke refreshed when the sun danced through the gaps in her Venetian blinds. Soon after I woke up, a bleary-eyed Nicole walked into the living room, dressed in a lilac silk dressing gown. Even tired and devoid of make-up she looked stunning.

'Should I go down to the nearest bakery and get some croissants and baguettes for breakfast?' I asked, trying to sound as helpful as possible.

Nicole smiled sleepily. 'That's a good idea, Louise.' She handed me some francs.

'I'll take Mitzi with me,' I said.

I hurriedly got dressed and walked to the corner of the road, where I had remembered seeing a bakery the night before. I bought some pastries and returned.

After we'd eaten breakfast, I washed up and cleaned Nicole's rather neglected kitchen until it shone. Having spent two months working for Monsieur and Madame Vert, I had become an expert kitchen scrubber. I could see that it was dawning on Nicole that I could be a help rather than a hindrance.

Nicole was now dressed in a smart trouser suit and had completely woken up. She seemed in the mood to chat.

'Tell me a bit about yourself, Louise. I can see that you're an adventurous girl, but when I asked you about yourself in Cannes, you were very secretive. Do you remember? I sense there's something going on with you.'

I nodded and trembled. Could I risk telling her the truth? I decided it was my only hope. If she felt sorry for me, she might let me stay at her apartment for a while.

'I . . . I've run away,' I said, almost in a whisper.

Nicole nodded sympathetically. 'I thought it was something like that because you're so young, *chérie*.'

Her compassion encouraged me to continue. 'I'm terrified that if I have to go back to England, the police will catch me and put me in prison because I'm underage. My mum and her boyfriend beat me all the time at home. That's why I ran away.' My voice began to tremble, and tears rolled down my cheeks.

Nicole couldn't have been more than twenty-one or so, but she put a very maternal arm round my shoulders. 'There, there, *chérie*, don't cry. You can stay with me for a little while and help me out with things around the house. I won't send you back to England.'

'Oh, thank you, thank you, Nicole. You're a good, kind person.'

She hugged me, and, determined to prove my worth, I jumped up and started tidying up the living room. I was delighted to have somewhere to stay again.

In Cannes I had never been quite sure what Nicole did. After a few days in Paris, Nicole explained to me that she was a model, but all her assignments seemed to take place in the evening, which I thought was odd. Sometimes she told me that I had to leave the flat for a couple of hours and not come back before a certain time. After a couple of weeks I guessed that she had the same job as the women I had come across in Soho and that she was selling herself to the richest men in Paris for large amounts of money. I didn't judge Nicole for what she did, even though the thought of doing it myself horrified me. I knew that it was hard to make money and that everyone found different ways to survive.

Whenever a customer was due to come round to her apartment, Nicole said, 'Go and sit with the dog on the terrace of one of the cafés on the Champs-Élysées.'

I took her advice and spent many hours outside various coffee shops watching the chic Parisian world go by. Sometimes when I was out with Mitzi, I decided to explore, and one evening I found myself in the Bois de Boulogne. I didn't know it, but it was a notorious place for sexually deviant behaviour. When I returned to Nicole's flat later that evening, I told her about some of the strange people I'd seen there.

'You're just a child – you shouldn't be going to those places,' she said, furrowing her brow. 'Stick to the terrace of cafés and the George the Fifth Hotel – they do the best hot chocolate in Paris there. You can get raped and kidnapped in the Bois de Boulogne.'

I had noticed that Nicole had seemed increasingly jittery in the few weeks since I'd arrived. She was making frequent trips to the bathroom and was then coming out sniffing. At the time I didn't know anything about cocaine and didn't understand that she was using it heavily, nor did I realise that the drug was at least partly responsible for her increasingly erratic behaviour.

One evening after I'd been staying with her for three weeks, she went out dressed in an exquisite pale-green silk dress, set off with a necklace of large diamonds. She threw a heavy mink coat over her as she walked out.

'Bye, *chérie*, see you later. I'm meeting a client for my modelling work.' She blew me a kiss.

I thought she looked rather sad. Her beauty seemed irrelevant to her.

She returned home late – it must have been after one in the morning – and I was in a deep sleep on the sofa. She turned on all the lights and I sprang out of bed. She staggered and then collapsed in a heap on the floor under her fur coat. I rushed to her side and helped her up.

'I need to go to the bathroom, *chérie*,' she said. Her speech was slurred and she could barely walk.

When she came out of the bathroom, a kind of madness seemed to have grabbed her by the throat. She threw off her coat, then started stabbing it with a kitchen knife, completely destroying it. She pulled a Cartier watch from her wrist and threw it across the room. Next she pulled the diamond necklace from her neck, breaking the chain the diamonds were on, and dramatically flung it out of the window. She seemed to be having some kind of breakdown. I had never seen anyone in this state before. I felt horrified and helpless.

Then she turned to me and grabbed hold of me. 'Do you know what I am?' she asked.

Her light-blue eyes were completely altered. They looked as if they might burst into angry flames at any moment. I was terrified of what she would do next. My instinct told me to try and stay, but my pulse was racing and I kept my eye on the front door in case I needed to make a hasty exit.

'You're a model,' I said, even though I knew she wasn't, trying to make my voice sound as quiet as possible in the hope that it would soothe her.

She laughed insanely. 'A model? No, I'm not a model. I'm a prostitute. Do you know what that is? I'm a woman who sells her body and sells her soul.' She began to cry hysterically. 'And I can tell you, *chérie*, it doesn't bring me happiness. All those fucking, fucking people, they have destroyed me. Don't you ever sell your soul. Never let a man have sex with you for money.'

She was becoming more and more hysterical, and began throwing ornaments around her apartment. Wailing loudly, she threw an ornament at the window, smashing it. Shortly afterwards, someone started banging on the door and I opened it. It was the police – one of the neighbours must have heard the commotion and called them. The police phoned an ambulance, and medics arrived, armed with various pieces of equipment. Nicole was injected with a substance that seemed to subdue her almost immediately. Then she was put on to a stretcher and carried out of her apartment. Her eyes looked dead.

I didn't know what to do. I asked the police and doctors if I could go with Nicole, but they shook their heads gravely.

'No, you must stay here for now,' one of them said. 'Let's wait and see how she is in the next few days.'

I was horrified at the scene I had just witnessed. It had been like watching an animal writhing in a trap. I had never seen a human being look so wretched and tortured. I was in a state of shock at the violence of Nicole's outpouring. I had thought she had everything in life, but now I realised that she had nothing. Once again I recoiled from the world of grown-ups. I had experienced so much pain throughout my childhood and had thought it would be different when I was older, but it seemed that things weren't much better for adults. Shards of ornaments lay scattered on the floor. I stood amongst them and cried for Nicole and for myself.

When my tears were spent, I began to wonder what I should do next. Should I tidy up and continue living here? I asked myself. There was a chance Nicole would return in a few days, and if so, life could continue for both of us. Or perhaps I was expected to leave right now and melt away into a different kind of life.

As I stood pondering, Harry, the man I had assumed was Nicole's boyfriend in Cannes but who I now knew was one of her sugar daddies, appeared at the flat. He opened the door with a key and found me standing dazed in the middle of the living room. He had been expecting to find the flat empty and jumped when he saw me.

'What on earth are you doing here?' he asked rather disdainfully. 'This is the last place I expected to bump into you.' He looked tired and drawn, and was dressed in a dark, elegant suit and white shirt. He had loosened his red spotted tie.

'It's a long story, but I came to Paris to see Nicole – she had given me her business card and I decided to look her up,' I explained. 'I've been staying with her for the last few weeks.'

He raised his eyebrows. 'Well, I'm afraid, young lady, that you can't stay here any longer. The flat belongs to me.' He took a bulging leather wallet out of his pocket and handed me a hundred francs. 'Here, take this money to help you on your way, then get your things together and off you go. You can use it to get a room in a hotel for the night.'

'Can't I go and see Nicole? I'm really worried about her,' I said earnestly.

He looked at me sadly. 'No. I'm afraid you can't help her now. She's in hospital. She's had a nervous breakdown.'

'Well, could you just tell me where they've taken her?' I asked.

'No. You must leave now,' he said firmly.

I had no idea where I would go. It was almost 2 a.m. I didn't feel like wasting the hundred francs on a room for the night, so instead I wandered around and ended up in Place Pigalle. I had never been there in the early hours of the morning. While during the daytime the area felt alive with interesting people, in the early hours of the morning it just felt dangerous and seedy. Various men were hanging around, and the atmosphere was very menacing. I could smell urine, and my shoes kept sticking to the spilt beer on the pavement. My instinct told me to get away, but I had no idea where else to go and I was too exhausted to walk any further. I wedged myself into a doorway in the hope that I could snatch a couple of hours' sleep.

I woke up at dawn to find that my bag had been stolen. Fortunately I had stored Harry's hundred francs in my shoe. I knew that my blissful extended summer had officially ended. I was back to square one. I had nothing and yet somehow I was going to have to find enough food to eat. I also had to stay below the radar of anyone who might send me back to England and into the arms of the police.

I had begun to get a very bad feeling about Paris and had a sense that if I stayed in this large, ruthless city any longer, something terrible might happen to me. I shivered as I sat huddled in the doorway. I felt very scared in case the people who had stolen my rucksack decided to come back. Where could I run to that would be safe and where I could find a way to survive?

I thought of getting a train to Italy and trying to track down Leo and Marco, but I knew I'd be looking for a needle in a haystack. Then I thought again about returning to the *pension* in Le Havre, but rejected the idea for the same reasons as before.

I stood up, stretched my stiff limbs and walked towards the train station with no clear plan. When I arrived, I decided that it didn't really matter where I went as long as I went somewhere away from my mother and Michael and children's homes. I screwed my eyes shut and then jumped on the first train that drew up alongside a platform. The train I chose turned out to be going to Brussels.

I bought myself a couple of croissants on the train and munched them miserably as I looked out of the window. I was tired of always having to run away. I wondered how Nicole was. Would she recover and go back to the life of prostitution she hated so much, or was the damage to her mental health permanent? I wanted to find somewhere I could be safe and happy, surrounded by kind people, a place where I could work hard and earn just enough to feed myself and have a roof over my head. At that moment it seemed like an impossible dream.

I crossed the border between France and Belgium in the train toilets and successfully dodged passport control. I decided I could write a comprehensive guide about the best and worst train toilets. Some were spacious, clean and had air-fresheners, while others were cramped, smelly and had damp lumps of toilet paper stuck to the floor. When it came to dodging border guards and ticket inspectors, though, there was no scope to be choosy. Avoiding detection was all that mattered.

When we arrived in Brussels several hours later, I jumped off the train and wandered around some of the nearby streets. I was trying to work out if Brussels was a place in which I could survive or not. The people seemed very cold and buttoned up. Something about them made me shiver. Everyone I saw was a businessperson carrying a briefcase. They scared me. Impulsively I ran back to the station and jumped on a train to another Belgian city, Antwerp. I stepped off the train there and felt this was a better place.

The thought of having to start again, though, made my heart sink. How would I find a job and a place to live? Even if I pretended to be older than fifteen, I would only be able to get a job cleaning or working in a café. And would I have to continue to tell the lie about taking a break from my studies? I was tired of running and tired of lying, but I knew that telling the truth could be disastrous for me. After all, if the authorities got any sense that I had run away, I could find myself taken back to the Blue Door Centre, or somewhere worse, in handcuffs.

A NARROW ESCAPE

I walked through the streets of Antwerp wishing I could be invisible. I felt as if everyone was looking at me and saying to themselves, 'What's that runaway doing here?' Of course nobody said anything, or even gave me a second glance, but I felt very self-conscious.

I wandered into a market where birds chirruped and cooed and cawed noisily. They were all shapes and sizes, and some had feathers in dazzling hues. Seeing the beauty of the birds lifted my spirits a little. I knew I couldn't just wander around, though; I had to find a job. I turned into a street full of cafés and bars. Standing up tall and pushing my shoulders back in the hope that I'd look more confident and mature, I started going into places and asking them if they needed help with cleaning or washing dishes. I was trembling. What if they guessed that I was on the run?

The third café that I walked into agreed to give me a job restocking drinks. I had to tidy up the drinks cellar, haul huge crates of Coca-Cola up the rickety cellar stairs and put them into the fridges behind the bar. The pay wasn't much, but I was extremely relieved. Nobody had asked me any difficult questions. They had accepted my story that I was a student looking for casual work. The money would be enough for me to rent a cheap room, buy myself a few new clothes and purchase enough food to keep hunger pangs at bay. They told me I could start immediately.

The work was manageable, and I enjoyed being in a lively place. Many of the customers seemed friendly, particularly after they'd had a couple of beers. Gradually I got to know more and more of the regulars. Most of them were nice people who lived locally, and many worked in the diamond trade. I discovered from talking to people that Antwerp was one of Europe's major diamond centres.

I rented a bedsit close to the café. It was sparsely furnished and quite shabby, but I spent very little time there. At work, I was able to smile and joke with the customers, but once I was by myself I felt as if loneliness was swallowing me up. I didn't miss my family in England, and apart from Monsieur and Madame Vert, my friendships in France had been quite superficial. I was passing through and so were the people I met, even Marco and Leo. We all viewed friendships as temporary, flimsy things that would disintegrate as soon as one or other of us moved on.

Rather than missing the people I knew, I longed for people I didn't know – the parents I wished I had, sisters and brothers I could be close to and good friends. I was determined not to be self-pitying, though, and told myself I was lucky to be free, to have a job and a roof over my head. I phoned Jay once again when I knew neither my mother nor Michael would be at home. He seemed neither happy nor sad to hear from me, and just said that he'd let my mother know I'd called again.

There was one customer at the café who seemed to take a particular interest in me. He drove an expensive sports car and dressed in a smart suit. His name was Pierre. He was tall and slim, and seemed very affable, often buying drinks for other customers. I was not yet sixteen, and although I was tough in some ways, I was still extremely naïve in others.

'Are you here alone? Do you have family nearby?' he asked one night.

'I'm a student from England. I'm on a working holiday, taking a break from my studies,' I said, breezily trotting out the story I'd told so many times it almost felt like the truth.

'And about your family? Are they coming out to visit you here?'

I shook my head. 'Nah, we're not really close. You know how it is with families.'

He nodded sympathetically. 'I do,' he said, grinning. 'I can't stand mine.' He then told me that he had a house in the country where he would take me to relax. 'I bet it's a long time since you've had a proper holiday, isn't it?' He smiled, though I thought I saw something in his eyes harden.

I wasn't prepared to commit myself, but I thought over his offer. He was right. I'd had very few holidays, and the idea of getting out of the city into the countryside I loved sounded great. He kept on badgering me to go with him, and eventually I agreed.

'Don't let the boss know I'm taking you. It must be our little secret,' he said.

Alarm bells should have been ringing loud and clear at that point, but for some reason they didn't.

'I won't pick you up straight from work. Go to the bird market and I'll pick you up from there,' he said.

Unquestioningly I agreed. He was probably in his late twenties or early thirties and I thought that the reason he wanted to pick me up away from work was because he was embarrassed about being seen with someone so much younger than him.

I waited at the bird market for Pierre, and at the appointed time he arrived and leant over to open the passenger door for me. As soon as I jumped in, he roared off before I had even had time to close the car door properly.

'Did you tell anyone you were going with me?' he asked. There was a slight edge to his voice.

'No, I didn't tell a soul,' I reassured him. I began to feel uneasy. 'Will it just be us at your place in the country, or will there be other people there too?' I asked.

'Just you wait and see,' he said tersely.

I decided that if I didn't like the look of the set-up when we arrived, I would simply make a run for it.

As we left the city behind and took a narrow country road, he began to ask me creepy, sexual questions: 'Have you ever whipped someone? Have you ever had sex while you've been tied up?'

I shook my head, my heart starting to pound loudly.

Then he began talking about biting off women's nipples.

Suddenly I was drenched with fear. Those were the horrible things he wanted to do to *me*, I realised with a jolt. I frantically began to work out how I was going to escape. The time when Jim had pinned me to the wall of the storeroom and tried to stuff his penis inside me flashed through my mind. I wondered if I'd be able to jump out of the moving car and make a run for it. But there were no traffic lights for him to slow down at, just a dark, open road. I glanced at the speedometer and saw that he was travelling at more than seventy miles an hour. If I tried to jump out, I'd be killed instantly. I sat quietly and tried to plot my escape.

A few minutes later we arrived at his house, which was an isolated place in the middle of a wooded area. It was pitch black and I was absolutely terrified. He gripped my hand firmly and led me inside.

How the hell am I going to get out of here? I wondered desperately. It's in the middle of nowhere.

I felt droplets of sweat dripping down my spine. My terror made them feel icy against my skin. I decided to try to talk him out of whatever he was planning to do and somehow persuade him to let me go. Maybe I could tell him that my father was a senior police officer in England and would leave no stone unturned to catch him if anything happened to me.

He unlocked the front door and, still gripping my hand, led me inside. Then he double-locked the door behind us and put the keys in his pocket. A wave of nausea swept over me. The place smelt damp and musty as if it had not been lived in for a very long time. He opened the windows because the mouldy smell was quite overpowering, then went to a cupboard and took out two glasses and a bottle. He poured something that looked like wine into the glasses, gave one to me and started drinking. My eyes were frantically scanning the room to see if there was any means of escape.

He put a Betamax video into a machine and a violent porn film started playing. I began edging towards one of the windows he'd opened in the hope that I'd be able to climb out. Talking him out of things was obviously not going to work. Suddenly he changed into a savage animal. He lunged at me, ripped off my shirt and started stabbing my breasts with a hat pin. I screamed with pain and shock, convinced that he wanted to kill me. My survival instinct kicked in and I fought like a wildcat against him. My terror gave me strength and I shunted him hard enough to make him lose his balance. He fell backwards on to the floor.

I knew that I had only a few seconds to escape. I could feel the blood draining from my face, but I knew that if I didn't act now, I might be dead in a few minutes. I bolted to one of the windows he'd opened, then quite literally dived out of it in the same way that I would dive into a swimming pool. As soon as my feet touched the ground, I began to sprint. Suddenly all the blood rushed back to my head and I felt a surge of confidence: I was going to get away.

Even if this man stabbed me a hundred times, I would still find a way to get up and fight for my life, I told myself, as I ran panting from my attacker's house.

I raced through bushes and hedges, oblivious to the thorns that scratched my arms and face. I looked round and saw to my horror that Pierre was running after me. How had he managed to pick himself up so quickly? I prayed that I would be able to outrun him, but I was no longer sure that I could. He was gaining on me. I was so exhausted and breathless that part of me wanted to sink down on to the ground, but I willed myself to keep going.

Suddenly I heard the sweetest music – the hum of traffic – and ran towards it. After a minute or two I reached a country lane and stood in the middle of the road, ready to flag down the next car that passed. I looked a total mess. I tried to button up my ripped shirt as best I could. It was covered in dirt and blood from the scratches, and I was so out of breath I sounded as if I was about to die. I looked round anxiously, but could see no sign of Pierre. A car came along, an old French jalopy, and I jumped in front of it, forcing the driver to stop. I climbed in, not caring who the driver was because I was so desperate to get away and get somewhere nearer to civilisation.

The driver was a man in his sixties. He was wearing farming clothes and smelt faintly of manure. He said little, but kept on looking sidelong at me. Evidently scenting vulnerability, he tentatively reached across the gearstick and put his gnarled, work-roughened hand on my thigh. Horrified, I screamed and scratched his face. He was so taken aback that he slowed the car right down. I grabbed the handbrake and jumped out of the car as it skidded to a standstill on the gravel.

As I hurtled away from the car, I couldn't believe that I had gone from one predatory man to another. I could see the lights of the village in the distance and bolted towards them.

Incredibly weary by the time I reached the village, I came across a little police station, which was closed. I found a scrap of paper and a pencil, and wrote a note saying, 'A rapist lives at this address,' and described Pierre and the house. I didn't know the right words to use in French to describe the attack, but tried my best. Then I posted the piece of paper through the letterbox and ran off.

I was overjoyed when I saw a sign for a railway station. Exhausted, I made my way there and sat huddled on a bench on the platform until a train arrived at 6 a.m. and took me back to Antwerp. My shirt was so badly ripped that I had to press a magazine to my chest to cover myself up. I was tired of my life on the run, tired of danger and people who wanted to take advantage of me. I just wanted to be safe and to have loving parents to put their arms round me and tell me that everything would be all right.

When I got back to my sparsely furnished little room and collapsed on to the bed, I finally allowed myself to think about the horror of the ordeal I had just been through. I had hardly cried since I was nine years old – I didn't like giving people the satisfaction of seeing how much they had hurt me – but now, in the privacy of my room, I sobbed and sobbed until I thought my heart would break. I was furious with myself that I had been so stupid and trusting, and vowed never to let anything like that happen again.

The next day I went back to work and told my boss what had happened so that she could warn other young women who might be tricked by Pierre's deceptively pleasant demeanour. But he never appeared at the café again.

I shuddered at the thought of what could have happened to me in Pierre's musty house. Maybe he would have murdered me after having his sadistic way with me and then buried me under the floorboards. Looking back, I realised that he had made sure that I was a runaway with no loving, anxious family hovering in the background before he had grabbed me, and he had checked and double-checked that I had told no one I was going away with him for the weekend. I felt like a fool as I replayed how easy I had made it for him, and how close I had been to being raped or worse.

Usually I had an inner confidence that I would find a way out of any problem, but not this time. I was incredibly shaken. For the first time I realised that my life could be snuffed out in an instant and that danger lurked everywhere.

Even more distressing than the fact that I could have died was the realisation that no one in the world cared about me. If my body had lain undiscovered under the floorboards of Pierre's house, would anyone have come looking for me? I doubted it. I was just an anonymous runaway who didn't mean anything to anyone.

DODGING BULLETS

I became suspicious of everyone after that terrible weekend. Every man I saw was a potential murderer.

I managed to shake off the advances of men in the café who tried to chat me up. 'You're very beautiful. Let me take you out for a drink,' became a familiar chat-up line. It was like trying to dust off grains of sand from the soles of your feet when you come out of the sea.

The last thing I was interested in was getting involved in a relationship with a man. I just wanted to work hard, earn some money and keep out of trouble. But Thom had other ideas. He was a very good-looking man in his early twenties and came into the café most weekends.

He didn't bother with the usual chat-up lines, but talked to me in a normal, friendly way. I didn't get the feeling that he wanted anything from me. He told me that he had a passion for bodybuilding and spent a lot of time at the gym. He seemed to know plenty about the world, and I found his easy confidence very appealing. He was strong and handsome, with fair hair and honest blue eyes. Subconsciously I began to feel that he could protect me against Pierre, should he ever return.

Thom was from Amsterdam, but had to travel to Antwerp regularly for business, although he was always vague when I asked him exactly what his work was. I presumed it was something high-powered because the hotel he stayed in was expensive and he always dressed in designer suits with crisp white shirts and bright ties.

Gradually a friendship developed between us. It felt very natural, and my instincts told me I'd be safe with him. One night he bought me a few vodkas when my daytime shift at the café had finished. I rarely drank and the alcohol made me drunk very quickly. The conversation moved from chatting about customers we both knew to flirting.

'You're a very beautiful girl, you know, Louise. Sometimes when I'm sitting in the bar I can't take my eyes off you. I watch you working hard, your strong, slim body lifting the crates of drink effortlessly. I'm incredibly attracted to you and would be so happy if you and I could get together.'

I gulped down the rest of my vodka. I was surprised that such an attractive, successful man wanted to be with me. I would have been happy for him to go on showering compliments on me for ever, it made me tingle with pleasure. I was very drawn to him. He seemed safe and gentle, and when he asked me to go back to his hotel with him, I said yes without a second thought.

We didn't sleep together that night. I'd had many men approach me and ask me to be their girlfriend, but I was determined that any man I was prepared to have a relationship with needed to know that my body wasn't just available to be pawed whenever they felt like it.

'I'm young, Thom,' I said as I perched on the edge of the hotel bed. I'd told him I was eighteen, though I was just sixteen and a half when we met. 'Relationships are special and serious things for me. I want to take my time and be sure.' Although the vodkas I'd drunk had made things slightly blurred, I hadn't lost control.

He didn't push me. In fact, my refusal to sleep with him seemed to make him desire me more. We shared his bed and he held me all night long. We continued to see each other whenever he came to Antwerp, and when I did finally agree to have sex with him, a month later, I was happy that I had made him wait. It made me feel that I was in control of the situation.

I enjoyed being with Thom, but although I wasn't exactly sure of what love was, I didn't think that this was it. He kept telling me that he was in love with me, though, and he sounded as if he meant it. Although I was flattered to get so much attention, I did sometimes feel smothered. I was so used to being by myself and relying on myself that I sometimes felt as if I couldn't breathe in his company.

One afternoon not long after my seventeenth birthday, Thom said, 'Come and live with me in Amsterdam, Louise. I don't just want to be with you just at weekends – I want to wake up next to you every morning.'

My face fell.

'What is it? Don't you want to be with me any more?'

'No, no, it's not that, Thom, it's just that . . .'

'What? I can't imagine you've got any terrible secrets. Tell me what's on your mind.'

I was slightly apprehensive about making the commitment of living with Thom, but there was another reason why I was hesitant.

'It's just that I don't have a passport,' I blurted out. 'I won't be able to get across the border into Holland with you. The one I used to get here was just a temporary one and it's run out.'

He smiled and seemed unruffled by my confession. 'Don't worry, Louise, it won't be a problem. I've got something to tell you too. I know you've wondered a lot what line of business I'm in. Well, I'm a diamond smuggler. I bring diamonds across the border in the boot of my car. I could smuggle you that way too, if you want me to. You'll be my very special diamond.'

I was shocked. I'd met a few shady characters but I'd never met a diamond smuggler before. 'It is just diamonds that you smuggle, though, isn't it?' I asked, suddenly wary. Although I was young, I knew that I didn't want to become mixed up in any kind of drug trafficking.

Thom looked into my eyes. 'It's just diamonds, Louise. No cocaine, no heroin. That's a completely different sort of business, run by a completely different sort of person.'

Then Thom opened his briefcase and showed me a tray of diamonds. I had never taken much interest in jewellery before, and certainly none in precious stones, but I was mesmerised by the dazzling display of different shades.

'Choose one. You can have any one you want,' said Thom.

I was delighted and chose a magnificent blue diamond. It was mounted on a ring, which I slid on to the third finger of my right hand. The ring fitted me perfectly, and the diamond winked every time it caught my eye. I didn't know any seventeen-year-olds who walked around wearing a diamond ring, and it made me feel very grown-up.

'So why not come back to Amsterdam tomorrow with me?' said Thom. 'There's nothing to keep you here apart from your bar job, and you can just hand in your notice.'

I shrugged. I couldn't think of any reason not to go with Thom, so I agreed to quit my job. That night I explained to my boss that I was going to go and live with Thom in Amsterdam. She accepted my sudden resignation with a smile, though she seemed sad to see me go.

'Come back to us any time, Louise. You're a real hard worker and a pleasure to have around. But I understand that affairs of the heart must come first.' She nodded in Thom's direction and beamed.

Once again I was delighted to receive praise and felt proud that she thought I had been useful and conscientious. She in turn had been a good boss and had treated me very well.

The following day, as arranged, Thom drove me to Amsterdam. About ten minutes before we reached the border, he pulled his BMW into a lay-by and I climbed inside the boot. Thom had sweetly provided a pillow for my head. At first curling myself into a ball in the darkness didn't feel too bad, but after being in this position for about fifteen minutes, I was desperate to stretch my limbs and gulp some fresh, clean air. Thankfully Thom stopped the car a few minutes later in another quiet lay-by and I sprang out like a cat, had a good stretch and returned to the passenger seat. Thom told me the border guards had not suspected anything and had waved him through without a second glance.

When we drove into Amsterdam, I was entranced by the prettiness of the city, the canals and the tall, thin pastel-coloured houses. Thom took me to his ultra-modern apartment in a converted warehouse. There were plates and pans neatly stacked inside pristine white cupboards, delicious cheeses, meats and fresh fruit in the fridge and racks of freshly laundered shirts and suits hanging in the wardrobe.

It felt marvellous to walk into someone's very comfortable home and to know that I would be staying for a while. I was unfamiliar with this kind of set-up. Running had become such a habit that I had forgotten that sometimes it was nice to have a break from being in constant motion.

I was completely dependent on Thom when I first arrived in Amsterdam, even though I picked up Dutch quickly. He seemed quite happy with this situation, although I was certainly less so. I was so used to only having myself to rely on and felt uncomfortable not being self-sufficient.

I knew for certain now that I wasn't in love with Thom. We had connected with each other in Antwerp, chatted about all sorts of things and were attracted to each other, but my heart didn't beat any faster when I heard his key turn in the lock. I was fairly happy with him, but I knew that things were unlikely to last.

Now that we'd moved to Amsterdam, I noticed that Thom was becoming increasingly possessive. He took care of every-thing, and gave me money to buy clothes and make-up and to get my hair done. He wanted me to look nice when we went out together, but when I got admiring looks from other men, he didn't like it and accused me of flirting.

'Don't be ridiculous,' I said irritably whenever he insisted that I was eyeing up another man. 'I'm not interested in anyone else. You know that. You know you're really driving me crazy behaving as if you own me. You need to give me some space.'

When he made trips to Antwerp and left me in the flat, he called to check up on me twice a day. I was totally faithful to him and rarely even left the flat when he was away. His calls made me furious. His jealousy led to more and more tension in our relationship. Whenever we went out to clubs or for meals he didn't want me to socialise with other people.

He seemed to resent me becoming friends with other women almost as much as with men.

One night he accused me of kissing another man in a nightclub. I hadn't and had simply had a brief chat with him. I stormed out of the nightclub.

'Stop it – you're suffocating me. If you carry on like this, I'm off,' I said. 'You're making me feel as if I'm in a cage.'

One evening he locked me in the bedroom to prevent me from going out. I was enraged. I had spent my whole life running away from people who tried to confine me and wasn't prepared to put up with a boyfriend who treated me the same way.

As I'd done so many times before, I jumped out of the window and went to stay at the house of a friend called Marie. As soon as my feet touched the ground, I felt a shot of joy run through my body. I was free again and didn't have to answer to anybody.

Marie was a young woman I'd met through Thom, and despite his interference we had become good friends. When I knocked on her door, she wasn't surprised to see me.

'Come on in, Louise. I didn't think you'd survive Thom's possessive ways for too much longer. He's always like that with girlfriends. I think it's because deep down he's very insecure. Smuggling diamonds is a precarious business. Anyway, you can stay with me for as long as you want. I never use the spare room.'

'Thanks, Marie, that's great. He was really getting on my nerves. It's not as if we're an old married couple. I'm not interested in other guys, but I want to be able to do what I want to do and not have to get permission to breathe.'

Marie nodded sympathetically.

At that moment her phone rang. It was Thom. He'd guessed that I'd run off to Marie's.

I took the phone from her. 'It's over, Thom. Let's face it, we're not really suited to each other. You want a girl who'll sit at home waiting for you, and I'm not that girl. We've had a good time together, but we need to move on now.'

To my amazement, he began to cry down the phone and begged me to come back to him. 'Please, Louise, stay. I love you, you're a great girl, and I want to be with you. I know I can be a bit jealous sometimes, but it's because I care so much about you and the thought of losing you scares me.'

'Thom, we're finished,' I said firmly, and put the phone down. I didn't feel sad that the relationship had ended, just relieved to be on my own again.

Maybe I'm just not suited to relationships, I thought. I was so independent and had done such a good job of building up a tough, protective shell over the years in order to survive the physical and emotional blows from my mother and Michael that there didn't seem to be any chinks to let in a person who cared about me. I felt sad that I had had to become so hard, but to me it was more important to protect myself from hurt than to risk opening up to another human being. Almost all the people in my life who were supposed to be my protectors had betrayed me in one way or another. I knew that Thom was not the right man for me, and as Marie had said, many girls were unhappy with his possessiveness, but I did wonder if I would ever be able to have a proper relationship with anyone. I felt sick at the thought of the damage my mother, Michael and the children's homes had done to me.

To deaden these emotions, I immersed myself in Amsterdam's craziness. It was 1978 and Amsterdam was really swinging. It was awash with sex and drugs and illicit money. Thom kept calling me at Marie's, but I always refused to come to the phone. Once or twice he came round with a big bunch of flowers in the hope of tempting me back. I shook my head and closed the door in his face.

Thom went to the upmarket clubs and wealthy areas of the city, so Marie and I and a few other female friends began to go to some of the seedier bars and clubs. One night we were drinking in an underground club when one of Amsterdam's most notorious criminals swaggered in. His name was Hank. I had heard many terrifying tales about him, but had never actually met him face to face. People said he controlled the entire underworld in Amsterdam – he ran drugs and diamond-smuggling rings, and pimped a variety of prostitutes. They also said that he'd served time in prison for manslaughter. He was a big man with a well-worn face and short hair, wearing an expensive suit with a white open-necked shirt. His eyes made a 360-degree sweep of the club like a hawk looking for prey.

I was very curious to meet this legendary figure and stared him boldly in the eye. The other occupants of the bar lowered their heads, frightened that they might be singled out if they met his steady gaze. He saw me immediately and walked over. I was conscious that he was looking me up and down, undressing me and assessing my body like a joint of prime beef.

'You're a goldmine – look at that body,' he said admiringly, fixing his eyes on my breasts. 'If you come and work for me, I can make you a fortune.'

I was revolted by his leering and was so angry that he was

ogling my body that I abandoned all caution. 'Go fuck yourself,' I said crossly.

I could see everyone staring at me open-mouthed. They were thinking, 'You don't know who you're talking to'.

He gave me a thunderous look, then shook his finger at me and said in a low voice that sounded like tyres crunching on gravel, 'I'm going to have you.'

His friends managed to distract him and he walked off.

Marie looked panic-stricken. 'I'm sure something terrible is going to happen to you. I think the sooner we get out of this place, the better.'

My other friends nodded in agreement, looking worried.

'OK, OK, let's go, but the night's still young – let's find another club.'

I didn't take my friends' warnings seriously. I'd had a few drinks and felt absolutely fearless. However tricky a situation I found myself in, I had always found a way to wriggle out of it: I had managed to prevent Jim from raping me; I had escaped from the supposedly high-security Blue Door Centre; and I had outwitted the psychopathic Pierre in Antwerp. I was sure that whatever Hank had in store for me, I would somehow be able to deal with it.

Reluctantly my friends agreed to accompany me to another club nearby. Little did they know what was to come. Hank had obviously been keeping tabs on my movements because almost as soon as we'd walked up to the bar and ordered a drink, he appeared, his face like thunder. He walked right up to me, pulled out a gun and placed it against the side of my head. I felt the cold, hard metal digging into me. I didn't know much about guns, but I knew the sound a gun makes when you're preparing to shoot someone.

'You're coming with me,' he said through gritted teeth. 'And don't go getting any ideas about asking anyone for help.' He was so close that I could feel his breath on my face.

Everything stopped and hushed in the bar. I think I was the only person in there who wasn't scared to death. I was so determined that this vile man wasn't going to get the better of me that there was no room for fear. The gun was digging insistently into my temple, yet I couldn't believe that he would possibly pull the trigger and splatter the contents of my skull across the bar. I reasoned that he wouldn't shoot me in the middle of a crowded club; surely the gun was either fake or empty and was being waved around out of bravado.

Convinced that my life wasn't really in danger, I grabbed the barstool I'd been sitting on and hurled it at Hank with all my strength. He had been drinking heavily and was a bit unsteady on his feet, but even so I was surprised at how easily he toppled over. As he fell, he dropped his gun. Like lightning one of the barmen jumped over the bar. 'Quick, get the hell out of here while you can,' he shouted to me as he grabbed the gun and emptied out a pile of bullets.

When I saw the bullets, I went into shock. The events of the evening suddenly hit me. I began to shake from head to toe as I realised how close I had come to being shot in the head. It was only by fluke that I was alive instead of lying dead in a pool of blood on the sticky floor. I didn't know it at the time, but just ten minutes earlier Hank had shot a man in the nose in another bar.

When I heard Marie say, 'Let's go,' I needed no persuading.

We hailed a taxi, and as we sat on the back seat, I began to shiver uncontrollably. 'Oh, my God . . . Oh, my God,' I kept saying over and over again.

'Believe me, Louise, Hank uses that gun a lot. He means business and you were probably the only person in that bar who didn't realise it. You need to leave town now, immediately,' Marie said urgently. 'You made him lose face like he's never lost face before, and in two bars where his associates drink. It will be a matter of honour for him to finish you off. If you want to stay alive, you need to get out of Amsterdam right away.

'I've got a friend called Jill in Rotterdam who has a big flat. She's used to having people crash at her place. I'll call her. I'm sure she won't mind you staying with her for a while. You need to lie low, at least until things cool down,' she added anxiously.

Two hours later, clutching my usual minimalist bag of belongings, I was on the train to Rotterdam. I knew that I was quite literally running for my life and that Hank might well come after me to settle a very serious score. I looked around the carriage nervously and pulled the hat I was wearing further down over my eyes.

The thought of dying by a bullet petrified me. I decided that my only chance of staying alive was to get out of Holland. I had no idea that before I could do that, I was going to find myself in a situation that was beyond my worst nightmares.

WORSE THAN DEATH

When I arrived in Rotterdam, I decided that I had to find a way to obtain a false passport so that I could move to another country. Rotterdam wasn't very far from Amsterdam, and I was sure that Hank could very easily track me down and reap his revenge. Terrified that I was being followed, I trembled as I walked through the streets of Rotterdam. I kept looking over my shoulder and tried to keep to busy, main streets, which I thought were likely to be safer. I had bought a map and found Jill's address quite easily. I sighed with relief that I had made it to her doorstep in one piece but I still had a terrible sense of foreboding that something awful was about to happen and was convinced that Hank had sent someone after me.

I knocked on Jill's door and prayed that she'd open it quickly so that I wouldn't be gunned down on her porch. I glanced up and down the street, but couldn't see anyone lurking suspiciously.

You're over-reacting, I tried to reassure myself. Hank just wanted to drive you out of town and now he's done that he'll leave you alone.

Jill was expecting me. She was a friendly hippie type in a long, swirly cheesecloth dress and wore lots of beads fashioned into necklaces and bracelets. The whole ensemble swished noisily as she moved. I guessed that she was a few years older than me.

She'd just cooked and offered me some food and a glass of wine. Marie had said that Jill was trustworthy, and she seemed very open and friendly. We chatted casually for a while. I had no intention of telling Jill everything that had happened to me in Amsterdam, or the chequered events of my life in England, but I decided it was time to come clean to her about what I needed to do.

I took a deep breath and blurted out, 'I don't have a passport. I ran into a few difficulties in Amsterdam and I may need to get out of the country in a hurry. Do you know anyone who could arrange something for me?'

Much to my relief, she nodded. 'There are some men who fix things for people, shady things. They work down in the docks, and people say they can arrange anything for a fee. I don't think they're particularly pleasant individuals, but I'm sure they can get hold of fake passports. Just ask for Hans.'

The next evening I went down to a warehouse in the docks in search of Hans. I asked around and eventually I found myself knocking on a filthy door which was opened by a shifty looking young guy who pointed out a mean-looking man. His face was pockmarked and he had thinning hair, which was combed back in lank strands. He was wearing a black shirt and black trousers, the kind of outfit I never liked seeing on a man. I walked up to him hesitantly. To this day I don't understand why, but my intuition completely deserted me during the following encounter.

'Are you Hans?' I said, trying to stop my voice from wavering.

'Who wants to know?' he snarled.

'My name's Louise. I heard you could arrange passports for people.'

He raised an eyebrow. 'I might be able to do that. You on the run or something? Children's home kid?'

He asked me why I needed a passport and because he was a shady character who wasn't likely to report me to the police, I looked him in the eye and told him I was a runaway. I remember he narrowed his eyes.

'Come with me to my office. I need to get some details from you, like date and place of birth, and a photo.'

I followed him out of the warehouse, relieved that he was willing to help me.

'The office is just a couple of streets away. It'll be quicker if we go by car,' he said. It had started to pour with rain, so what he said seemed to make sense. 'My car's parked round the back. Come this way,' he said.

I followed him round the corner. I couldn't see a car, just a deserted, rubbish-strewn wasteland.

'Where's your car?' I said anxiously. I felt tense and considered making a run for it.

'Shut up, bitch!' he shouted, swiping me suddenly across the head.

I fell to the ground. Then he beat and kicked me in the stomach and carried me round another corner to his car. He threw me on to the back seat. I was in too much agony to move and lay there moaning. I was absolutely terrified. He had locked the car doors and was driving fast. Every time I moaned he turned round and said the same words irritably, 'Shut up, bitch.'

He drove me to an anonymous-looking building, which was

set back from the road and didn't have any other houses next to it. The only thing I remember about the exterior was that it had a thatched roof and was very run-down. I was barely conscious as he dragged me out of the car and threw me over his shoulder like a sack of potatoes. My head told me that I should run, but my body had turned to painful lead. I could do nothing. I was too petrified to cry and lay slumped over his shoulder, not moving a muscle.

He pressed the intercom bell and spoke quietly into it. 'I've got a girl for you,' he said gruffly. 'Young and sexy.'

The person inside buzzed the door open and he carried me into a sparsely furnished room that contained just a bed and a sink. He threw me down on the bed. It had grubby sheets and smelt of stale sweat. Another man handed him a thick bundle of notes. Later, but not then, it dawned on me with horror that I had been sold. Hans left without saying a word to me, and the new man, my jailer, approached me with a pill and a glass of water.

'Here. Swallow this if you know what's good for you,' he snarled. He was a thickset man with small, piercing blue eyes. He was wearing a faded black leather jacket and had brown hair cropped so short that a roll of fat was clearly visible at the back of his neck, just above his collar.

I refused to swallow the pill, thinking it contained some deadly poison. He crammed it into my mouth, but I spat it straight on to the floor.

'OK, so you want to do things the difficult way, do you?' he said in a quiet, dead voice. 'Makes no difference to me.'

He opened a cupboard under the sink and took out a hypodermic needle, which he plunged into a vein in my arm. I wanted to scream, but I suddenly felt too woozy to make any sound. I slumped back on to the pillows. The man then tied me to the bedstead by my wrists and ankles. I felt that I was no longer a human being but a bruised punchbag.

Whatever my captor had injected me with did something to dull the pain from Hans's beating. It made me feel strangely there but not there. I was aware of what was going on, but although I could move my limbs, I felt paralysed, as if my clothes had been stitched to the bed. The drug seemed to deaden my emotions. I couldn't cry and I couldn't shout. I was sure I was going to die sooner rather than later and that my death would be gruesome. Tied up and drugged, I could only scream inside.

My guard threw the hypodermic needle casually into the bin and turned to me. 'And now you need to get to work. We've paid Hans good money for you and you need to earn your keep.'

I had no idea what he was talking about. How could I do any sort of work in this state?

'Many men will be coming. They will be in search of – what shall we say? – special services. And those you must provide. Yes?'

A wave of nausea overwhelmed me. I knew now I was going to be raped. It occurred to me that I was in some sort of brothel. The place I was in looked nothing like the prostitutes' flats in Soho, with their soft-focus pictures of girls in underwear on the walls and transparent crimson drapes at the windows. I had also seen girls posing in the windows in Amsterdam, waiting for customers to pick them out and buy sex. Sex for sale in those places was very much out in the open. I never imagined that girls could be drugged and chained to beds.

How was I going to survive this? Whenever I'd been in a difficult situation before, I'd always managed to use my ingenuity to get out of it, but here I was utterly helpless. My guard was in the room with me, so even if I could wriggle free from the cords binding my hands and feet to the bed, I wouldn't be able to run very far. I lay back, closed my eyes and prayed for a quick and painless death.

After I had been attacked by Pierre in Antwerp, I had realised that nobody would have missed me if he'd killed me. And now I was in the same situation. Who would notice I was gone? I doubted my family would care what happened to me. Hank may be looking for me, but if he was, he certainly wouldn't do anything to save me. I'd heard from Marie that Thom already had a new girlfriend, so he wouldn't be interested in knowing where I was. Jill, in her vague and dreamy way, would probably assume I had got my passport and decided to move on immediately when I didn't return to her flat. All in all there wasn't a single person in the world who might raise the alarm about my disappearance.

The bleak realisation that there was nobody who cared about me was almost as bad as being held prisoner and being powerless to fight back. It is hard to explain how deep my despair was. I had completely lost hope. Terror and paralysis overwhelmed me.

And then the rapes started. My guard ushered in a cruel-looking man of about forty. His thin mouth looked as if it had never smiled. He pulled off his trousers with lightning speed, ripped off my clothes and climbed on top of me, brutally forcing himself inside me. I squeezed my eyes shut as he pushed and pummelled at my body. I felt as if I was being ripped inside.

He said nothing to me before, during and after the rape. Then he got off the bed, coldly spat at me, dressed quickly and walked out. The guard, who had left when the man had come in, instantly reappeared.

It wasn't long before the guard ushered in a second man. I decided to try to keep my eyes closed as much as I could. It was bad enough seeing the face of the first man and looking into his icy blue eyes. I didn't want to have any more faces like that imprinted on my memory. A procession of men came day and night. I had a curious sensation of things being simultaneously speeded up and slowed down.

Twice a day one hand was untied so that I could spoon some foul-tasting porridge into my mouth and drink a little water. Then I was injected again and another man would come, sometimes two, rolling me between them like a piece of processed meat. All of them beat me and inserted various implements into me. I was trying to keep my eyes shut, but the objects they shoved up me felt sharp and painful. I was constantly vomiting from the drugs I was being injected with, but the men didn't seem to care.

I couldn't keep my eyes screwed shut constantly and it was hard not to catch glimpses of the men's faces. After a while they all started to look the same. I had stopped seeing their features and instead my eyes were X-raying them. All I could see underneath their eyes and their skin and their skulls was the bottomless blackness of their souls.

I soon lost track of time. Days and nights bled into one long nightmare. Sometimes I wondered if I had died and was now in hell. I didn't know what I was being punished for, though. All I had done was run away from bad things and bad people.

I knew there were other girls being held in the house because I heard their desperate cries and moans, but I had no way of communicating with them as I never once left the room.

Then one day, after I had been pinned to the stinking bed for about nine days, I heard a commotion. My guard ran out of the room and I strained to hear what was happening. It was a different sound from the cries and moans coming from other rooms. There was a loud battering on the front door and then the sound of heavy boots clattering up the stairs. I heard shouting: 'Police! You're under arrest.'

I never thought I would be so pleased to see the police, but at that moment I could have kissed every one of them. I wanted to weep in relief, but my battered, drugged body wouldn't let me.

The door to my room burst open and a policeman untied me. I could see by the shocked expression on his face that I looked terrible. I was wearing my by now filthy and tattered T-shirt and jeans, and could detect the metallic taste of blood in my mouth.

'We must take you to the police station,' he said softly. 'You have to make a statement. You're an important witness. We can look after you. We'll get a female doctor. You look in a bad state.'

'OK,' I said weakly, my whole body trembling uncontrollably.

He put a blanket round my shoulders and led me gently into another room. I experienced a feeling greater than joy at being freed. I felt as if my heart would burst with relief, yet part of me still felt numb from the drugs. I felt as if the great happiness I felt inside couldn't penetrate my heavy skin and bones to produce a smile.

There were four or five other girls in the room. All looked wild-eyed and had matted hair. A couple were Asian, and one looked as if she was South American. There was one other English girl in the room.

'What's happening?' I murmured in a daze.

'I pretended I was falling in love with my guard,' the English girl whispered hoarsely. 'I begged him to untie me so that I could kiss and cuddle him. The idiot agreed and I ran down the stairs and raised the alarm. I found a port official and he called the police. The rest you know.' She smiled weakly. 'I thought I was going to die in this hellhole. I can't believe we're safe at last.' She broke down and started sobbing.

'You did an amazing thing,' I said, choking back tears. 'You saved all our lives.'

My head was beginning to clear. The combination of knowing I was free and the fact that the drugs were beginning to wear off made me think lucidly for the first time in days. I started to worry what was going to happen next – the police were going to ask me questions. As grateful as I was to them, I couldn't face being sent back to England.

As soon as they find out I'm a runaway, they'll send me home, I thought, panicking. I need to get away.

The police were still checking the other rooms in case there were more girls tied up there. I had no idea whether they had arrested the guards or not, but I could hear angry voices and thought that they probably had.

To the amazement of the other girls, I jumped up, threw the blanket off my shoulders and ran out of the front door before I could be taken to the police station. Once again I was on the run, though I was far too weak to go very fast. A combination of hunger, dehydration and the cocktail of drugs I'd been given made my body feel leaden, but I managed to stumble in the direction of the railway station, which I knew was not far away.

It was too soon to think about the horrific things I had been subjected to. All I could feel was an unbearable wall of pain inside my head, bruises all over my body and a gnawing hunger. Even in my hazy state, however, I knew that the procession of men who had assaulted me had killed something deep inside me. I couldn't imagine ever trusting another human being again, and certainly no male. My spirit was crushed, and my optimism gone.

As I staggered to the station, I saw a little lost kitten mewling. Normally my instinct would have been to pick it up, cuddle it and find a saucer of milk, but my own pain was so all-encompassing that I had nothing left inside me to care about another living creature.

'Life's tough,' I said to the kitten as I lurched past it.

That night, I decided to sleep on a bench at the station because I felt too weak to travel. A cleaner saw that I looked starving and unwell, and offered to share her sandwiches with me. So often, it seems, the people who have least in life are most willing to share everything they have. The food and her kindness restored some strength to me.

I slept badly that night, haunted by a restless mind. Perhaps surprisingly, the thoughts that filled my head were not of the horrendous ordeal I had just been through, but of my mother. In my despair, I blamed her for everything. If she hadn't been such a lousy parent to me, I never would have fled over and over again, getting myself into all kinds of messes and culminating in this one, the biggest mess of all.

I was seventeen now, but still longed to have a mother who

loved me and supported me. I remembered the envy I had felt when I had seen my friends being nurtured by their mothers. I could see that another way of living was possible, but it wasn't something that was ever going to be on offer to me.

The more I thought about my mother and the way she had let me down, the more hatred for her boiled inside me. After my parents had divorced, I had prayed that I could live with my more easygoing father, instead of my mother. I had got my wish, but for too brief a spell. If only he had been more involved in my life, things might have turned out very differently.

If I called my mother now and told her what had happened to me, I reflected, she would probably still send me straight back to the Blue Door Centre, or maybe somewhere worse. I was not yet eighteen after all.

I tried to twist my body into a more comfortable position on the bench, but my mind refused to give me peace. The trauma inside my head was so bad it felt like it was consuming me. I longed for someone to rescue me, but I had never had such a person – someone kind, empathetic and loving. At this point in my life I had never needed a protector more, and yet I had never felt so utterly and completely alone.

I woke up the next morning stiff and in agony after the countless beatings. Usually I managed to recover quickly from traumatic experiences, but this time I felt I had no spirit left to fight against the relentless brutality of the world. The men who had visited the house where I'd been held had broken me completely. They had leached all hope from my bones and my soul. I felt wrung out and empty. I had nowhere to go, and I no longer wanted to live.

For the first time ever I no longer cared whether I lived or died. I had lived through the days and nights of rapes and beatings, but coping with the aftermath was too much to bear. The men had taken me to a dark, bad place where no human being should ever have to go. After what I had been through, there was only one thing that I wanted and that was death. My ordeal was too enormous to block out. If I continued living, I was destined to replay the nightmare for the rest of my life.

I decided that I might as well go back to Amsterdam, where Hank would be waiting for me to settle his score. I was sure he would do me one final favour and blow my brains out.

THE TEENAGE SMUGGLER

As I wandered wearily from Amsterdam Station, I pondered what I should do next. Rather than prolong the agony, I wondered whether I should go straight to one of the underground bars and let it be known that I was back in town and ready to face whatever punishment Hank wanted to dole out to me. I knew I wanted to die, but I felt it would be more courageous to stand tall and take a bullet than to slit my wrists.

I didn't have the energy to move very far. My ribs and abdomen ached, and my head was pounding. I sat down at an outdoor table of a café. I didn't have any money, but I was starving and decided that I'd have to do a runner as soon as I'd eaten. I hoped I'd be able to lose myself in the crowds before any of the waiters noticed that I'd slipped away. I ordered the most calorie-laden meal I could think of: a huge burger in a bun and a big pile of greasy chips cut as thin as matchsticks. I thought of the men on death row in America. I'd watched a TV programme about them once. They were interviewed about what they were going to choose for the last meal. Most of them chose the kind of junk food that I'd just ordered.

I wolfed it down, waited until none of the waiters was looking in my direction, then calmly walked away. Nobody followed me, and I knew that in the general scheme of things such a large café would not suffer a dent in its bank balance through my failure to pay for one cheap meal.

I began to walk aimlessly down the Lieserplane. It's an area for trams in the middle of the city. Cars are not permitted to drive down it, but suddenly a large American saloon roared towards me. It screeched to a halt a few feet away and Hank jumped out. How had he managed to track me down so quickly? One of his henchmen must have spotted me at the train station or when I was sitting in the café.

I felt surprise but no fear when I saw him. An eerie calm came over me, a gratitude that at last someone was going to put me out of my misery. So this was where my life was going to end – in the middle of the Lieserplane next to a flash American car.

'OK, you've got me. You can kill me now,' I said hopelessly. 'I know you've been waiting for me, and here I am. I'm ready to take the bullet, but try and make it a clean shot. I don't particularly want to be lying moaning on the Lieserplane with my brains hanging out.'

Hank laughed throatily.

I wondered where his gun was. I could see both of his hands, and neither was holding a gun. I peered into his car, wondering if he was going to get one of his henchmen to do the job for him. Giggling on the back seat were three scantily clad women.

What happened next stunned me. He extended his hand. I thought at first that he was going to strike me, but he was smiling and instead he shook my hand and placed a fatherly arm round my shoulder.

'I'm not going to shoot you. You're the first woman who's ever stood up to me and I respect that.'

I looked into his eyes and to my amazement saw a softness there.

'Actually, you remind me of my sister, who died. She was tough like you,' he said. 'There's something about you that I like, not like those stupid hookers sitting in the car. You've got guts, and I like that in a woman. Anyway, what the hell happened to you? You look like shit.'

When he said that to me, my chest started heaving with dry sobs. It was a surreal moment, standing in the middle of the city's busiest tram route, overwhelmed with emotion because Amsterdam's most ruthless gangster had just shown me some kindness. After everything I'd been through, I couldn't believe that I had found such an unlikely protector. He hugged me to him and I knew that this wasn't a ruse; he really did want to help me. Tram drivers were beeping to Hank to get his car out of the way.

'Come on – we better go. Jump into the front seat,' he said to me with a conspiratorial wink.

I was numb to the core and I no longer trusted anyone. But I didn't care what happened next, so I climbed in. The three women in the back, all of whom had bleached-blonde hair and unnaturally pronounced cleavages, looked at me open-mouthed. They didn't know what to make of me.

Hank dropped them off in the red-light area and said he'd see them later. Then he took me back to his luxury apartment.

'You look terrible,' he said, gesturing for me to sit down on his plush sofa. 'What's been happening to you?'

I looked at him, saw that he was genuinely concerned, and decided to tell him everything. The fog in my brain started to clear and I suddenly felt safe having Hank as my protector instead of my enemy. I still didn't want to carry on living, but I knew that before I died, I wanted to get my revenge on the men who had made me suffer. Because I was a runaway and wanted by police in England, I never could have gone to the police in Holland and acted as a witness in a trial. But even if I could have done that, I wouldn't have considered it to be justice. Seeing my aggressors jailed wasn't what I wanted; I wanted them to suffer mentally and physically, the way I had.

I poured out the whole terrible story to Hank. I assumed that as an A-list gangster himself, he would not be shocked by what I told him, but he looked aghast.

'Jesus,' he said, shaking his head. 'I know those guys. They're into really nasty stuff. I've got my code of honour, like a lot of gangsters. That kind of sexual brutality, snuff movies, that whole scene gives us all a bad name. Don't worry, you'll get over it – you're young and you're tough. I guess you should have stuck with me in Amsterdam,' he said ruefully.

I managed a watery smile. 'Hank, I need to get my revenge. I don't think I can carry on living unless I do. Can you help me?'

He nodded grimly.

I knew he would have his own way of dealing with it and I asked for no details. I began to feel a bit better. The crushing weight of misery had lifted a little and wasn't pushing quite so heavily on my soul.

The next few days passed in a daze. Hank gave me some sleeping pills and said that it would be better for me to try to sleep through the worst of the trauma. I gulped them down gratefully, craving oblivion.

After a couple of days I half-heartedly tried to eat, but I had no appetite. I knew I was alive because I was still breathing, but I felt as if I were dead. My mind was in tatters, my faith in mankind decimated.

'Have you made any arrangements yet to get those bastards in Rotterdam?' I asked Hank over and over again. Nothing else mattered to me or interested me.

'Don't worry, I'm working on it,' he said quietly. 'Something will happen very soon.'

A few days later I was lying on the sofa in Hank's apartment feeling wretched when he walked in and said casually, 'We've shot Hans, the ringleader, in the kneecaps. I don't think he'll be walking anywhere for at least the next thirty years.'

When I heard this news, my heart leapt. For the first time since I'd been held captive, I saw a tiny glimmer of hope. I was not a cruel person; throughout my life the thought of hurting anyone else had appalled me. I had always sprung to the defence of children who were weaker than me and had always cared for animals, but for the first time I needed to know that someone who had destroyed a part of me was suffering. As far as I was concerned, justice had now been done and although, now, I am appalled at the cycle of violence, at the time it felt as if I had a way to carry on living.

'Thank you,' I said, hugging Hank. 'You've helped me more than you'll ever know.'

He smiled. 'I told you I'd protect you and I meant it. Hans broke every rule in the book and that has been made very clear to him.'

Suddenly for the first time in days I felt hungry. I walked over to the fridge and loaded food on to a plate.

'I feel a whole lot better now I know that bastard is writhing in agony,' I said between mouthfuls.

Hank was still extremely angry about my treatment at the hands of the Rotterdam gang. It made him gentle towards me. 'You need to be taken care of. I'm going to book you in with the best doctor in Amsterdam. He knows what he's doing, and he won't ask any difficult questions.'

The next day I went to see the doctor, who gave me a thorough check-up. I was terrified about letting a man touch me, but the doctor was professional and put me at my ease. I explained to him that I'd been injected with a drug that made me feel sleepy and woozy and unable to even think about fighting back against my captors.

'It may well have been heroin,' he said, shaking his head in disgust at the way I had been treated. 'It's extremely addictive. You're lucky you got away when you did, before it could do too much damage to you.'

He told me that my injuries from the beatings were superficial but that I'd picked up a sexually transmitted infection. I confided that various men had inserted objects into me.

He gave me a detailed examination and said gravely, 'Judging by what I've found after examining you, those men were complete animals. I'm very sorry, Louise, but the damage done to you could interfere with your chances of having children.'

I hadn't been expecting such a bombshell. While I had no immediate plans to have children, no seventeen-year-old girl wants to have that choice permanently taken away from her. I lay on my back on the examination couch staring up at the doctor's pristine white ceiling. I was choked with rage and grief, and couldn't stop tears rolling down my cheeks. There are many small deaths in life before the final one, and this was such a moment. I mourned the loss of the part of me that could give life to another human being.

The doctor gave me some strong antibiotics to cure my infection and told me to come back if there was anything else I needed.

I walked out feeling bleak. The news that Hans had been shot had lifted my spirits, but the discovery that I probably wouldn't be able to have children had shredded my spirit once more.

I hurried back to Hank's apartment. I was relieved to discover he was out as I needed to mourn alone. I collapsed on the sofa sobbing. How much more damage could those bastards do to me? I asked myself in my despair.

By the time Hank came home, I had dried my eyes, washed my face and combed my hair. I didn't tell him what the doctor had said.

I vowed that nobody would ever be able to damage me again, either emotionally or physically. I had always been a closed book emotionally, but now I felt as if a cage of reinforced steel had formed around me. I wanted to make sure that nobody could ever penetrate my defences again.

Hank looked after me very well in the weeks following my escape from Rotterdam. When I walked through the streets of Amsterdam, I knew that everyone in the underworld was aware that I was protected. Associating with Hank was like having an invisible bodyguard. I knew that he could be a cruel and dangerous man, but at this extremely vulnerable point in my life it was in my interest to allow him to shelter me.

Slowly I began to get back in touch with my old friends in Amsterdam. All of them noticed a major change in me. Before, people had often told me that I had beautiful eyes, which sparkled so brightly they looked as if they were dancing. After Rotterdam the light in my eyes died. I was no longer a cocky, lively teenager with everything ahead of me. I had suddenly aged. I felt like a troubled grandmother.

I no longer wanted to go out to nightclubs because they were full of men. Any man who tried to make a move on me received a sharp reprimand. 'Get lost. Don't you dare touch me!' I found myself yelling at any man who paid me even the slightest attention. Men violated women; I completely understood that now, and the thought of a man being close to me made me feel physically repulsed.

I spent a few weeks smoking cannabis heavily in an attempt to numb my pain. Eventually I emerged from my stupor with a plan to earn as much money as I could; it would be a way of sending out a signal that I could thrive without men, and neither needed them nor wanted their attentions. While I had never been interested in having lots of material possessions, I knew that having money was one way of protecting myself.

I also wanted to make sure that I was ready to run at a moment's notice, so I was still keen to get a passport. Hank said that he would arrange everything for me and that the safest kind of passports were the ones acquired legally.

'I'm going to find a Dutchman to marry you and then you'll get a passport no problem. Because you're only seventeen, you'll have to forge your parents' signature giving consent to the marriage.'

'I'm used to forging signatures, so that won't be a problem,' I replied, grinning.

A short while later Hank introduced me to a man called Paul. He was a few years older than me and Hank said he was going to be my husband. He was unremarkable-looking with blond, neatly combed hair and was wearing a pale-blue shirt and jeans.

'Hello, wife-to-be,' he said, smiling. 'It's a pleasure to meet you.'

'You too,' I said.

Beyond the initial pleasantries we didn't talk to each other much. He was happy to marry me because he would receive tax breaks. Tax was a big issue in Holland. Hank told me that tax inspectors had more clout than the police and that people who evaded paying their due ended up in serious trouble.

'Try to look like you're madly in love with each other during the wedding ceremony,' Hank said. 'I've booked the registry office for next Saturday.'

The wedding passed off smoothly. It was the perfect non-event. The registrar seemed blissfully ignorant of the fact that he was presiding over a marriage of convenience. We went to a bar after the ceremony to toast our union, and a couple of days later I applied for my Dutch passport as Mrs Louise van Eyck. I received it quickly and without fuss.

Hank had been keen to get my passport not only to help me out but also because he wanted to recruit me to do diamond runs for him. Like my ex-boyfriend Thom, Hank was heavily involved in Antwerp's flourishing black-market diamond trade. Because I was young and fresh-faced, he assumed (rightly, it turned out) that I would be able to cross the Dutch–Belgian border without attracting suspicion. I agreed to help him out and he asked me if I was interested in doing other work, like carrying cocaine into Europe from Colombia.

'No way would I get involved in smuggling drugs,' I said. 'Just forget that. Diamonds are OK because they don't ruin people's lives the way drugs do.'

'OK, OK, Louise. No need to get on your high horse. We'll concentrate on the diamonds. I won't mention it again, my little firebrand.'

I nodded unsmilingly. I was angry that Hank had thought I would even consider smuggling cocaine.

These days the terrible things associated with the mining and sale of diamonds are well documented – people know how diamonds have fuelled conflicts across Africa and how those who mine them, often children, suffer terribly. But in 1978, when I was in Amsterdam, such things were not known. I was very naïve and wrongly thought that smuggling diamonds was a victimless crime.

Once I had my passport, I was ready to learn more about diamond smuggling. I was eager to find out as much as I could because I knew how lucrative it was. I had watched Thom work and already understood something about the stones and what kind of prices they sold for.

My job was to hire an anonymous, middle-of-the-road car and drive it across the Belgian border to Antwerp with a wad of cash strapped round my waist. I would then meet up with a diamond dealer in an anonymous hotel room and swap the cash for handfuls of diamonds. Then I had to drive back across the border into Holland with a briefcase that had a false bottom, which of course contained the diamonds.

I always crossed the border at around 5.30 p.m., when the border guards would be changing shifts. The old shift of guards would be catching up on news from the new shift and so they were less interested in checking people in the cars. I never once got searched, even though I made trips about once a fortnight. At first I found the whole thing thrilling. After I'd done a few runs, however, it became rather routine and I grew very nonchalant.

Hank started me off with relatively small amounts of cash to buy diamonds – around £10,000. Gradually I was trusted with larger and larger amounts. I earned good money for smuggling and soon began to see the business opportunities for myself. If Hank sent me to Antwerp with £20,000, I would add £3,000 of my own money and buy £23,000 worth of diamonds from the dealer. I'd then sell on £3,000 of diamonds myself, often to the prostitutes who worked in Amsterdam's elite brothels. This discreet little sideline was extremely profitable.

Over a period of a few months I had gained myself a reputation as a top diamond smuggler. I was smart, careful and quiet. The world of diamond smuggling was entirely male, so as the sole female trader, I stood out and impressed my male counterparts.

Before long I was able to afford to buy myself a nice apartment and a Porsche, not something that most seventeen-year-olds could even have dreamt of possessing. Sometimes when I stepped out of the driving seat, people said, 'You're so lucky that your dad lets you drive his car.' I'd just smile and nod. I also bought myself a huge round bed and installed a state-of-the-art stereo system, from which I blasted the likes of the Police, Joe Cocker and Fleetwood Mac.

Although I had bought myself expensive possessions, my car, my apartment and the diamonds ultimately meant nothing to me. I never expected anything in my life to be permanent. Just as I had gone from living a life of luxury in Nicole's

Parisian apartment to sleeping in a doorway in Place Pigalle, I knew that my car and my apartment could vanish in a flash and I could end up back on the streets without enough money in my pocket for a cheap meal. I knew instinctively that until I found some part of the world where I could truly rest, the cycle of rags to riches and back to rags was likely to continue. I had gone from living rough in the woods in Southampton to immersing myself in the gangster lifestyle and embracing material goods. On the surface, things appeared to be going well, but really I was simply a wandering spirit in search of an anchor.

In my heart, I was uneasy with the lifestyle of gangsters. The only thing that held me to this underground world was the money I was making. I had little education and even fewer skills that would make me attractive to an employer. Because of my horrific experience in Rotterdam, I had a fear of being left without money. It would have made me feel stripped bare at a time when I needed to protect myself.

When I wasn't working, I got into my car and drove out of Amsterdam into the countryside. I knew of a forest with bungalows that could be rented, and I often stayed in one of them for two or three nights. During these trips I spoke to no one and spent my days walking, lost in thought. As I ambled along the shady paths, I felt comforted by the breeze on my face and the smells of wood and earth. It helped to heal my shattered spirit. I had been walking through treacly darkness since my nightmare in Rotterdam. During these walks through the forest I felt as if once again I had light around me.

THE BIGGEST DIAMOND I EVER SAW

I knew that my profitable career in diamond smuggling couldn't last for ever. I was beginning to get nervous. For protection against rival gangsters, I took to carrying a little silver handgun with a white handle known as a 'lady gun'. I also had a safe in my apartment and sometimes had several hundred thousand pounds worth of diamonds in it.

I knew how highly Hank valued me when he asked me to deliver a rare and expensive diamond to a buyer in Paris. It was worth hundreds of thousands of pounds and had been stolen from somewhere.

'I think you're the only person who could pull this one off,' said Hank. 'I trust you to find an appropriate way to get that goddamned diamond across the border into France. There's a room booked for you at the George the Fifth Hotel. The two people collecting the diamond from you will phone reception and say, "We've come for the collection," and mention my name. When you hear those words, you can let them in. I will then call you. As soon as I get word that the diamond has been successfully handed over, the men will transfer the money to me.'

I nodded. I didn't for a moment consider the enormous risks I was taking and the very serious consequences if I got caught smuggling such a valuable jewel. After Rotterdam, it was as if I felt that nothing would ever scare me again.

I racked my brains trying to think of the safest way of transporting the diamond. I sometimes hid money in my shoes, but knew it would be too painful to walk with a hard diamond digging into the sole of my foot. One day I was walking through one of Amsterdam's clothes markets because I wanted to buy myself a new shirt. At the time the fashion was for denim shirts with lots of diamantés sewn on, like a shower of raindrops. As I took a couple of them off the rail to examine them, an idea popped into my head. I remembered hearing someone say, 'The best place to hide is in plain sight.' Inspired, I grabbed one of the shirts, paid for it and rushed home. Now I knew exactly how I was going to transport this priceless diamond. Very carefully I stitched it in among the diamanté beading on the shirt. No one would never notice.

The next day I set off for Paris. I knew exactly how to get to the George the fifth Hotel. The last time I'd been there, all I had been able to afford was a hot chocolate on the terrace while I dog-sat for Nicole. Now I'd been booked into one of the best suites in the hotel, all expenses paid.

I strode confidently towards reception. The ornate hotel lobby was polished to a high sheen and decorated with lavish displays of flowers. The man behind the hotel reception desk gawped when he saw this very young, casually dressed girl approach. I was wearing the diamanté denim shirt, a pair of jeans and cowboy boots, and my hair was tied in a loose ponytail. Presumably the staff had been expecting an elaborately coiffed woman of at least twice my age wearing a tailored business suit.

'Hello, I'm Louise van Eyck. I'm booked into one of your suites,' I said calmly.

'Yes, of course, mademoiselle.' The receptionist became deferential when he saw that the name on my passport matched up with the name on the booking. 'One of the bell boys will show you to your suite.'

I could see the bell boy looking me up and down, doubtful that he would receive a tip from a young upstart like me. He showed me to my suite and I casually took a hundred francs out of my purse and handed the money to him. He looked amazed.

'*Merci*, mademoiselle.' He kept turning it over in his hand to make sure it was real; then he folded it carefully and clutched it in the palm of his hand as if afraid I would change my mind and try to whisk it away from him.

After he'd left, I lay on the blissfully soft bed and ordered the two fanciest items on the room-service menu – lobster and champagne. I thought of all the hard, dirty, uncomfortable beds I'd slept on in my time, and the nights when I'd slept out in the woods or on the doorsteps of tower-block flats and woken up starving. I doubted that many people had experienced the same extremes.

As I lay there revelling in my current good fortune, images of what had happened to me in Rotterdam flashed unbidden into my mind. Over the last six months I had tried my best to block out the memories, but however much I tried to stuff them to the recesses of my brain, they would still jump into the front of my mind like a devil hopping on to my shoulder.

Many bad things had happened to me throughout my life, but until recently I had always had the gift of resilience and had somehow emerged fighting. I could bear all the other things because in a lot of cases the cruelty had been casual, accidental almost. This time was different; thoughts of the men who had tortured me in Rotterdam could not be disposed of that way. These men had assiduously planned their brutal assaults on young women and had worked hard to make us suffer to an extraordinary degree. I hadn't known that bodies could be ransacked in the way that they had ransacked mine. I felt as if the memories were strangling me.

I drifted into a fitful sleep and was woken by the phone. I jumped up, straightened my ruffled hair and answered it.

'Who is it?' I asked.

'We've come for the collection. We're here for Hank,' came the reply.

'Come on up,' I said. I quickly called Hank to tell him the men were on their way up to my room and left the receiver, with Hank waiting on the end of the line, on the bedside table.

I opened the door and let two bland-faced, grey-suited men enter. These two would certainly not elicit a second glance in the street, I thought.

I was very cautious and hadn't even taken the diamond off my shirt. They were shocked by how young I was.

Then one of them picked up the phone and spoke to Hank. He passed the phone to me, and Hank said, 'It's OK – you can go ahead and hand over the diamond.'

I picked up some nail scissors and cut the thread that was holding the diamond to my shirt. The men gaped – I don't think they could quite believe that I'd chosen such a bold way to hide the diamond. They were put out that I hadn't transported the gem in my vagina wrapped in a condom, as instructed by Hank.

Carefully, I handed the diamond over to one of the men. He picked it up, gasped at its size and beauty, and tested its authenticity. Then he nodded and passed it to the second man, who repeated the test.

'Yes, it's the one,' he breathed.

Then he made a call, instructing for the money to be released to Hank. I could see that now they had the diamond in their hands, they had almost forgotten that I, the courier, existed. The two of them swiftly left my suite.

I spent the rest of the day shopping in Paris's luxury boutiques, then headed back to Amsterdam to await instructions on my next assignment.

Hank was full of praise for me when I returned. 'You handled that assignment perfectly, Louise. It's hard to believe that you're not yet eighteen.'

I shrugged. I was glad that I hadn't messed up the deal, but beyond that the expedition to Paris meant little to me. After Rotterdam, nothing I did had very much meaning.

I made a few more trips to Paris for Hank after that, but the diamonds were never again of such high value. I felt unsettled in Amsterdam and began to think about moving on, although I had no idea where I would go. Just a few weeks later the decision was taken out of my hands.

Joanna, a friend of mine in Amsterdam, became pregnant, and she and her boyfriend, Heinz, were struggling financially. She asked if I could find some work for Heinz so that they could save up for the baby. Although I took my instructions from Hank, I was given lots of leeway to conduct my business as I thought fit.

'I could probably use some help,' I said to Joanna. 'A kind of diamond-runner errand boy.'

She laughed. 'That sounds perfect.'

Heinz began working for me. He seemed to be trustworthy, and apart from a couple of minor mistakes, he did well. I didn't know, however, that idiotically he had continued signing on and receiving the dole. Social security officials noticed that his standard of living had improved dramatically and launched an investigation. When he was hauled in for questioning, he gave the tax inspectors my name. Up until that point I had been entirely invisible in Holland except for my marriage and passport application.

I too was questioned. A small, hard-faced man with suspicious eyes paid a visit to my apartment.

'Where did you get so much money from?' he said. 'You're only a kid.'

'My grandmother died a few months ago and left me a substantial inheritance,' I said, desperately trying to think on my feet.

The inspector looked unconvinced. 'Where are the documents that prove this inheritance?'

'They're in a safe at my grandmother's lawyer's office in England,' I said.

'OK. You have seven days to produce these documents, and if you can't come up with them, we have a right to confiscate your assets and will serve you with a writ.'

Obviously I knew I could produce no such documents. My heart plummeted. What on earth was I going to do now?

After the official had left, I quickly did some research and discovered that I needed to be on Dutch soil in order for them to serve me with a writ. I was determined not to be. The feelings of being like a trapped animal flooded back. I knew that this was one thing Hank couldn't help me with. If he got involved, he risked being dragged down too. It was time to run.

TRUE LOVE

Having come to the conclusion that I should flee Amsterdam, I was now faced with the difficult decision of where to go next. I thought and thought about what to do. Eventually I decided to go back to Paris. At least no one was looking for me there, and it was less risky than returning to England.

I wasn't sorry to cut my ties with Hank. I was grateful that he had helped me get revenge on Hans in Rotterdam and that he had offered me protection, but I could see what a hard and dangerous man he was and was relieved that I would no longer be reliant on him.

I packed a few belongings, several thousand pounds in cash and a few diamonds, and once again boarded a train that would take me to a new life. On arrival in Paris, I rented a modest apartment and got in touch with some diamond contacts whom I had met when I had made trips to Paris for Hank. Many of them were models and I quickly became drawn into their brittle, beautiful lifestyle.

I was relieved to be out of Amsterdam and liked being in the familiar surroundings of Paris. I knew that sooner or later my money would run out and I would have to find a way of earning more, but for the first few weeks I did very little. Usually things happened to me without me having to go and seek them out and I decided that sooner or later something would present itself to me.

At the end of my third week in Paris, one of the models I was friendly with gave me a front-row ticket for a prêt-à-porter show. A model who came on to the catwalk threw me a rose. I had never seen her before and I thought nothing of it, but after the show she made a beeline for me. I was wearing a white jacket with tassels on it and the first words she said to me were, 'Oh, your jacket's really cool.' Her name was Natalie and she was an exquisite creature, tall and willowy with incredibly smooth black hair and olive-coloured skin. She told me that she was eighteen, the same age as me, half French and half Indonesian, and had spent a lot of time in Amsterdam. She invited me to the after-party and I accepted.

The party was oozing with female youth and beauty and shady-looking older men. Everybody drank copious amounts of champagne, but nobody ate any of the dainty canapés that waiters endlessly circled the room carrying. Natalie and I chatted away for a while about people and places we both knew in Amsterdam, and then she darted across the room and came back with two friends, a man and a woman.

'It's getting tiresome here. Would you like to join us at another party at my friend's apartment?' Natalie said.

'OK, sure – why not?' I replied.

I was feeling very miserable. Memories of my nightmare in Rotterdam were not fading. If anything, the pictures that flashed through my mind were becoming more vivid. The experience hung over my head like rancid smoke. Wherever I went and whatever I did, I could smell it on me. I had no idea whether I could trust Natalie and her friends, but I didn't care too much what happened to me any more. It was easier to let the tide carry me wherever it wanted to go.

The party turned out to be just the four of us. Her friends paired up and she placed her hand on my knee. I jumped. I had never been approached by a woman before and wasn't sure what she wanted. Then she started flirting with me, whispering in my ear that I was very beautiful. Her long hair brushed against my cheek.

We ended up going back to my apartment. I hadn't considered a relationship with a woman before, but after Rotterdam the thought of going near any man still filled me with revulsion. I felt utterly lost and decided that maybe a woman who treated me tenderly could act as some sort of salve. I didn't understand how a physical relationship with a woman would work, but I was sure that a woman wouldn't be able to inflict the kind of pain on me that the men in Rotterdam had.

At my flat, Natalie started kissing me and we ended up making love. It was a very gentle experience, and after our first night together we became inseparable. Natalie was like a drug for me; I was mesmerised by her and seemed to have the same effect on her. She soon moved into my flat and we spent every moment together. I wasn't working and went with her to fashion shows and photoshoots.

We talked about everything under the sun – our childhoods, our opinions about the world, the kind of food we liked to eat. With Natalie I felt that I had found my soul mate. With every other person in my life – not only boyfriends but also female friends and family members – I had often felt claustrophobic, but with her I never did. For the first time in my life I didn't get the urge to run away and be by myself.

There were no secrets between us. I told her about my family, about Jim the milkman, the children's homes, the diamond smuggling and, haltingly, about what had happened to me in Rotterdam. She listened intently to everything I said, and without saying much I felt that she completely understood my pain and why I was leading such an itinerant life. Spilling out my secrets to her brought us even closer. In her company I always had a warm, safe feeling, something I had never experienced during my childhood or with any boyfriend.

I had never been attracted to women, but decided that rather than being attracted to either a male or a female body, I was attracted to a person's soul. Natalie had a pure and beautiful soul, and I felt that being with her nourished my damaged spirit.

After a couple of months I got evicted from the flat I was renting for playing music too loudly. Natalie was stunning to look at, but her modelling work seemed to be drying up. The cash I had brought with me from Amsterdam was running out, so money was tight.

At exactly the right moment we met a photographer called Jean at a party who told us he had a spare room we could stay in. I couldn't believe it when he said his apartment was in Avenue Foch. Of all the streets in Paris I wondered why I had been drawn back to that one. Jean moved in model and celebrity circles, and we tagged along to endless parties.

My relationship with Natalie continued to be intense. She was the first person to whom I unlocked myself and explained my whole life. I had always thought it was normal to keep all my thoughts and feelings bottled up inside me, and it was a real joy for me to discover that spilling out my innermost thoughts and feelings to someone I trusted and who understood me, felt far better than keeping everything to myself.

As time went on, my love for Natalie deepened, but the more I adored her, the more terrified I became. I was used to behaving like a clam. Natalie painstakingly prised my emotions open. But opening myself up to her bright sunlight became too much for me. Such honesty is hard when you're not used to it. In the end I felt so scared of it that I could see only one solution, the same one I'd always seen – to run away.

'I'm running out of money. I have to go back to Amsterdam for a while and try and get myself re-established in the diamond business,' I lied. 'Hopefully the taxmen have stopped looking for me by now.'

Natalie wept and didn't believe my feeble excuse about getting back into the diamond business. She loved me, knew I was running away from her and she couldn't understand why. As far as she was concerned, the relationship was perfect. She had led an open, trusting life with a caring family and found my excessive distrust and fear of intimacy hard to understand.

'I'll be back,' I said, trying to sound nonchalant, although we both knew I wouldn't be. 'Goodbye, Natalie. I'm so sorry,' I said, embracing her with tears in my eyes.

She was sobbing too much to reply.

I hurried to the Gare du Nord, desperate to get away from the terrible mess I'd made. I didn't particularly want to go back to Amsterdam, but at that moment I didn't have the energy to start again in a new and unfamiliar place. My

plan was to look up some old friends and stay in Amsterdam for a few days, recover some emotional strength and
then move on.

As the train pulled out of the station, I was overwhelmed
with sadness and self-reproach. I felt desperately confused
about my sexuality and didn't know how to handle the
relationship at all. I did know that Natalie was the best thing
that had ever happened to me. Nobody else had ever shown
me such love, kindness and gentle attention. With her I knew
that whatever I did she would be by my side, supporting me,
yet I had thrown it all back at her.

I ran as fast as I could to escape bad situations, but why did
I also flee good ones? Was I so damaged that I couldn't sustain
a healthy relationship when it fell into my lap? Natalie and I
had been under each other's spell, but I had destroyed that and
rubbed Natalie's face in the debris.

I often forgot that I was still young – I had just turned
eighteen. I had already crammed more experiences into my life
than some people had in an entire lifetime. I usually thought
of myself as a grown-up, but the way I had behaved with
Natalie made me realise that in many ways I was still a little
girl, too overwhelmed by the intensity of adult love to cope
with it. Most girls of my age would probably confide in their
mothers or in a best friend about the battery of emotions that
drench the senses during a love affair, but I had no one.

In this time of deep despair, my thoughts once again
returned to my mother and all the ways she had let me down.
I imagined that a consistent and selfless mother's love could
prepare children for other kinds of love. I had been so
determined to be independent, to virtually bring myself up
and show that I could do everything on my own that I hadn't

realised that there was more to life than just clothing and feeding myself.

As I leant back into the train seat, I found myself doing something I hadn't done for years. I screwed my eyes shut and appealed to my imaginary fairy godmother to produce some perfect parents for me, parents who could show me love.

FALLING INTO THE MOVIES

When I arrived back in Amsterdam, I booked myself into a cheap bed and breakfast. I didn't have much money left, but I had a handful of diamonds, which I could sell if I needed to. Despite what I'd told Natalie, I knew it was too risky to start smuggling diamonds again, but I couldn't think what else to do. I mooched around, unable to think of anything but Natalie. I was so used to walking, talking, eating and sleeping with her by my side that I felt as if I had lost a limb. I had no interest in doing anything, and I hoped that somehow an adventure would fall at my feet and take my mind off my loss.

I wondered if my mother thought about me much or if she was just relieved that her wild, difficult child was out of her hair at last. Was she hungry for information about me when Jay passed on news of my occasional calls? Although I had no desire to be reunited with her, I felt totally desolate and alone. I had gone through my childhood showing everybody that I didn't need adults to survive, but as time went by, I craved parental love more and more.

One evening I was sitting in a bar by myself with my fingers wrapped tightly round a glass of wine. Before my experience in Rotterdam, I had never really drunk much alcohol, but since then I had found that alcohol helped me to blot out the fear and loathing I experienced when the memories of my ordeal became too much to bear.

Suddenly I spotted Janette and Marieke, two girls I had known vaguely when I had lived in Amsterdam. They sat down and started chatting to me.

'Oh, I'm just back in town for a couple of weeks,' I said, trying my best to sound breezy and confident. 'I was in Paris for a while, but decided to come back here. I'm on my way to somewhere, but at the moment I've no idea where,' I said.

'Sounds like you've met the right people,' said Marieke. 'We're off to Hollywood to try our luck in the movie business.'

My eyes lit up. I had absolutely no interest in finding fame and fortune in Tinseltown, but I was still feeling very confused about Natalie and needed some space. I still needed to get away from enthusiastic tax inspectors and the authorities in England, too. America sounded a healthy distance away. I'd heard that there were some very good beaches in the area and decided that while Marieke and Janette strutted in front of the silver screen, I could teach myself to surf.

They had air tickets booked for the following week and had organised an apartment to rent.

'Mind if I join you?' I said tentatively. 'I can't see myself as a movie star, but I hear the beaches are pretty good. I don't have any other plans at the moment and I like the sound of going somewhere new.'

'Of course,' said Janette. 'The apartment is small, but I'm sure it'll be fine.'

The following week we set off for Hollywood. On the plane, Janette and Marieke chattered animatedly about the fame and fortune that lay in wait for them. They were very excited, while I had no interest in Hollywood beyond the fact that it was on a different continent and would give me a chance for a fresh start. Mixed-up thoughts about Natalie, Rotterdam, Michael and my mother swirled round my head – when I pushed one thought away, it was replaced by another. I closed my eyes and tried to sleep. I envied Janette and Marieke. Their minds seemed to me like white, trusting sheets of paper, not full of dark splodges like mine. I longed to have my innocence back.

When we arrived in Los Angeles several hours later, I felt more cheerful. The sky was a brilliant shade of blue, the sun was strong, and the ocean looked perfect. I felt that this would be a calm and soothing place for me. I planned to spend as much time as possible in the sea or on the beach, perhaps picking up a job as a waitress in one of the beach cafés so that I could cover the cost of food and rent.

The apartment the girls had rented was on the edge of Hollywood in a slightly down-at-heel street full of other young hopefuls who waited on tables and held their breath for their big break. It was very liberating not to care about things like that. The town didn't appeal to me – it was all a showy façade – but I loved the beach.

I bought a cheap surfboard and spent my days on Venice Beach rolling into the shore on the creamy waves. I enjoyed the feeling of the hot, gritty sand. Out in the open air, with the sun warming my skin, I thought less about Natalie, the children's homes, Hans, Hank, my mother and all the other things that had caused me grief. Not thinking about these incredibly painful memories seemed to be the only way I could cope with them.

As I lay on the sand with the sound of the sea in my ears, I thought of the other parts of nature that I adored and remembered my days spent climbing trees in the New Forest, caring for the orphaned lambs and riding ponies. Unlike Janette and Marieke, I saw Los Angeles as a place of rest and recovery. I knew little about the lifestyle of the inhabitants of Hollywood, but what I saw of the brittle, ego-drenched existences didn't appeal to me. I was happy to keep away from people who worked in the film business, to laze around on the beach and let Janette and Marieke push themselves forward onto the silver screen.

I got into a routine of rising late and wandering down to Venice Beach, where my surfing quickly improved. I loved the excitement of being carried by the waves, and submerging myself in the natural world had always given me enormous pleasure.

One day a young man who wouldn't have looked out of place as the leading actor in a Hollywood movie approached me on the beach. He was tall with a slim, athletic body and tousled hair that was streaked blond in the sun. His eyes were a clear bluish-green and looked almost translucent. I had seen him surfing and he obviously knew a lot more about it than me. He was fast and graceful as he curved his tanned body into the waves.

'Hi,' he said, grinning. 'I'm Jack. I've been watching you surf. Looks like you're new to this, but you've taught yourself pretty well. Want me to show you a few tricks?'

'Sure – why not?' I said, returning his smile. 'I'm Louise, by the way. Good to meet you.'

And so we surfed and drank coffee and ate toasted sandwiches from the beach café together. Things fast-forward when you're spending long outdoor days together. After a few days, when we were lying side by side on the beach and I was laughing at one of his jokes, he leant over and kissed me. Without much fanfare or discussion, Jack and I began a relationship.

Jack was my first relationship with a man since Rotterdam. Despite my terrible experience, I didn't hate all men and I continued to have friendships with them. He was kind and gentle, and I thought we could have a light-hearted fling, cemented by our mutual love of the beach and surfing. The relationship cheered me up. I certainly wasn't in love with Jack, but it did me good to be with someone with whom I didn't need to think about anything serious. It was a welcome break after the intense passion of my relationship with Natalie.

Jack was an actor and he told me that his brother, Warren, worked at Universal Studios training stuntmen for the films.

'It'd be easy enough for him to get us a couple of passes. We could meet him for lunch one day and see how the stunts are done,' he said.

'Sounds fun,' I said. I had no burning desire to get into a Hollywood studio and see its inner workings, but I was always keen to have new experiences.

A few days later Jack and I went up to Universal Studios to meet Warren. Jack told me that his brother was considered to be Hollywood's top stuntman.

In my mind I had imagined that a big Hollywood studio would be impossibly glamorous, stuffed with actresses in slinky gowns. The reality was far more prosaic. The studio looked like an industrial complex. There were white airport-style hangers everywhere, and the actors were standing around in heavy make-up smoking cigarettes and chatting to each other.

Jack led me to the back of one of the lots and I saw a track where someone was practising spinning a car.

'Oh, I used to do that,' I exclaimed, suddenly remembering all the fun I had had with the gypsies spinning cars on the rough ground in the New Forest. 'Would Warren let me have a go?'

'I think they're pretty strict about these things, but we can certainly ask.'

Jack introduced me to Warren, an older, broader version of himself.

'Great to meet ya,' said Warren in that enthusiastic, vigorous, American way. He pumped my hand up and down in a firm handshake.

'Louise tells me she's a secret car spinner,' said Jack. 'She wants to know if she can have a try on the track.'

'Sorry, honey, insurance rules are very strict – I'd be crucified if I let you anywhere near one of the cars.'

'Never mind,' Jack said, shrugging his shoulders. 'Listen, we'll see you in a few minutes and we'll eat,' he said to Warren.

His brother nodded and I gave him a big wave. Just then I saw that Warren had carelessly thrown the keys down on a nearby table.

'Jack, we've got to have a go,' I said.

He shook his head. 'It's too risky. We'll get thrown out and Warren could lose his job.'

'Jack, I'm dying to have a go – please, please, please.'

He looked into my eyes and buckled. 'OK, come on, then, but we need to be quick.'

I decided that if there was any fuss, I would tell the studio managers that I had stolen the keys from Warren and that the whole thing was nothing to do with him. I grabbed the keys, ran down to the track where the car was parked and swung into the driving seat. Jack jumped into the passenger seat, looking slightly worried. There was a cross painted further down the track where the car was supposed to land after a spin. I got the car up to about forty miles an hour and then did a perfect four-point spin, landing precisely on the cross. I couldn't believe that I'd managed it so well first time round after not having done anything like it for years. I felt elated. I had been dozing since I'd arrived in Los Angeles, but suddenly I had woken up.

Jack looked at me admiringly. 'You're certainly a woman of hidden talents. That was absolutely amazing!'

I looked out of the car window and saw Warren running down to the track. Oh, no, I'm in really big trouble now, I thought.

But he was beaming.

'That was unbelievable! Who the hell taught you to do that? I've been trying to teach the guys to do that for months, but we're not there yet. When you said you wanted to have a spin in the car, I assumed you were just an amateur.'

'I kind of taught myself,' I said. 'I used to hang out with a group of kids in a woodland area in England and we practised with old cars.'

'Hollywood is crying out for stuntwomen. I'll train you properly if you like and I'm sure you'll get lots of movie work.'

I agreed enthusiastically, hardly able to believe my good fortune. Apart from the casual work I'd done in bars and restaurants, I'd never had a proper job before. Now for the first time in my life someone was going to employ me. And it wasn't just any old job either; it was a prestigious job in Hollywood. I wondered if my mother and Michael were still living on the council estate in Southampton. This would certainly be the last thing they'd have expected a girl like me to end up doing.

POWDER, POWDER EVERYWHERE

Jack was amazed that I'd secured myself a job just like that. 'People spend years trying to break into the studio system, you know,' he said, shaking his head in astonishment as we wandered around Universal Studios.

We sat down and ate lunch with Warren, who talked excitedly about all the things he was going to teach me and all the upcoming films he thought he would be able to use me in. Although I'd had no interest in getting involved in the movie business up till now, listening to Warren made me feel excited about the kinds of things I'd be doing. I had always been a thrill-seeker, and from what he was saying, I'd be able to do lots of daring things and actually get paid for them. I decided that my run of bad luck must be over.

When I returned to the apartment I was sharing with Marieke and Janette that evening, both of them looked glum.

'We've been going to auditions for weeks and neither of us has got anywhere. Our money's running out and I think we're going to have to go back home,' said Janette despairingly.

Marieke in particular seemed devastated. She had really pinned her hopes on making it in the bright lights of Holly-wood. I didn't want to rub salt into the wound, but I had to tell them that I wouldn't be getting on the plane home with them.

'Jack took me up to Universal Studios today to meet his brother, who trains the stunt guys. He offered to take me on and train me up, so I'm going to give it a go,' I said, trying to play the whole thing down, but their mouths dropped open.

'You don't even *want* fame and fortune and you've got yourself a plum job with a top Hollywood studio,' said Janette. 'Life is full of ironies.'

After their initial shock and disappointment, Marieke and Janette wished me luck and said they really hoped things would work out for me. A couple of days later they climbed aboard the plane back to Amsterdam with heavy hearts.

I spent the following month training with Warren and a group of stuntmen. I learnt how to fall properly, how to do combat training, how to leap from one building to the next and how to do a whole range of car stunts, including plunging a car off the edge of a cliff – the car was hauled back just in the nick of time.

Warren had a guest apartment at the bottom of his garden and he said that I might as well stay there rather than pay rent on an apartment that was now too big for me. He had an enormous garden full of tropical blooms and chatty parrots. I loved waking up and stepping out into somewhere green and natural, even though it was a manicured version of nature.

My relationship with Jack had fizzled out by this point, as I had thought it would, but we remained good friends.

One evening Warren said he wanted to see if I was as fearless as I seemed. 'Come on, jump on the back of my bike – we're going for a ride,' he said.

He tossed a helmet to me and I clambered on the back of his 1,000 cc CRB racer bike. He roared off through the streets of Los Angeles and when we got out into the country as far as Death Valley, he got up to about 180 kilometres an hour. I was too scared to find the ride thrilling, but I managed to keep my mouth clamped shut and not scream. When the ride finished, Warren gave me an approving nod. I sensed that the mere fact that I'd survived in silence meant that I'd passed some kind of test.

While I was doing my training with Warren, I began to mix with various Hollywood celebrities including John Belushi, Warren Beatty and Jack Nicolson. Unlike Marieke and Janette, though, I wasn't remotely star-struck. I met Mickey Rourke at a party and started drinking tequila slammers with him. As our inhibitions loosened, we both climbed up onto a table and started dancing. I wouldn't have dreamt of doing something like that sober, but alcohol makes you do all sorts of things. The other guests at the party didn't bat an eyelid; they were used to seeing outrageous behaviour.

As the night wore on, Mickey bet me that he could out-drink me. I was determined to prove him wrong. After ten tequila slammers apiece, we agreed to call it quits. I could barely stand up, but somehow I managed to walk out of the room before collapsing in a heap on the floor and being violently sick. My stubborn streak was still getting me into trouble. I knew it wasn't safe to get so drunk, but I just couldn't resist challenging such a famously party-loving guy.

When I had completed my training with Warren, I got a part in a film in which I doubled for an actress whose car rolled off the edge of a cliff. I was padded up with a leather bodysuit under my film clothes during rehearsals. At lunchtime I decided to go for a swim and had only just got myself dry when I was called back to the set. I didn't have time to put my protective bodysuit back on and so simply pulled on my film clothes. In the stunt, the car rolled a bit too far off the cliff and I got quite battered and bruised. I vowed not to take any shortcuts after that.

Despite a few close shaves, I loved doing the stunt work and was very grateful to have a well-paid job that I enjoyed so much. While everybody worked hard during the day on film sets, they partied even harder at night.

The longer I spent in Hollywood, the more dysfunctional and crazed I realised the town's inhabitants were. Of the minority who made it, most were destroyed by their fame, while the majority who didn't make it were destroyed by their lack of fame and often descended into drug abuse, alcoholism and terminal bitterness. I soon realised that Hollywood was the land of broken dreams.

It was 1980 and mobile phones were not yet around. One night I found myself calling a cab after a party from a phone box. A man walked up to me sobbing and said, 'Zizi's left me.'

Trying to be compassionate, I said, 'Don't get too upset about it – there are plenty more fish in the sea.'

To my horror, he opened his trousers and began masturbating. He was obviously trying to use any possible ruse to engage me in conversation.

'Put that away. I'm an undercover cop and I'm going to arrest you,' I said in a flash.

I must have selected an appropriately stern tone because he seemed to believe me, fastened up his trousers and ran off.

Another time I walked out of Warren's house and saw someone being gunned down in the street. I wondered if perhaps the flasher and the shooter were both people who had arrived in Hollywood young and full of hope and their failure to achieve their dreams had brought out the worst in them.

Hollywood was a very insular place. The inhabitants were programmed to work in movies, but when it came to other areas of life, most were deficient in knowledge and skills. Many had never travelled outside of America and shuttled between New York and Los Angeles, completely disregarding the vast expanse of country in between.

One C-list starlet was so ignorant about things beyond Hollywood that even I was surprised: 'Oh, my God, you're from England. That's so cute! London's still how it was in Victorian times, right – with no electricity and gas lights and lots of fog?'

One evening I was invited to a particularly big and fancy Universal Studios party. I felt uncomfortable there because the ratio of plastic to human was too high. I had made friends with another young woman called Jill, a bit-part actress who was also not keen on the artifice of the party scene. Most of the guests were in the garden or around the swimming pool. Jill and I decided to go and sit with a bottle of wine in a quiet part of the garden.

A certain industry big-cat with connections to one of the top executives at Universal Studios, wandered up to us. He was an ugly man with a paunch and a face reddened by alcohol. He obviously fancied Jill and was flirting with her very unsubtly. She wasn't interested, and both of us wanted to stay as far away as possible from people like him. He was quite drunk and didn't seem able to comprehend that a man of his power and stature wasn't automatically irresistible to us. After a few minutes he wandered off and we hoped that we'd been left in peace. To our dismay, he returned with a huge bottle of vintage champagne.

'You have to drink this with me, ladies,' he slurred.

He went on and on, and closed his ears to our polite refusals. In the end I couldn't bear to hear any more words of rubbish dribbling out of his mouth.

'Just fuck off will you,' I shouted.

He seemed to snap out of his drunken ramble almost immediately. In those days the 'casting couch' was a way of life for young women who wanted to make their way in Hollywood. They were dependent on men like him to make things happen for them. I couldn't bear men throwing their weight around and was getting more and more irate.

He poked me sharply in the chest and said, 'You don't know who I am. I'm going to get you thrown out.'

Suddenly, a memory of Michael poking me in the chest popped into my head. I couldn't stand any more and I exploded. Impulsive as ever, I jumped up and punched him on the nose. In an instant all the vacant people who had been staring into the distance swivelled their heads in our direction and gasped. I thought about all the revolting men in the world, men like him, who had complete power over women. I hadn't punched him just because he was buzzing irritatingly around Jill, but also because I hated the way men like him took advantage of women.

I walked out of the party proudly with my head held high. I knew that what I had just done would probably end my career in Hollywood, but at that moment I didn't care. I couldn't play the Hollywood game anyway and felt that if I didn't speak my mind, I'd burst.

The incident didn't quite finish things off for me, although after that I was made to operate as if I had one hand tied behind my back and one ankle bound to the back of my knee. While some people whispered to me that they admired my boldness and courage, they were reluctant to step out of line. I still got stunt work on a freelance basis, but didn't work on Universal films as much as before.

I know that many people in my position would have been devastated, but I really didn't mind about losing my contract. I felt lucky that I had got myself a job in Hollywood without making any effort, but it wasn't work that I cared passionately about and I disliked many of the people who had power in Hollywood. Part of me was relieved not to be tied to Universal Studios. I had fallen into this line of work by accident, and if it dried up completely, I was sure that something else would come along.

Although not many people wanted to employ me, everyone wanted to meet me. It was big gossip because I had humiliated such a key player. The *Hollywood Reporter* called me and asked if I'd do an interview with them. I was happy to oblige, but the article was pulled. I had my suspicions about the timing of that decision.

I was invited to lots of A-list parties, where endless verbal action replays were demanded of me. I began to feel like a performing monkey. It was at these parties that I saw some of Hollywood's worst excesses. Cocaine was everywhere. It was piled high in big dishes on coffee tables alongside nibbles like crisps and peanuts. I had always been very opposed to drugs. Some of the people I knew in Amsterdam were addicted to drugs and seemed absolutely wretched, and I couldn't forget how powerless and paralysed the drugs I'd been injected with in Rotterdam had made me. I wanted to be in control and hated the idea of being dependent on anyone or anything. But because it seemed so normal to use cocaine, and because I didn't have to pay for it, I decided to try it. It made me feel confident, alert and happy. I didn't plan to keep on using it, but after a week or two I was suddenly reaching for it as often as everybody else.

One of the people I met in Hollywood was a man called Bernie Cornfield. He was an enormously wealthy business-man and a huge playboy. He was small with a beard and was very affable. I soon discovered that he was only truly happy when he was surrounded by beautiful young women. He lived in Douglas Fairbanks Junior's old house, Grayhall Mansion, a ten-bedroom place with secret passageways that was deco-rated in the old Hollywood style.

I had no idea who he was when I first met him. He invited me to his house one afternoon and I turned up casually dressed in jogging trousers as I'd just finished training for a stunt. He welcomed me warmly and insisted that I go to a party he was holding that evening. I was one of the few people in Hollywood who didn't have a car.

'Sure I'll come to your party, but I need to go home and change – I can't turn up like this. Do you have a number for a cab firm?'

By way of reply he threw me a bunch of car keys. 'Here, you can borrow my Bentley – no need to call a cab – but make sure you bring it back.'

'Wow,' was all I could manage. Although I could do all manner of fancy car stunts, I'd never actually taken a driving test and I had a fleeting moment of apprehension before I climbed into the soft brown leather driving seat.

As I was about to drive off, Bernie came up to the passenger side of the car and jumped in. 'Where are you heading?' he asked.

'My apartment's in Maria del Ray,' I said. By this time I had moved out of the flat at the bottom of Warren's garden and was renting an apartment in Maria del Ray, right on the beach.

'I'll hitch a ride. My girlfriend lives there,' he replied.

I knew Bernie was married, but I said nothing. I found out later that he was the world's worst driver. He was keen to be driven around rather than risk his own life and the lives of other people by getting behind the wheel.

Like everyone else in Hollywood, Bernie had heard the story about me slapping the studio exec.

'So you really did it then, kid? Good on you,' he said.

We talked very easily and told each other jokes. Then I dropped him at his girlfriend's house and agreed to pick him up in an hour's time, which would give me chance to go home, have a shower and get changed.

When I returned to pick him up, he winked and said, 'This is a secret between you and me. You won't let it get back to my wife that I've been with my girlfriend, will you?'

'Of course not, Bernie. It's none of my business what you do.'

Although I had only just met Bernie, something had clicked between us, not a sexual attraction, although later he often tried and failed to get me to sleep with him, but a very instinctive friendship. He trusted me and I trusted him.

I became Bernie's unofficial driver, and after a few weeks he suggested that I moved into Grayhall Mansion with him, his wife, Louise, and their daughter, Jessie. I agreed and got on very well with the whole family. As I got to know Bernie better I did more and more odd jobs for him. I became a kind of Girl Friday although driving him around was my main task. He really was a terrible driver. Both his wife and I received a lot of phone calls and it got very confusing not knowing which Louise people wanted to speak to.

I had recently got a job on a film called *Sky High* and Bernie said, 'This Louise business is ridiculous. I'm going to call you Skye – it suits your personality and it'll end the confusion between the two of you.'

I loved the name, infinitely preferring it to Louise, and from that day on everyone in Hollywood referred to me as Skye. Even after I left Hollywood, I introduced myself to everyone I met as Skye.

Bernie adored women: he was always surrounded by Hollywood bimbos and hung around with Hugh Hefner, who held the best parties. He and Bernie had the most beautiful girls at their dos, which attracted all the A-list male stars. Hugh had a rule that all his girls had to be under twenty-five. In the end Bernie's wife got fed up with his serial philandering and moved out with their daughter. I stayed on good terms with both her and Bernie. I was doing more and more for Bernie and had become a fully fledged minder for him.

My existence was becoming increasingly soulless, though. I spent a lot of my time at parties taking cocaine, swimming in pools filled with champagne and dining on lobster. Now that I'd joined the ranks of the coke snorters, I had begun to understand why so many people in Hollywood were so edgy and cranky – because I had started to feel that way myself. The drug was making me increasingly paranoid. I started thinking, What are all these people looking at me for? I began taking Valium at bedtime because the cocaine made me so wired that I couldn't sleep naturally. I had only been using the stuff for a couple of months, but it was terrifying how quickly it had taken me over. The feel-good buzz I had experienced when I had first taken the drug had vanished. Now I just used it to dull the irritability I felt when I wasn't using it. A lot of the time my brain felt addled by the drug, but one morning I woke up with a start, sat bolt upright in bed and said to myself, I've got to get out of this town now. I'm not going to survive if I carry on like this.

I knew I had to leave quickly before I changed my mind. I got out of bed, threw a few things into a suitcase and then grabbed the keys to one of Bernie's cars. I drove myself to the airport, then called Jill, told her I'd left the car unlocked in the airport car park with the keys hidden under the sun visor.

'Something urgent's come up. I've got to get back to England fast. Could you do me a big favour and pick up the car and drive it back to Bernie's?'

Jill agreed. 'Will you be back soon?'

'Yes, I'm sure I will. I'll call you.' I said. I had no intention of returning to Hollywood, but it seemed easier to say that I'd be back.

Now that I was over eighteen, no social workers could lock me up in a children's home. After my years of roaming, I suddenly wanted to see England again.

Bernie had given me lots of film-industry contacts in London just a couple of weeks before. 'You never know when you might decide to go back home, Skye. Take them. These people are all friends of mine and I'm sure they'd give you some stunt work if you needed it.'

At the time I had no plans to return to England, but I had

made a careful note of the names and phone numbers in case I ever did need them. I hadn't expected that I'd be getting in touch with Bernie's friends quite so soon.

At the airport, I managed to buy a seat on a plane that was leaving in a few hours. As I handed my money over, I was flooded with relief. There was no going back now.

On the plane, I craved cocaine. I felt fidgety, irritable and miserable, but I knew that the feelings would pass. Simply having physically removed myself from temptation made me feel better. By the time the plane landed, I felt much improved. I was sure that I had made the right decision to leave Hollywood.

I hadn't wanted to tell Bernie of my plan before I left Hollywood in case he managed to talk me out of leaving, but once I arrived in London I called him and explained. As ever, he was laid-back and understanding.

'I'll miss you, Skye. Keep in touch and make sure you call my movie contacts. They'll sort out some work for you.'

'Thanks, Bernie, I will. Take care and I'll definitely be in touch.'

It felt very strange to be in London again after more than four years away from England. The capital didn't seem very different from when I'd left it – busy and dirty and full of people wrapped up in their own lives. I hoped that I would be able to stay here anonymously. All I wanted to do was live a good and calm life, free from violence.

I'd spent most of my money on the airfare to London. I took the Tube into Central London. When I arrived there, the only place I could afford to stay was in a run-down hostel in the King's Cross area. It was full of drug users who tried to entice me into using heroin and benefit fraudsters who wanted to share their knowledge of scams against the state with me. It was certainly a long way from Hollywood and Bernie's mansion. I firmly turned down all offers to lead me away from the straight and narrow.

The next day I made my way to Soho, where Bernie's friends were based. It was strange being back in Soho so many years after I'd hidden in vegetable sheds and worked as a runner for sleazy cinema bosses. I looked around to see if I could see any young kids hiding in the nooks and crannies where I used to lurk, but couldn't. Maybe Soho was no longer a target destination for runaways, I thought.

The first film company that I walked into welcomed me with open arms when I mentioned Bernie's name.

'Of course I can find a job for you,' said Alastair, the balding man who ran the company. 'Any friend of Bernie's is certainly a friend of mine.'

I was relieved to have found a job and was employed as a 'Jill-of-all-trades'. I did some stunt work for them, but when things were quiet, I ran errands, made phone calls and did anything else that was required of me.

I began a relationship with a wealthy Dutchman called Philip, and when I told him that I'd run away from England more than four years before and hadn't seen my family in all that time, he urged me to get in touch.

'They can't touch you now,' he said. 'You're over eighteen, you're not living at home, and you're not reliant on them. If you meet up with them, you may lay a few ghosts to rest.'

I decided he was right and picked up the phone to call my mother.

She sounded shocked and wary when she heard my voice. 'Louise, where on earth have you been?' she said.

'Well, I had to run away, Mum. You know I was never going to accept being locked up in an institution when I hadn't done anything wrong.'

'Suggest we all meet up for dinner in London,' Philip hissed in my ear.

I asked my mother and she agreed and said she would come, along with Michael.

When I met up with her and Michael one evening soon after, it felt very strange. My mother had only just turned forty and still looked attractive and well groomed. She and Michael were noticeably impressed by Philip's obvious wealth – he was wearing an expensive suit and a Rolex watch – and so both were on their best behaviour. There was no hugging or any sort of emotional reunion. I looked at my mother and felt that she was a stranger to me. I couldn't believe I had grown inside her, because I felt absolutely no connection to her. We spent the evening making small talk. It was a fantastic feeling knowing that I was now at a point in my life where neither of them could touch me either physically or emotionally. It made me feel very strong.

Although Michael had been the cause of so much misery in my childhood I felt no bitterness when I saw him. In fact I welcomed the chance to see him again because I could show him that despite his constant put downs when we lived under the same roof I had done extremely well for myself, had made some money and had a wealthy boyfriend on my arm while he was still struggling and hadn't made a success of his life. It was a kind of therapy to sit across the table from him, knowing that he couldn't touch me and that I'd proved him wrong about his predictions that I'd never amount to anything. My relationship with Philip fizzled out soon afterwards but I was delighted that I'd had the opportunity to show off someone like him to my mother and Michael.

After that first meeting we saw each other infrequently. The relationship was neither loving nor full of hate; it was perfunctory and mainly consisted of brief phone calls.

I heard through Jay that my mother's relationship with Michael continued to be volatile. It took a long time for them to finally part, though. The sexual attraction seemed to thread itself through the rancour. What really held my mother to Michael was the ongoing seduction of the wonderful life together he kept promising they were going to have in Spain. I suppose that like many people my mother was disappointed with the way her life had turned out, and one of the few things that sustained her was the belief, however deluded, that something much better was round the corner. Her Achilles heel was her lousy choice in men. The sexual chemistry she shared with Michael and various other unsuitable men prevented her from achieving her true potential. If she had chosen more shrewdly, I could have imagined my mother married to some lord of the manor, graciously hosting large parties for other wealthy folk in a perfectly judged silk evening dress and a string of pearls. Instead she got stuck with Michael and his pipe dreams.

My mother didn't love me. I don't believe she knew how to love her children. I, in turn, didn't love her, because she did nothing to earn my love and throughout my life I felt she was a stranger to me. She never showed any interest in the detail of my life as I had seen other parents do with their children.

At our occasional meetings she constantly urged me to

marry a rich man. I had never been interested in money and
the thought of relying on a man for cash was abhorrent to me.
I always knew that I was resourceful enough to find my own
ways to earn a living.

'Stop saying that to me. I'm not interested in getting
married, and I'm not interested in sponging off someone
wealthy. If I found myself a rich man, I'd be like a butterfly
in a bell jar, desperate to fly away. You can't put a price on
being free,' I said to her over and over again.

But she genuinely didn't seem to hear my objections. It was
the same when she urged me to change the way I dressed.
'You've got a good body,' she often said. 'Why on earth don't
you show it off a bit? High heels, short skirts and plunging
necklines don't go amiss when you're trying to reel in a
wealthy man, you know.'

'Mum, you're just not listening to me,' I said. 'You know
I've never liked exposing my body, and I'm comfortable in
jeans and T-shirts and cowboy boots.'

It was as if she wasn't capable of seeing beyond a cardboard
cut-out of what she wanted her daughter to be. I was an
enormous disappointment to her because I didn't conform to
the qualities she wanted me to have – a younger, firmer replica
of herself. Beyond her disappointment in what I wasn't, she
had no interest in what I was.

There are only a handful of times in my life when I have
become so engorged with rage that I have lashed out. One
of those times was with my mother a couple of months after
our meeting in London, when I visited her and Michael in
Southampton. As we sat talking about nothing very much, I
was overwhelmed with a familiar sense of injustice about
how she had abandoned me throughout my life. She had

never been there for me at the times when I needed her most, and often she would humiliate me both at home and in front of other people. We were standing in the kitchen and once again she made a snide, derogatory remark to me. Suddenly I was set alight by anger. I threw a bottle of whisky at her and she stumbled and fell. My anger gave me superhuman strength and almost as if I was lifting a stray feather I picked her up off the ground and flung her against the wall. Years of rage gathered into a gigantic ball of energy inside me.

'Why have you messed up my life? Why have you never been there for me? Why did you never protect me or defend me against Michael?' I screamed.

'I just wanted peace in the house,' she whimpered feebly.

'Well, it didn't work did it?' I said grimly.

I stalked out, still boiling with fury, but as I walked away, my rage began to dissipate. The further away from her I walked, the more I was bathed in a cooling feeling of peace. I had waited a long time to vent my anger. I never returned to my mother's house again.

My mother and Michael bought a property in Spain a few years later and moved there. Ironically it was there that the dream of a rosy future together finally soured. My mother caught Michael *in flagrante* with another woman and dumped him.

Meanwhile I continued working for Bernie's friend Alastair at the Soho film company. To my enormous relief, I didn't come across cocaine in London. My work for his company was a calm and peaceful period in my life, just what I needed after the madness of Hollywood. It didn't last long, though. The films I worked on were not always shot in London. Sometimes they were filmed in other parts of the UK and sometimes in other countries. One of the films I worked on took me to Thailand and what happened there was to change the course of my life for ever.

BABIES: DESPERATELY SEEKING PARENTS

Travelling from place to place with my stunt work suited me well. I was so used to moving around that I actually didn't know how to stay in one place for more than a month or two at a time. My job on the film in Thailand was to wrestle with crocodiles in a film called *Cry Tang*, which is based on a Thai legend about a boy who turns into a crocodile. The crocodiles I had to fight were mechanical ones, but they looked extremely lifelike. The stunt was quite dangerous because getting accidentally tangled in their snapping mouths could lead to serious injury.

I loved Thailand. The people were gentle, and the scenery was beautiful. I was only required to work on the film for a week and I decided after that to go off exploring. I'd heard that there was a wild, unspoilt island called Koh Samet and took a boat there. It was virtually untouched by modern civilisation, a paradise inhabited by fishermen, who lived in simple bamboo huts. The island looked like the sort of snapshot you could find in a holiday brochure – unnaturally blue sea and sky, soft, bleached sand and shady palm trees.

I met a group of young Thai men who were camping out on

the island to avoid national service. We dined on papayas, mangos and bananas, and joined the fishermen, netting a delicious variety of fish – stingrays proved to be the exception and were exceedingly tough and chewy. We bought a few essentials like oil and mosquito nets with us from the mainland, but for the most part lived off the land. I stayed a few weeks and wore no shoes the whole time I was there. It may sound like a minor detail, but if the soles of your feet connect with nature, it's like the completion of an electrical circuit. I felt very much part of the land, rather than something superimposed on it. The sea became my shower and my washing machine. Stepping out of my bamboo hut in the morning to watch the sun streak the sky orange as it rose out of the sea, and then seeing the same thing in reverse at the end of the day, gave me a feeling of pure joy.

I met a Buddhist nun on Koh Samet called Lin. She came from a wealthy family in Bangkok but had tired of the lifestyle. I learnt a lot from the depth and simplicity of her spirituality.

Something about Thailand got under my skin, and though I returned to England after a few weeks, I itched to return. Island life was particularly appealing to me. I began to spend a couple of months of every year in Thailand when I wasn't working on films. I also had to return on occasion for work. I particularly loved exploring unspoilt islands, including Phuket, which is now extremely developed, but when I first visited it, twenty years ago in 1988, it had little more than a few makeshift bars accessed by dirt tracks.

I had always loved children, and the words of the doctor in Amsterdam, who had told me I may never be able to have babies of my own, haunted me often. I had never got to the point of actually planning a child, nor did I have any particular man in mind to have a child with. My marriage of convenience in Amsterdam had been annulled a few months after it took place on the grounds that it had never been consummated, and I had not met a man that I wanted to share my life with.

But after all the horrible things I'd experienced in my childhood and adolescence, I had a massive desire to protect children from the things I'd suffered.

People say that some abused children go on to become abusers themselves, which I know is true, but many more are very aware of the dangers and want to protect innocent children from the harm and damage cruel adults can inflict. The cruelty I had experienced as a child made me feel fiercely protective towards other children who were being abused. If I saw a parent hitting their child in the street, I used to march up to them and say, 'Please don't do that. My mother used to beat me like that and it can really destroy a child's life.' Often I received a mouthful of abuse for interfering, but sometimes the adults I spoke to looked ashamed and stopped hitting their children. I knew that I was making myself very unpopular with the parents by wading in, but I just couldn't stand by and do nothing.

During one of my trips to Thailand to work on a film, various members of cast and crew went out drinking one evening to celebrate the end of filming. I was twenty-four years old and had settled into the life of films – periods of frenetic activity punctuated by lots of hanging around wait-ing. I felt rootless, the way I had for most of my life, but I was happy because my stunts were praised by the film crews I worked with, I wasn't short of money and I had my freedom. There was very little love in my life, though, and although I wasn't particularly interested in seeking out someone to a have relationship with, I often felt lonely.

I was the only English person working on this particular film; everyone else was Thai. On the way home, I was bursting to pee and asked my friends to stop for a minute while I darted into the nearest alleyway to relieve myself. As I crouched down, I saw various rubbish bags and then in amongst these bags I heard a rustling, whimpering sound. My first thought was that it was an abandoned puppy. I pulled up my trousers and went to investigate. I couldn't believe it when I saw that it was not in fact a puppy but a baby with a mop of black hair. I let out an involuntary scream, which set the baby off.

I picked her up and held my breath. She stank of stale faeces and urine, and her hair was terribly matted. Her eyes were red from crying and neglect. I guessed that she was six or seven months old. When I emerged from the alleyway carrying this filthy, shrieking baby, my friends were horrified. Sadly people did from time to time abandon babies in Thailand if they couldn't afford to look after them, and when these babies were discovered, sometimes alive but often dead, nobody made much of a fuss. My friends came from the wealthier classes in Thailand, and poverty was a fact of life that rich people often turned their backs on.

'What on earth are you doing with that filthy creature?' said one friend.

'Put it back,' said another. 'It's none of your business if someone decides to abandon their baby. I wouldn't touch her if I was you – she's probably got leprosy, AIDS and all sorts.'

I looked at them incredulously. 'Sorry, there's no way I'm going to put her back in that filthy alleyway.'

Another friend, Ji Mai, chimed in and said, 'Yes, let's take the poor little thing down to the police station.'

So Ji Mai and I trooped down to the police station with the baby. I had expected that the police would be amazed that I'd found a baby in the rubble in an alleyway and that they would be very grateful to us for averting loss of life, but if anything they were irritated that I'd destroyed a quiet evening at the station for them. Two of the officers were engrossed in a card game when we arrived.

They seemed to have no clue about what to do with the baby.

'Can you wait with it in the station until nine tomorrow morning, when the children's home opens?' one of the officers asked me.

It was about 4 a.m. and there was no way I was going to sit with this stinking, distressed child on my lap for the next five hours.

'Look, this child is suffering. She needs milk and nappies and a good bath. I'm going to take her back to my hotel with me and clean her up. Contact me in the morning to let me know what you're going to do.'

The police officers looked relieved that I was at least temporarily taking this sticky problem off their hands. Ji Mai and I went to an all-night supermarket and bought nappies, baby milk and bottles, and then I took the baby back to the hotel with me.

First of all I stripped off my own clothes, which by now smelt as foul as she did. Then I bathed her in the sink with lots of the hotel's complimentary bubble bath, wrapped her in a big, white towel and put a nappy on her. I followed the instructions on the tin of powdered baby milk, tried as best I could to sterilise the bottle by pouring lots of boiling water into it from the kettle in the room, and fed her. I had never had anything much to do with babies and was terrified that I might do something to harm her. She was so tiny and fragile. I didn't want to do anything that might add to the pain she had suffered in the alleyway, and no doubt before she was dumped there.

After the poor little girl had been washed and fed, she looked like a different child. She gazed up at me with her glossy, dark eyes and cooed. She couldn't have been in the alleyway for more than a few hours. When I held her, instinct took over. I began rocking her rhythmically and she seemed to like that. I remembered how insecure I had felt as a young child when I'd witnessed all the rows and violence between my parents. I held her gently but firmly in the hope that that would make her feel safe.

I laid her carefully on my bed and ran a long, hot bath for myself. It was such a curious chain of events that had led me to her that I was sure that some higher power had intended me to find her and rescue her. I lay back in the bath and splashed hot water over myself like a wave. Looking after this helpless little girl had awakened something in me that I hadn't experienced before. Although she was a stranger to me, and although I had only spent a very short time with her, I believe I felt a kind of love for her. It wasn't like the love I had felt for Natalie, but a very pure and selfless love, an urge to protect this little brown-skinned bundle from harm. I had never understood how a mother could fall in love with her baby immediately after giving birth, when the baby was still a stranger to her, but now that I'd looked after this tiny, defenceless creature who was entirely dependent on me for her survival, I understood perfectly well.

I named her Mai, after Ji Mai, and carefully climbed into bed beside her after my bath. She didn't stir until nine the following morning. It was lovely to have a smiling, gurgling little companion. She never cried once but looked around the hotel room in wonderment. Perhaps even at her tender age she knew that she had had a lucky escape from the stinking alleyway and was grateful. I started tickling her stomach and she giggled.

I expected the phone to ring at any moment and for a police officer to say he was on his way to pick her up, but no call came. I tried repeatedly to call the station, but every time I called the officer who answered the phone kept on saying, 'Not our problem, not our problem – you picked child up, you sort out.'

I was due to go back to England in a few days' time and knew that it would be impossible for me to take Mai with me. Although I felt a powerful bond with her, I knew that I couldn't keep her myself. I was jumping on planes to different countries all the time to work on films and it would be a miserable life for her. I wanted her to have the kind of love and security that I had never had as a child.

I made up another bottle of milk for her, changed her nappy and crooned a lullaby to her.

'Don't worry, little Mai. I'm going to make sure you don't end up in one of those horrible children's homes,' I whispered.

I racked my brains trying to think what I could do to make sure that Mai would be properly loved and cared for. Having had my fill of horrible institutions as a child, the last thing I was going to do was dump her in one of them. Then suddenly the perfect solution flashed into my mind.

I remembered that Lin, the Buddhist nun I had met on the island of Koh Samet, looked after abandoned children now and again. She was a kind and loving woman and lived in one of the most beautiful places on earth. I decided that I would take Mai to Koh Samet and ask Lin to look after her.

I cuddled Mai all the way to the island, a journey of three hours. She never cried once on the bus journey or on the boat. She drank her milk eagerly and lay quietly when I changed her nappy. I sang her every song I could think of, made different noises that made her laugh and talked to her quietly about my life working on films and visiting many different countries. Although of course she couldn't understand what I was talking about, the sound of my voice seemed to soothe her. She nestled contentedly against me and slept peacefully.

When I arrived on the island with Mai, Lin greeted me warmly. She was a very intuitive person, looked at the baby in my arms and knew without words what I wanted her to do.

'OK, Skye, I'll take her, poor beautiful soul. Where did you find her?'

I explained what had happened and she smiled.

'You have good karma. You were meant to find this helpless child, save her and bring her to a better life.'

I hugged her, gave her all the money I had and promised to send over regular sums for Mai's upkeep when I returned to England.

Mai is twenty-two now and I visit her as often as I can. She doesn't know the story of the early months of her life and believes Lin to be her real mother. She thinks that my only connection to her is that I'm a friend of her mother's.

Although I did not bring her up, I love her like a daughter. Every time I see her I feel overjoyed that I helped to direct her life on to a better path. She has become a beautiful, serene and very loved young woman. Lin brought her up with kindness and consistency, and taught her the importance of the simple beauties of nature. I often wonder how different my life would have been if I had been brought up by someone like Lin on an idyllic island like Koh Samet.

Finding Mai in the rubbish increased my awareness of the terrible plight of some of Thailand's children. While my own childhood was filled with different problems, I strongly identified with their suffering and very much wanted to help.

Several years after I scooped up Mai in the alleyway, another vulnerable child came unexpectedly into my life. It was 1997 and I was 36 years old. I loved being in Thailand and had decided to establish a base for myself on the beautiful island of Phuket. It was relatively wild and unspoilt, not the tourist magnet it is today.

I bought a beach bar for £1,000 from a German woman who wanted to go off travelling, and it became very popular and successful. I also set up a motorbike business. These businesses occupied all my time and a few years before, at the age of 32 I had given up being a stuntwoman. I employed an eighteen-year-old Thai girl called Achara to help me out with cleaning the motorbikes and my house. She told me that she had moved to Phuket from Bangkok in search of work and had no accommodation, so I offered her a room in my house. She had not been to school and struggled with reading and writing, but I helped her to learn and paid for her to go to night school. With support she became a good assistant.

One evening I received a call from a hospital in Bangkok. A nurse said to me, 'Your baby is very sick – she's in a coma. You need to come to the hospital right away.'

'What are you talking about? I don't have a baby,' I responded. Then it dawned on me that it was Achara they wanted, not me.

I handed the phone to her and she started sobbing as she spoke to the nurse.

'What's going on, Achara?' I asked when she had put down the phone.

'I had a baby when I was very young. I didn't want to tell you this in case you didn't give me the job. I left her with my neighbours to look after, but they treated her very badly and now she's in hospital. They have injured her. She won't wake up.' She was in floods of tears and felt enormous remorse for having left her baby.

'OK, Achara, don't cry. We'll travel to Bangkok together and see what's happening at the hospital.'

She gave me a watery, grateful smile.

The next day we arrived at the hospital. One of the doctors explained that police were investigating and what appeared to have happened was that the baby, Sarakit, who was eighteen months old, had been in a car with the neighbours and had peed on the back seat. The husband had become enraged with her for damaging his car, had pulled over, grabbed her and punched her so hard that she had fallen out of the car on to concrete and lost consciousness.

By the time we arrived at the hospital she had come out of the coma but looked groggy and disoriented. Achara looked at her but made no move to pick her up and cuddle her. Suddenly the infant turned towards me, looked me in the eye and weakly stretched out her little arms towards me. I looked into her frightened eyes, picked her up and cuddled her very gently so as not to aggravate any bruises she had received. She clung to me tightly and looked into my eyes. I was sure she was saying silently, 'You've got to help me.' I could feel her spirit crying out to me. I felt the same surge of love I had felt when I had cared for Mai.

Sarakit was small and skinny for her age and looked as if she had barely been fed. Her hair was cropped unevenly, which gave her a lopsided appearance, and she was covered with old and new bruises. The beating she received in the car was apparently not an isolated incident. Every cell in her body seemed to be begging for love and protection. I wondered if I had sent out the same signals when I was her age.

I looked into her eyes and replied to her in the same silent way that she had spoken to me, 'I promise you, Sarakit, that I will never let anyone hurt you ever again.' I'm sure that she relaxed visibly the longer I held her.

As Achara hovered uncertainly in the background, some seismic shift was taking place inside my brain. It was as if finding Mai in the rubbish had been a practice run for me and now, holding Sarakit, I was facing the real thing. I knew that Achara was unlikely to be able to take good care of her, and I also knew that this time I wasn't going to run to Lin and ask for her help. I was 36 now and ready to take on responsibility for bringing up a child.

I had spent my life as a restless soul, wandering, searching and running from place to place. I had been starved of love and stability, and had never had a parent to nurture me. As I stood in the scruffy hospital ward surrounded by sick babies in bleeping incubators, a peculiar sensation came over me. It was almost like the description people give of having their whole lives flash before them when they're drowning. Suddenly I knew that all my life experiences up to this point had been for a reason. They had been to prepare me to care for children like Sarakit whose parents had let them down as my parents had let me down. Perhaps I could bond with such children in a way that others who had led smooth and even lives could not.

'There's no way Sarakit is going back to those cruel neighbours,' I said decisively to the doctor and Achara. 'She's coming back to Phuket with us, and we'll bring her up in a safe and loving environment.'

Achara nodded, and the doctor was more than happy to let Sarakit go with us when she was discharged from hospital the following day. One of the doctors filled me in on the horrific abuse that poor Sarakit had experienced. The couple who Achara had left her with were both heavy drinkers and often didn't have enough money for food. They had children of their own, who were fed first, while Sarakit was just given the scraps. Every time she cried she was punched and beaten. I thought of my own brutal childhood and I wept for her. I was determined that nobody would ever hurt her again.

As before, I bought nappies, milk and bottles, but this time I also bought her a wardrobe of cute baby clothes. Sarakit clung to me on the journey back to Phuket. It was as if she knew instinctively that her mother was unable to care for her. Achara seemed hugely grateful for the support I was offering to her and her child but there was no maternal bond there. I think she was simply not equipped to take on the responsibility.

In my arms Sarakit was always quiet, and now and again she smiled up at me. I felt completely elated. All my life I had focused on my own survival and pursuit of happiness, however temporary. Now my emphasis had shifted entirely to the survival and happiness of this small, vulnerable bundle of humanity. I was overwhelmed by how much love I felt for her. The gaping void I had felt for so much of my life had suddenly been filled. I had not understood why I had felt there was something missing before, but Sarakit had suddenly become the centre of my world and it felt wonderful to focus entirely on making sure she was safe and happy and that she could thrive.

Back in Phuket, Achara told me she didn't feel able to bring up Sarakit. She hadn't bonded with her at all and just seeing a helpless child made her feel uncomfortable. I had seen during the first few moments in the hospital that Achara didn't want to take on full responsibility for Sarakit and had already planned to ask her if I could bring her up.

'Look, Achara, I know it would be very difficult for you to keep Sarakit. I'm happy to bring her up for you if you'd like me to,' I said to her. I felt that it was my destiny to care for Sarakit.

Achara agreed and signed papers making me Sarakit's legal guardian. Soon afterwards she stopped working for me and took up another job elsewhere on the island. She visited Sarakit occasionally, and has stayed in touched sporadically.

At first Sarakit sat and rocked and pulled her hair out. If anyone made a sudden movement, she flinched, convinced that someone was going to strike her. I bought her a puppy and somehow caring for that puppy and enjoying his innocent frolicking on the beach helped her to get her troubled thoughts out in the open.

We ran along the beach with the puppy, the sea licking our ankles and toes. I encouraged Sarakit to shout and scream as we ran because I sensed there was a lot of pain locked inside her that she needed to release. I shouted and screamed by way of demonstration, my voice lost in the sound of the tide, and after a little while she copied me. I was sure that my instinct was right. She shouted and screamed a lot over the next few weeks, and afterwards was serene, as if she had exorcised demons. I hugged her and cuddled her all the time and did my best to reassure her that she could stay with me for ever.

The little girl bloomed under my care. As she recovered from her ordeal and inched towards trusting me, her face opened like a flower. She was a very slight, quiet child with large almond-shaped eyes. When she was four, I paid for her to go to one of the best schools on the island and she proved to be a good and conscientious student. I was convinced that if I hadn't found her, or rather if she hadn't found me, her fate would have been a violent, miserable childhood with no education. Later she would probably have progressed to one of the few job opportunities available to her – working as one of Thailand's many bar girls. I hope that being with me has provided many emotional and material benefits for Sarakit, but what she has given to me is beyond measure. The selfless love that a parent – whether birth or adopted – has for a child is like nothing else. Having Sarakit in my life has enriched me more than I ever thought possible. We have shared simple pleasures like swimming in the sea and running along the sand, and I have helped her to learn her Thai and English alphabets.

I never taught her to call me mummy, but she sponta-
neously called me it, much to my delight. One day when she
was four years old she looked up at me and said, 'I love you so
much, Mummy.'

I thought my heart was going to burst with happiness when
I heard her say those words. She was gazing at me with her
trusting, intense eyes.

'And I love you too, Sarakit. My love for you is as big as the
world,' I said, bending down and scooping her up in a huge
hug.

I knew that Thailand had huge numbers of abandoned
children living on the streets and that I could have taken
in any number of them, but I had never gone out looking for
anything or anyone in my life. Circumstances had come to
me and Sarakit was no exception. The same thing happened
with Niran, the second child I'm bringing up. Niran's young
mother, Dok, worked as a bar girl in Phuket. She met
Niran's father, a Scandinavian called Gus, while she was
working and began a relationship with him. He agreed to
support her and she left prostitution. She became pregnant
with Niran, but she came home one evening when she was
three months pregnant to find that Gus had hanged himself.
He had many money problems, as well as a wife and
children back home, and everything seemed to have become
too much for him.

Dok was grief-stricken and left in a financial mess. Her
sister tried her best to support her, but when she was six
months pregnant, Dok went to the toilet and Niran popped
out. In shock, she left him lying in the toilet. Her sister picked
up the baby and rushed him to the nearest hospital. He was

placed in an incubator and doctors said his chances of survival
were slim.

Against the odds, though, he made it. He was given steroids
to build his lungs up, and after three months in an incubator
was well enough to go home. Like Achara, Dok had little
bond with her child, and having enjoyed her three months of
freedom, was uncertain about the prospect of caring for him.
A week after bringing him home, she went back to bar work.
He was looked after by various babysitters and sometimes by
bar girls when she was forced to take him to work with her.

I knew nothing of Niran's fate, having never met Dok, but
one day our paths were to cross. I had to go to a tailor's shop
to have a fitting for a shirt.

'Hi, Skye. I'm just finishing something off. Go and have a
coffee and come back in twenty minutes, then I'll do your
measurements, if that's OK,' said the tailor.

'Sure, no problem,' I said, and wandered round the corner,
where there were many bars.

I decided that I would order myself a coffee and sit in the
sun. Logically I should have stopped off at the nearest bar, a
place I'd been to before and where I knew some of the girls,
but something propelled me to the far end of the street and I
entered a bar I'd never been into before and ordered myself a
coffee.

As I sat outside in the sun, I saw a baby lying in a crate. I
was horrified. The baby was screaming. I watched as a bar
girl came up to him with a bottle of milk. I saw her unscrew
the teat and pour in some whisky from a miniature bottle.

I was appalled and ran up to her. 'What the hell do you
think you're doing feeding a little baby whisky. Are you mad?
Is this your child?'

The girl, who was probably about eighteen, very small and skinny, and dressed in a low-cut, strappy top and tiny miniskirt, shook her head. 'No, his mother's over there with a customer.' She gestured to a girl who was dressed almost identically to her and had a similarly diminutive frame.

I ran across to the mother and beckoned her away from her customer. 'Do you know that your friend is feeding your baby whisky?'

She seemed unsurprised and unperturbed. 'Well, he cries a lot and I can't have him making a noise while I'm working,' she replied, shrugging.

'Don't you want him or something?'

She shrugged again.

I looked at the poor neglected little boy, who was covered in mosquito bites and scabies, and looked as if he had been living in a hedge. He appeared to be about eighteen months old. Turning back to the girl, I explained that I was legal guardian for another Thai child, that signing guardianship papers was relatively simple to do and that I'd take her baby if she wanted me to.

'Sure, why not? You can take him,' she said.

I picked up the baby and cradled him in my arms. Something has led me here at this moment, I thought. I was sure it was my destiny to care for Niran.

Just a few days later Dok signed the forms and Niran joined the family.

Niran was not to be the last child I rescued. Like both Sarakit and Niran, the third child I agreed to look after, Sugunya, was eighteen months old when I found her. It was as if eighteen months was a make-or-break time for the fate of these children. Sarakit, Niran and Sugunya were permitted to perform a sharp U-turn on the trajectory their life was expected to follow.

Sugunya was Achara's daughter by another man, and once again she was unable to look after her. Achara came to me and asked me if I could take her. I looked into Sugunya's wide, trusting eyes and said yes right away. She has blended in well with our unorthodox family. A local woman called Mem helps me look after the children. She has a little boy of her own who I support financially and is like a second mother in the family.

The horrific tsunami in 2004 underlined to me just how precious my children are to me. I know of many people who lost loved ones, including children, in the disaster and I feel very blessed that all of our family survived. That fateful Boxing Day was a beautiful sunny day. All my ex-pat friends had arranged to meet up for a barbecue on the beach. We planned to meet at 9.30 a.m., so we could eat before it got too hot. I was taking Sarakit and Niran; Mem was going to look after Sugunya for me. I was running late that morning because some people who were renting a villa I own didn't arrive until after 10 a.m. The villa was en route to the beach, so I'd brought the kids with me on the back of the motorbike. When we'd finished there, we rode to the beach. I had a weird sensation that things weren't quite right. As we approached, I saw the first wave. It just kissed us and went back out. Luckily I was on the bike and could move out of the way quickly.

Then there was mass hysteria. My friends were in a quieter part of the beach with lots of rocks, which thankfully protected them. I spun the bike round, the kids still on the back. I drove up to my office, told Mem to get her young son and

Sugunya. Then I jumped into my pick-up truck, threw in the kids and some of the neighbours' children, and drove to the highest point on the island, fearful that there would be another wave. The roads were completely jammed because everyone had the same idea. The local police told us all to stay calm and asked anyone with pick-ups to come down to the beach and help to rescue people.

Once my kids were safe, I went back to the beach with one of the policemen and helped people who were injured. One man had his hand cut off by the propeller of a boat, and lots of debris had hurt people. One woman had a punctured lung.

Then somebody screamed, 'Tsunami!' The second wave was massive and powerful. It came in so fast that by the time you blinked it was upon you. I had all these people in my truck when the second wave chased us off the beach. There were fridges, tables and other items of furniture from hotels floating down the street. I got about ten injured tourists off the beach and into my truck. It was a state of emergency and I knew I had to help. Having no fear of death helped me to act swiftly and practically. I had a strong feeling that this wasn't my day to go.

Because there were only a couple of roads out of the beach, there were many accidents caused by motorbikes and cars smashing into each other in the chaos. My stunt skills came in handy dodging all the cars coming towards my truck.

We went to the highest point on the island and stayed there all day. People kept on saying, 'There's another one coming,' but luckily they were wrong. A few people had their car radios on and the news trickled through to us gradually that we could venture back down.

We went back to Phuket town that night, which is in the middle of the island. The wave hadn't touched that area. No mobile phones were working, but I managed to get hold of a friend who lived there. There were twenty people camping out in her house. I decided to take the children up a mountain to spend the night. It was the highest point on the island. I parked the car and we all curled up on the seats and slept fitfully there.

There was a huge black cloud over Phuket after the tsunami. The smell of death was everywhere. Then we received warnings about disease and bacteria. People began to walk down the streets with masks on. We drove down to Samui, which is on another coast where I had another house and we stayed down there for a week. We didn't want to return to Phuket until they'd cleaned up all the dead bodies. I felt I could feel lost spirits floating around, and the place still stank of death even after the corpses had been removed. It was a very weird time.

A couple of months later things were ostensibly back to normal. It was a year and a half before I swam in the sea again, though. I didn't fancy swimming where dead bodies might still be tossed through the waves.

I am enormously grateful that me and the children survived this terrible disaster unscathed. It has made every day I spend with them even more precious.

I have tried to give the children huge dollops of the love and security I missed out on and to teach them the value of honesty and hard work. One time I gave them all a one-bhat coin and told them to plant it in the garden to see if it would grow into a money tree. All three dutifully planted their bhats, but they were disappointed when several weeks later there were no green shoots appearing from the soil.

I sat them all down and explained to them why nothing had grown. 'There's no such thing as a money tree, and I thought this was a good way to explain to you that money doesn't grow on trees. The only way you will get money when you're older is by hard work and honesty.'

I am extremely proud of all the children. They are growing up like straight, tall trees. My love for them is boundless, and it gives me enormous comfort to think that they are having a childhood that is so different from mine. Sarakit is 13 and is doing well at a private girls' school on the island. Occasionally I see flashes of temper from her which I think are linked to her early, traumatic experiences. For the most part though she is a kind, gentle and quiet girl and like me she adores animals. Niran is eight now, he is a free spirit like me and loves adventures. Sugunya is almost three and is settling down well.

Niran's health has remained precarious because of his poor start in life. He is very susceptible to fevers and I have lost count of the number of nights I have sat up with him mopping his brow in a bid to cool him down.

I adore spending time with the children teaching them how to surf, ride bikes and play football. One of Sarakit's favourite things is to feed stray dogs on the beach. We have a very peaceful house; there are no fights and arguments. It is a wonderful contrast to my life growing up. The only noise is the sweet sound of children playing.

My heart bursts with joy when Sarakit comes up to me, cuddles me and whispers, 'Mummy, I'm so glad you found me. I can't imagine life without you.'

When the children came to me, they had the same mistrust of adults that I had. Helping them learn to trust and open up their hearts to someone who they have gradually learnt will protect them is the best feeling I've ever experienced.

I've got all the time in the world for children and animals, and my aim in life now is to help abandoned children in any way possible. When I travelled to Cambodia a few years ago, I got chatting to an American aid worker on the plane who told me about the children who lived and worked in the capital Phnom Penh's stinking municipal rubbish dumps. I visited and couldn't believe my eyes. Young children dressed in rags were scavenging for things they could sell among a mountain of putrefying rubbish that stretched as far as the eye could see. They seemed to accept their fate stoically, but every child deserves to have a childhood and I longed to help. I knew I couldn't take on all the children clambering up and down the rubbish mountain, but I was determined to do something. I spoke to Amanda, a wealthy friend of mine in Spain. She too was moved by their plight and has now set up a refuge for rubbish-tip children in another part of Cambodia. I'm very proud to be associated with it and to have acted as the catalyst for such an important rescue centre.

I am constantly looking for new ways to help children who are suffering. I know that I won't be able to change the fate of many, but I am determined to do everything I can. I truly believe that if there is a job I was put on earth to do, it is this one.

EPILOGUE

I'm often amazed that I'm still alive. My life has been stuffed full of adventures and traumas, and given the risks I've taken, I'm convinced that someone or something has been watching over me and has decided that it is not yet my time to die.

Maybe we all live many lives and our souls are constantly recycled on a loop. If there's a reason why I've survived despite the precarious life I've led, I'm sure it's so that I can look after Sarakit, Niran and Sugunya.

I know that living with my mother and Michael has had a profoundly corrosive effect on me, although I have tried my best to shake off the memories of them and their influence. My mother died of cancer a few years ago and I regret that we were not reconciled. We didn't ever have a chance to get close. I have no idea what has happened to Michael. I'm still in touch with my dad and Jay but we don't get to see each other very often because we live so far apart.

The biggest sadness that will stay with me throughout my life is my lack of a loving mother and father. People who have that are very blessed. I have not allowed it to make me bitter, though.

My life as a child was perpetually eventful. I was never

quite sure whether I found the adventures or the adventures found me. After the extremely traumatic incidents of my life, I had no fear left inside me. I surrendered myself to experiences, allowing them to take me into all kinds of uncharted waters. I reasoned that I would deal with negative consequences if and when they arose. When they did, I invariably found a way to wriggle out of them, like shedding a troublesome skin and slipping away in a bright, shiny new one. Until I found my beloved children, I lived my life shot through with a sense of isolation, of not belonging. They changed everything for me. They gave me roots and now I belong to them.

I've never led a conventional nine-to-five life, and I wouldn't know what to do with it if it was offered to me. I've never been on a monthly wage in my life; I've always lived off my wits and have never tolerated anyone telling me what to do. I don't have a GCSE, an A level or a degree to my name, but somehow I've survived. Despite these gaping holes in my CV, I believe that I can slip with ease from one social circle to another. I'm just as at home chatting to down and outs on London's Strand as I am mingling with Chelsea's smart set. I fit in anywhere but belong nowhere. Although my children are everything to me, my soul is still restless. I travel a lot and have an urge to be forever on the move.

My life so far has been richer in experience than most people's are in three lifetimes. I've travelled the world several times over. I hope I have many years left, but I don't fear death. For me, it represents a return to the earth that I love so dearly, and while I wouldn't do anything to hasten my departure, I feel that whenever death comes to collect me, I'll be ready to go.

I don't doubt that there will be other dramas and crises in my life, but I hope there will be many joys in store too. I have been on a very long journey to reach the point where I am able to offer Sarakit, Niran and Sugunya a stable and loving home.

My most fervent wish is to be able to help more children whose childhoods are wretched. Lousy childhoods impact on people for the rest of their lives. I believe that my years as a troubled rebel have not been wasted and have provided me with vital insights into ways to shore up young, fragile lives.

I now work building houses and my main motivation is to provide for my children. I firmly believe that children are the most precious thing we have, and if I can help as many of them as possible to avoid the kind of damage that I experienced in the early years of my life, then I will rest peacefully. I know that although I never learnt how to do my times table or pass an exam, I understand how to help damaged children and how to protect them. I have learnt how to give them infinite love, and I believe that is the most important thing in the world.